Small Claims Court
for the Everyday Canadian

Milena Celap, B.Sc., LL.B., and Pamela J. Larmondin, B.A., LL.B.

Self-Counsel Press
(a division of)
International Self-Counsel Press Ltd.
Canada   USA

Self-Counsel Press acknowledges the financial support of the Government of Canada through the Book Publishing Industry Development Program (BPIDP) for our publishing activities.

Printed in Canada.

First edition: 2000

Canadian Cataloguing in Publication Data

Celap, Milena.
    Small claims court for the everyday Canadian

    ISBN 1-55180-311-9

    1. Small claims courts — Canada — Popular works. I. Larmondin, Pamela J. II. Title.
KE8276.Z82C44 2000 347.71'04   C00-910516-6 KF8769.Z9C44 2000

Self-Counsel Press
(a division of)
International Self-Counsel Press Ltd.

1481 Charlotte Road	1704 N. State Street
North Vancouver, BC V7J 1H1	Bellingham, WA 98225
Canada	USA

Contents

APPENDICES

GLOSSARY

CHECKLISTS

FIGURES

SAMPLES

TABLES

Notice to Readers

Laws and court procedures are constantly changing. Every effort is made to keep this publication as current as possible. However, the author, the publisher, and the vendor of this book make no representation or warranties about the outcome or the use to which the information in this book is put and are not assuming any liability for any claims, losses, or damages arising out of the use of this book. The reader should not rely on the author or the publisher of this book for any professional advice. Please be sure that you have the most recent edition.

Note: The information contained in this book does not apply to the province of Quebec.

Prolegomen

Wait! The rest of our book is nothing like the title to this preface. It is written, not in the Latin of lawyer-speak, but in plain English for the everyday Canadian. After all, doesn't it make sense that a court system designed for everyday people should be understood by everyday people? This book offers you plenty of explanations, examples, and tips, all written in plain English.

When presenting a case in small claims court, more often than not, you have a lot to learn and little time to spare. This simple, thorough guide with quick references will lead you in your journey through the small claims court system. Let us help.

Both authors have appeared as advocates before the small claims court. We have also attended court for observation purposes. Throughout these experiences, we have kept detailed notes on what to do to prepare for an appearance in small claims court, and when, where, and how to do it. More important, we noted how not to appear in small claims court. This book presents our notes, observations, and opinions in a simple, practical manner.

We also had the benefit of learning and receiving feedback from people more experienced than us. Since we can't return the favour, we're passing it on.

Good luck, and remember: Don't plan your case or leave for court without this book!

Acknowledgements

Many thanks to the following people for contributing to this publication:

Judges and Clerks, Small Claims Court, Windsor, Ontario: For being patient with us and educating us when we were taking our first steps in court.

John W. Whiteside, Deputy Judge, Small Claims Court; Professor Emeritus, Faculty of Law, University of Windsor: For your interest in this book, your willingness to share your perspective from the Bench, and, moreover, your commitment to and enthusiasm for enhancing access to justice.

Staff of Legal Assistance of Windsor: For being our first teacher on small claims court.

Mira Columbro: For providing your nonlegal perspective on this book. The everyday Canadian will benefit tremendously from your time and effort.

Anne Pappas: For editing an early draft of this book as Student-at-Law (as you then were). Your contribution is immeasurable.

William A. Bogart, Professor, Faculty of Law, University of Windsor: For sharing with us your insights into the world of publishing, for your encouraging words, and for your commitment to access to justice.

Canadian Bar Association — Ontario Student Initiatives Programme: For showing support for this project through your award programme. We've now gone national!

Staff of Self-Counsel Press: For seeing the potential of this book and for your hard work in delivering the final product. Special thanks to Richard Day, managing editor.

Family Celap, Stoney Creek, and Family Larmondin, and Thornbury, Ontario: You were our first teachers. Your influence will never cease, your support is unending, and our appreciation can never be adequately expressed.

1
Overview of Small Claims Court

1. What Is Small Claims Court?

Small claims court is a court of equity. In other words, the court applies general principles of justice in addition to common and statute law, in the interests of fairness and impartiality. Small claims court was created to increase access to justice for the average person. Almost anyone can attend at the court without the assistance of a lawyer or law student. Sometimes, however, people are uncomfortable representing themselves and choose someone with legal training to represent them. Other times, people are quite comfortable presenting their own cases but hire a lawyer for legal advice before attending court.

Small claims court rules set out how a lawsuit must proceed. These rules are different from those of other courts. Small claims court rules also differ in small ways among the provinces and territories. The rules for most provinces and territories may be found using the links to government Web sites posted on the Self-Counsel Press Web site at <http://www.self-counsel.com/canlaw/smallclaims/resources.html>. You can use these as a starting point for gathering more information about small claims court. The rules deal, in part, with the following major issues:

> The kind of claims that are allowed

> How to bring a lawsuit

> How to defend a lawsuit

> How to settle a lawsuit without going to trial

> How to bring a lawsuit to trial if settlement fails

> How to conduct a trial

> How to get judgment

> How to collect money owed as a result of a judgment

2. Who Are the Players?

Before entering a small claims court action, you should become familiar with the people involved in the small claims court system and the overall course of a lawsuit. Table 1 outlines the various players you will encounter at small claims court, as well as their function.

Note: A single judge or adjudicator presides over a trial in small claims court. Jury trials are not held in small claims court.

Criminal versus civil actions

A *criminal* action is a court action brought by the government or state, also known as the *Crown*. A Crown attorney represents the state in a criminal action, which involves the prosecution of a person charged with an offence under the Criminal Code. The goal is to convict the accused if there is sufficient evidence that he or she committed the crime and to acquit the person if there is insufficient evidence that he or she committed the crime. Examples of criminal charges are assault, theft, forgery, and perjury.

A *civil* action is a lawsuit about any matter that is not criminal. The purpose of a civil action is to correct a wrong through an award of money or an order for the defendant to do something. Examples include tort, breach of contract, and landlord and tenant actions. (**Note:** Not all civil actions are available in all small claims court jurisdictions. For example, in Ontario, landlord and tenant matters are handled through a tribunal. Some landlord-tenant matters can be brought to the small claims court only when the landlord-tenant relationship has been terminated. Examples of civil actions include personal injury, failure to pay rent, failure to pay for goods, failure to perform a contract, or failure to pay for goods purchased (e.g., NSF cheque).

Criminal actions are dealt with not in the small claims court but in the higher court. However, civil actions arising out of criminal activity may be brought before the small claims court. Examples of such civil actions include personal injury, property damage, or trespass to property or person. As well, the criminal courts may grant restitution orders to repay for damage done through a criminal act. Restitution orders are enforceable in small claims court if they fall within its monetary jurisdiction.

TABLE 1
SMALL CLAIMS COURT PLAYERS

PLAYER	ROLE
Commissioner of oaths	A commissioner of oaths (or a lawyer) must be present when an affidavit is sworn. A small claims court office may have a staff member who is appointed as a commissioner of oaths.
Court clerk	The court clerk sits in front of the judge, calls the court to order, swears or affirms witnesses, labels exhibits, keeps order in the courtroom, and otherwise assists the judge. A prothonotary is a senior clerk of the court.
Court officer or court staff member	A court officer or court staff member works in the court office. He or she processes claims, defences, and other court documents; schedules appearances; and deals with other administrative matters.
Court reporter	A court reporter is present at trials and motions and records the players in attendance, takes notes at or records the proceedings, and keeps transcripts. In some jurisdictions, the court reporter performs the duties of a court clerk as well.
Court interpreter	A court interpreter translates witness testimony from a foreign language into English or, in some cases, into French.
Defendant	The defendant is the person being sued and is also referred to as a *party*.
Judge or deputy judge	The judge is the decision-maker who presides over motions, hearings, examinations, pre-trial settlement conferences, and trials. The deputy judge is a practising lawyer who performs the duties of a judge.
Lawyer or agent	A lawyer or agent represents a party who is either a plaintiff or defendant. An agent may be a law student, articling student, a paralegal, or any other person. Note that plaintiffs and defendants may represent themselves.
Plaintiff	The plaintiff is a person who initiates an action and is also referred to as a *party* or *claimant*.
Referee	The referee is a decision-maker who may preside over pre-trial conferences, judgment debtor examinations, and hearings ordered by a judge. The referee may be a lawyer or mediator.
Witness	The witness is a person who tells the story to support one or more of the parties in the lawsuit.

3. How Does Small Claims Court Work?

A typical lawsuit or action in small claims court unfolds as follows:

(a) A dispute arises between two or more parties relating to a civil matter.

(b) The case is suitable for the small claims court because it is within limits set by that court.

(c) The plaintiff starts a lawsuit by preparing a claim in which the plaintiff explains the dispute and the events surrounding it. This claim puts the defendant on notice that he or she is now a party to a lawsuit.

(d) The defendant replies to the allegations in the claim by preparing a defence. The defendant may also file a claim against the plaintiff or any other person. This is called a *defendant's claim*, *counterclaim*, *crossclaim*, or *third party claim*, depending on whom is being sued. (See chapter 4 for more information on the defendant's claim.)

(e) Any number of events may then occur:

　(i) The parties may negotiate a settlement.

　(ii) A party may request an order of the court by bringing a motion.

　(iii) The case may proceed to trial.

　(iv) A verdict at trial may result in an appeal or in collection procedures.

This is a simplified big-picture look at the small claims court. Many other things could happen depending on the type of lawsuit and the parties involved. Other steps may become necessary, such as —

▸ filling out forms and leaving them with the court,

▸ delivering documents to another party,

▸ summonsing witnesses,

▸ drafting affidavits, offers, and agreements, and

▸ swearing affidavits.

Although the rules will outline the steps you need to take, you will find some exceptions. This is because in small claims court judges have leeway in applying those rules. This judicial discretion makes the small claims court system more flexible than that of higher courts, allowing the judge to make a decision that is most fair for a particular case.

4. How Should You Use This Book?

Each chapter of this book focuses on one major aspect of the processes involved in the small claims court system. Numerous explanations, examples, and tips will help you through your lawsuit properly and efficiently.

Be aware that procedure differs in some ways among the provinces and territories. We have highlighted these differences whenever necessary, but you may also wish to confirm procedure with your local small claims court staff. In any event, the overall principles are the same from province to province and from territory to territory. Understanding these principles will make a world of difference between a good experience and a bad experience in starting a lawsuit or defending yourself against one.

Note: To the best of our knowledge, at time of publication, the small claims court rules for the Northwest Territories also apply to Nunavut.

Read this book thoroughly if you have never before been involved in the small claims court process. To get the most out of the book, use the detailed table of contents and appendices to provide you with a quick reference to the particular stage of the case with which you are dealing.

If you do not understand any words or phrases in this chapter, look them up in the glossary. If you need more information about the legislation for your province or territory, consult the links to legislation and law-related Web sites posted on Self-Counsel Press's Web site at <http://www.self-counsel.com/canlaw/smallclaims/resources.html>.

Note: The samples used in this book use addresses which may change. Even if an example letter or other document in this book uses a court address in your province or territory, you are strongly advised to check that the address is correct before using it.

2
Before You Sue

1. Should You Sue?

A dispute can be resolved in several ways. First, try resolving the dispute by sending a complaint letter or demand letter to the offending party as described in chapter 12.

Consider mediation if you feel that all parties would be willing to meet before a neutral third party. The neutral third party is called a *mediator*, and his or her role is to facilitate discussion between the disputing parties. The benefit of going to mediation rather than to court is that the parties can more readily preserve their relationship, retain their privacy, and settle the issues much faster than the court system permits. However, a cost is associated with mediation. If you wish to consider mediation, look for a mediator in your *Yellow Pages*.

If neither a demand letter nor mediation is appropriate, consider whether small claims court is the right way to resolve the dispute. You will need to think about many things before starting even the simplest lawsuit. A lawsuit takes time, costs money, demands effort, and affects personal and business relationships. It should, therefore, be the last method used to solve a problem. Think carefully about the next series of questions before deciding, and then read the rest of this chapter, which explains each of these considerations in greater detail:

(a) *Have you done everything possible to stay out of court?* Have you tried to resolve the dispute in other ways? Have you asked the defendant to pay you? Have you sent the defendant a demand letter? Have you considered mediation? Is suing the only way to regain what you lost as a result of the dispute?

Court should be the last resort for resolving a dispute. See chapter 6 for a discussion of alternatives to court.

(b) *Why do you want to sue?* Are you trying to recover losses or are you trying to get revenge? If you are thinking of suing as a way of getting revenge or venting your anger, think twice. The old cliché, "Don't bite off your nose to spite your face," couldn't apply more.

(c) *What solution are you seeking?* What do you want at the end of the day? Do you want money, an apology, return of goods, or the performance of a service? Is the solution available by law? If you want money, how much do you hope to win if the action is successful?

(d) *Does your claim have a legal basis?* Does the law support your case? In other words, is your reason for suing one that the courts recognize?

(e) *What is the amount of your claim?* Is the value of your claim within limits set by the small claims court?

(f) *Can you prove your case?* Do you have evidence to prove your story? Can you prove that the defendant did you wrong or ought to pay up? Are you sure it was not the act of another individual? Review the facts carefully before deciding to sue.

(g) *Have you contributed to your damages?* Have you mitigated (minimized) your damages? Are you coming to court with clean hands; that is, have you come to court without having done something immoral, unethical, or illegal? If you have engaged in any bad faith dealings concerning this claim, don't expect the court to be sympathetic toward your situation, even if you are fully entitled to demand payment from the defendant.

(h) *How might the defence react?* Do you expect that the defendant will file a defence? Can you imagine what that defence might be? Will the defendant have compassionate reasons for having behaved in a certain way? Will the defendant reveal to the court any bad faith dealings on your part? How might the defence affect your chances of winning?

(i) *Are you within the limitation period?* Time limits apply within which a suit must be filed. If you miss a time limit, you can lose your right to sue. If you bring your action within the appropriate limitation period, will you be able to locate evidence and witnesses to prove your case?

(j) *If you wish to sue the government, have you acted within the notice period?* Special requirements for suing the government may apply in addition to adhering to the limitation period. For instance, you must generally give notice that you intend to sue.

(k) *Do you have the time and money to sue?* The court process is lengthy. Documents must be prepared, appearances made, and errands run, almost all during business hours. Can you spare the time? Documents must be prepared, photocopied, filed with the court, and delivered to those involved in the lawsuit. Each step involves spending money and the cost increases with each defendant. You may even be required to take time off work on more than one occasion, thus incurring a loss of income.

(l) *How will a legal action affect you personally or in your business?* Are you willing to allow your confidential records to become part of the public record, as would be the case with medical records in a personal injury lawsuit? Would a lawsuit threaten your privacy? Do you wish to maintain a positive relationship with the person you want to sue or his or her friends or relatives? How will going to court affect your relationships with the parties? These questions are especially critical in small communities.

(m) *Can you collect if you win your lawsuit?* Winning does not necessarily mean that you will collect your award. If you win your case, will the defendant have the means to pay you or is the defendant judgment-proof (i.e., they cannot afford to pay if judgment is given against them)? Will the defendant want to pay you? Will you have the time, energy, and money to keep track of the defendant should they make efforts to avoid paying on the judgment?

2. Is Small Claims Court Suitable for Your Case?

Numerous issues need to be considered when deciding whether to present your case at small claims court, including the type of claim in dispute and the amount of the claim.

2.1 The type of claim

The small claims court can hear only civil actions. However, if you are seeking damages for personal injury, property damage, or trespass arising out of a criminal offence, you may sue in this court. The following cases are not suitable for small claims court:

▸ Construction lien cases (these should be heard in the higher court such as the Superior Court of Justice or Court of Queen's Bench)

▸ Family cases, including separation, divorce, custody, and adoption (these should be heard in the higher court such as the Superior Court of Justice or Court of Queen's Bench, but most provinces and territories have special family divisions within these courts to deal with family issues)

▸ Cases within the jurisdiction of the Federal Court (e.g., copyright violations; income tax cases; appeals under the Canada Labour Code; CRTC, railway, telephone, and communications matters; and immigration cases)

Federal statutes

Matters dealing with federal statutes (e.g., Income Tax Act, Immigration Act, and Copyright Act) cannot be brought before the small claims court. Therefore, if you wish to enforce a section of a federal statute or have someone punished for violating a federal law, you must do this in the federal court, not the small claims court.

Table 2 lists some of the claims that can be brought in the small claims court. If your type of case is not listed there, check the applicable legislation (e.g., Construction Liens Act, Negligence Act, or Occupier's Liability Act). (You may find the relevant legislation for your province or territory on one of the legislation and law-related Web sites posted on Self-Counsel Press's Web site at <http://www.self counsel.com/canlaw /smallclaims/resources.html>, or consult with a lawyer.)

2.2 The amount of the claim

Small claims court processes claims up to a certain dollar value. This is referred to as monetary limit or monetary jurisdiction. Costs for filing, service of documents, preparation, and attendance are not included in this

> If you have questions about any part of the small claims court process, consider consulting with a lawyer. You may seek assistance from a lawyer on a retainer (agreement) limited to an opinion on issues you feel you are not capable of handling.

TABLE 2
ACTIONS SUITABLE FOR SMALL CLAIMS COURT*

The defendant owes money to the plaintiff	▶ loans and credit lines that have not been repaid (e.g., personal, institutional, even student loans and student credit lines) ▶ transaction fees for loans that are promised but never happen ▶ bouncing (NSF) cheques ▶ payment for goods purchased ▶ payment for services provided but not paid for (plaintiffs may be tradespeople such as carpenters, plumbers, electricians, renovators, consultants, builders, lawn maintenance workers) ▶ payment of rent arrears if the tenant no longer resides with the landlord ▶ payment on a lease of any kind (for the use of a car, condominium, apartment, office space, etc.) ▶ payment on a promissory note
The defendant published or publicly said something to damage the plaintiff's reputation	▶ defamation (untruths in print) ▶ libel and slander (untruths on television or radio or spoken untruths)
The defendant was negligent and did something or failed to do something that caused damage to the plaintiff or the plaintiff's land or property	▶ damage to goods due to cleaning, renovations, repairs, accidents, crimes, bad deliveries ▶ personal injury ▶ damage to property ▶ poor quality of work (e.g., renovations, repairs) ▶ personal injury
The defendant intentionally did something to cause damages to the plaintiff or the plaintiff's land or property	▶ damage to property ▶ wrongful dismissal ▶ libel and slander ▶ personal injury ▶ breach of contract (refusal to pay on an insurance policy, refusal to return or provide goods belonging to the plaintiff) ▶ false imprisonment or false arrest ▶ intentional infliction of mental suffering

*Note: Your province's or territory's rules may specifically allow or prohibit certain actions listed in this table. Consult the govenment Web sites posted on Self-Counsel Press's Web site at <http://www.self-counsel.com/canlaw/smallclaims/resources.html> for the relevant legislation for your province or territory.

amount. Those amounts may be awarded by the judge after making a decision at the trial.

Table 3 lists the monetary limits imposed by each province and territory.

Fees for frequent filers

Generally speaking, small claims court fees are kept under $100. Fee schedules (lists of fees) are available from your local small claims court office.

Note: In some areas, frequent filers (people or businesses that frequently file claims) must pay higher filing fees. Some frequent filers include the following:

➤ A bank or loan agency collecting on bad debts

➤ A leasing company collecting payments

➤ A tradesperson hoping to get paid for services rendered

➤ A landlord frequently suing for rental arrears

If your claim is higher than the monetary limit of the small claims court, you may do one of the following:

(a) *Take the matter to the higher court.* This option may not suit you because it is more expensive to resolve an action in a higher court, even though you may sue for higher amounts. This is because costs in a higher court are higher than those in the small claims court, and include items such as the filing fee, fees for summonsing witnesses, and lawyer's fees. Also, by law, only the parties themselves or lawyers may appear in the higher court. Generally, unless you have had considerable exposure to the higher court, you may not wish to risk trying your own case without the assistance of a lawyer.

(b) *Waive the amount over the monetary limit and bring the action in the small claims court.* If you waive any portion of the claim in excess of the monetary limit, you cannot bring an action for the remainder of the money in any other court. This concept is called *res judicata.* It simply means that the matter has already been put to rest by judgment or settlement and cannot be reopened as a new action.

If your claim is worth more than the monetary limit of the small claims court, you cannot split the action into two or more actions to keep

TABLE 3

PROVINCIAL MONETARY LIMITS FOR SMALL CLAIMS COURT

British Columbia	$ 10 000
Alberta	$ 7 500
Saskatchewan	$ 5 000
Manitoba	$ 5 000
Ontario	$ 6 000
Nova Scotia	$ 5 000
New Brunswick	$ 3 000
Prince Edward Island	$ 5 000
Newfoundland	$ 6 000
Yukon	$ 5 000
Northwest Territories	$ 5 000

Common law is also referred to as case law.

the matter within the court's monetary jurisdiction. The *cause of action* means the reason for bringing the claim. It refers to the whole cause of action, not portions of it. If you are claiming damages for several items arising out of the same act of wrongdoing, you cannot claim the items in separate claims.

 **Example**

Suppose two rather unruly individuals were engaged in a fist fight in Saskatoon, Saskatchewan. You, the innocent bystander, just happened to be in the wrong place at the wrong time. As a result, you received a few punches yourself. Your brand new imitation Elvis suit was ripped in several places. The suit cost you $4 900. Your cool shades were also broken, and you had paid $200 to purchase them. Your total damages are now $5 100.

The police report gives the names and addresses of the two rogues. You write them each a demand letter but, after several weeks, hear nothing. You have no insurance coverage, so you decide to sue.

Since you decided to bring your action in Saskatchewan where the cause of action occurred, your small claims court monetary limit is $5 000.

You can do one of two things:

(a) Sue in small claims court for $5 000.

(b) Sue in Court of Queen's Bench for $5 100.

You cannot do any of the following:

(a) Sue for $5 000; then start another action in any court for the balance.

(b) Sue for the Elvis suit and glasses separately, as the damages arose out of the same incident or same cause of action.

3.   Limitation and Notice Periods

If the amount of your claim is suitable for the small claims court in your province or territory, then you can begin the action provided you are within the limitation period.

Beware of deadlines for bringing a claim

You must take certain steps within a certain time frame to ensure that your lawsuit is brought according to law. If you are considering bringing a claim, either do it immediately or get legal advice right away. Only a lawyer can advise you on deadlines for bringing a claim. If you bring an action out of time, it will most likely be dismissed and you will not be able to recover the money you feel is owed to you. Do not procrastinate.

3.1 The limitation period

Limitation periods are deadlines for bringing claims. These may be specified in legislation, judge-made law (common law), or both.

Different limitation periods may apply to different causes of action. An action for breach of contract may have a different limitation period than a tort action (an action that causes damage to person or property, including personal injury, trespass to property, or negligence). Limitation periods may differ for various tort actions as well.

Lawsuits may also be brought to recover damages as a result of the defendant violating a provincial statute. The limitation periods for such actions are usually set out in the particular statute violated or in the statute that sets out limitation periods generally. Consult the government and legislation and law-related Web sites posted on Self-Counsel Press's Web site at <http://www.self-counsel.com/canlaw/smallclaims/resources.html> for the statutes for your province or territory.

Limitation periods are seldom enforced for the time that a plaintiff is a party under disability. For example, if a plaintiff is age 16, the age of majority is 18, and the limitation period is 3 months, the limitation period would not start to run until the plaintiff turned 18.

If you are unsure about how to determine the appropriate limitation period for your particular lawsuit, check with a lawyer. A paralegal is not qualified to give this advice. This is one consultation fee you should not begrudge yourself.

What's in a name?

A *lawyer* is a person who has been specially trained in the study of law. A lawyer is also known as a *barrister and solicitor*. A *barrister* is a lawyer who spends a great deal of time in court. In contrast, a *solicitor* spends a great deal of time solving legal problems and performing legal services in the office. Most lawyers enjoy a blend of activities; hence, *barrister and solicitor*.

A *paralegal* is a person who may appear in court or may assist a party in completing the forms required for court. Some practising paralegals have formal schooling, while others rely on personal experience alone.

An *agent* is a person who appears in court on behalf of a litigant. The agent may be a law student, paralegal, friend, or relative of the litigant. The agent may or may not have formal legal training.

Agents and paralegals are permitted to appear only in the lower courts. Indeed, they are often seen in small claims court and traffic court. They are not qualified to give legal advice but may assist clients in completing paperwork to be used in court.

Example

Julia, an Ontario resident, lost her top-of-the-line television through a break and entry of her house while she was touring Bali. She filed an insurance claim, but the insurance company denied her claim. As a result, a year and one day after discovering the theft, she decided to start an action in small claims court to try to recover what she could not recover through the insurance company.

Unfortunately, Julia is out of time. According to the *Insurance Act*, her court action must have been made within a year of her discovering the theft.

Example

Barnie just obtained his dog licence at the municipal office in the City of Slippery Slopes in British Columbia. As he walked out of the municipal office, he slipped on some ice at the foot of the exit stairs. Barnie broke his collarbone and sustained other injuries. Barnie is furious that the ice wasn't removed and wants to sue the City.

After getting treatment at the hospital, he immediately wrote a letter to the City putting them on notice that he would be starting a lawsuit. Barnie served his letter within the required time (which is two months). Barnie can now start the action any time within the appropriate limitation period (which is six months) after the fall or after discovering injuries resulting from that fall.

Example

Elijah, a New Brunswick resident, read an article in his local newspaper. It stated that Elijah stole money from his employer. Elijah feels that this is completely untrue and wants to sue for defamation. Elijah finds out by reading the New Brunswick *Limitation of Actions* statute that he must bring a claim within two years of learning of the article.

> Limitation periods tend to be quite short for government defendants, utility commissions, and government agencies. Do not procrastinate.

The court may, in extremely rare circumstances, grant an extension of the limitation period if the plaintiff brings the appropriate motion. However, there must be a compelling reason for such an order to be made. Claiming ignorance of your particular limitation period as a reason for delay will not sway the court to grant an extension unless it would be a grave injustice for a claim not to be allowed. If the court grants such an order, it will likely set a stringent date by which the claim must be issued. Read chapter 11 for more on the procedure for bringing a motion or application to request an extension.

3.2 The notice period

In certain situations, a plaintiff is required to bring notice of his or her intention to bring an action *before* actually commencing an action. Most actions against government institutions require that the plaintiff provide notice of his or her intention to sue the government before a claim is commenced. In such cases, the claim would still have to be issued within the appropriate limitation period.

Check specific legislation relating to your cause of action to determine whether a notice period applies to your action. If you are suing for defamation, you would check your province's or territory's legislation relating to defamation (also known as *libel* or *slander*, depending on whether the defamatory statement is written or oral). In doing so, you would ascertain whether you must provide notice of your intention to sue.

If you fail to provide notice within the time allowed, you may not bring a claim even if the limitation period has not expired. Therefore, where necessary, immediately provide notice that you are going to bring a claim and then think about whether or not you still wish to sue within the limitation period.

Notice is required by law in a number of instances. A lawyer should be consulted to give you an opinion on this. Chapter 12 describes how a notice should be written and provides an example.

🍁 Example

Jeremy Tyrol sued Betty Monduc and her employer, *Ontario Whimsical News*, for libel and slander over an article Betty wrote about him in the *Whimsical News*. The *Libel and Slander Act* states that notice must be given to the defendant within six weeks of the time the alleged libel came to the knowledge of the plaintiff. The notice must be in writing, must describe the libelous event, and must be served to an adult at the head office of the defendant in the same manner as you would serve a claim.

If Jeremy did not give her the required written notice, Betty and her employer, *Ontario Whimsical News*, would, in their defence, plead that the action is statute-barred, because the plaintiff failed to provide sufficient notice under the *Libel and Slander Act*.

4. Parties to Sue

You can sue just about anybody except some government officials acting in an official capacity. Your defendants in such cases will be their employers. For example, if a police officer impounds your vehicle or takes your belongings as part of an investigation or the laying of a charge, and your belongings (other than those that are proceeds of crime) are not returned, you would sue the local police department and the officer. Generally, you would name the Chief of Police as a defendant rather than the individual police officer. However, this may vary between provinces and territories, depending on the legislation governing police services and statutes governing the protection of public authorities. You may also need to name a municipality if it is responsible for that police force.

Other than exempted government employees, you can and should (where appropriate) name both an employee and his or her employer as defendants in the same action. Keep in mind that the employer may be able to pay more than the employee and may make collection easier. Likewise, in a partnership, you can and should name as defendants each business partner as well as the partnership itself.

5. The Proper Court Office

Once you have established that small claims court is right for your case, you must determine the appropriate court office in which to start the action. This is known as *establishing territorial jurisdiction*.

Territorial jurisdiction is an important concept because, if you sue in the wrong territory, your case can be transferred to the proper jurisdiction. This transfer causes a delay in the proceedings. If the transfer is ordered as a result of a motion (a hearing at which the request is made) brought by the defendant, you may be responsible for paying the defendant's costs of the motion in addition to those of your own. Worse yet, some courts won't even allow a claim to be issued in their offices if their staff is of the opinion that the claim would be brought in the wrong jurisdiction.

5.1 Determining the correct territory

The general rule for determining the territory in which to have your claim issued is in either the territorial division —

(a) where the cause of action arose, or

(b) where the defendant or any one of the defendants resides or carries on business.

If there is no court office in the town where the defendant resides or carries on business, then the claim must be issued in the court office nearest the place where the defendant resides or carries on business. In such a case, it is probably a good idea to call the court office where you intend to initiate an action and ask if that is, in fact, the appropriate jurisdiction.

If you are not sure where to start an action, ask a clerk at the court office before you act. This will help you avoid having to respond to a motion brought by a defendant to move the case to another jurisdiction. If the trial judge finds that the territorial jurisdiction is incorrect, he or she may order that the matter be tried in the appropriate territorial jurisdiction. Imagine having your witnesses at the courthouse ready to testify, only to be ordered to testify at a later date in another jurisdiction. Sue in the right place!

🍁 Example

The plaintiff lives in Calgary, Alberta. The defendant lives in Edmonton, Alberta, and carries on business in Banff, Alberta, where the plaintiff was employed. The plaintiff is bringing a claim for wrongful dismissal. The plaintiff should bring the action in Banff where the cause of action arose, that is, where the firing took place. However, since there is no small claims court in Banff, the plaintiff would have to bring the claim in the nearest court location, Calgary.

🍁 Example

The plaintiff lives in Winnipeg, Manitoba. She is suing three defendants. One defendant lives in Brandon, Manitoba; the second, lives in Riverton, Manitoba; and the third lives in Thompson, Manitoba. The cause of action arose in Thompson. The plaintiff can sue in Brandon or Riverton where the defendants reside if Thompson is inconvenient for all parties.

 # Example

The plaintiff lives in Thornbury, Ontario, and the defendant lives in Stoney Creek, Ontario, a city within the Region of Hamilton-Wentworth. The plaintiff formed a contract with the defendant in Stoney Creek, but the defendant failed to honour the terms of the contract. The plaintiff wants to sue. He or she can do so in Hamilton, the nearest court office in the Hamilton-Wentworth region. However, the plaintiff would not be able to bring a cause of action in the courts of Niagara Region or Peel Region, even though they are easier to access from Stoney Creek.

5.2 The case of many territories

Sometimes many different cities or towns are involved in different aspects of the interaction between the plaintiff and defendant. For example, a contract may have been formed in one city, acted on in another city, and breached in yet another. In these cases, when it is more complicated to determine territorial jurisdiction, a judge may order a change in venue or jurisdiction.

 # Example

The plaintiff carries on business in Windsor, Ontario. The defendant lives in Hamilton, Ontario. The plaintiff and defendant formed a contract in Toronto, Ontario. Under the terms of the contract, the defendant was to have made payments in London, Ontario. He failed to make payments and the plaintiff wants to sue. Where does the plaintiff commence the action? In London, where the contract was breached? In Toronto, where the contract was formed? Or in Hamilton, where the defendant resides?

The court may order that the action be tried in a particular jurisdiction if it is satisfied that the *balance of convenience* substantially favours holding the trial at a place other than those stipulated by the small claims court rules.

The general practice is to bring the claim wherever the plaintiff deems appropriate. If the defendant is not content with the choice of jurisdiction, the defendant may request a jurisdictional hearing or an order for a change of venue. The procedure for a jurisdictional hearing is discussed in chapter 11.

6. Are You a Person under Disability?

As a general rule, anyone can sue and be sued. However, the court has established special rules for any plaintiff or defendant who is a *person under disability*.

This term is defined in the rules of your particular court. Generally, a person under disability is one of the following:

> ❯ A minor
>
> ❯ Mentally incapable
>
> ❯ An absentee (a person who has disappeared, whose whereabouts are unknown, and about whom no knowledge determines whether he or she is alive or dead)

A person under disability requires a litigation guardian to commence and conduct his or her action.

If a litigation guardian is not required in your case, skip the remainder of this section.

6.1 Who may be a litigation guardian?

Any adult who is not a person under disability may fulfil the role of a litigation guardian. If there is no suitable parent, guardian, or other individual known to the person under disability, a government official may fill that role. **Note:** Legal counsel cannot also fulfil the role of a litigation guardian.

6.2 Role of the litigation guardian

The litigation guardian stands in the shoes of the party suing or being sued. Therefore, it is critical that the litigation guardian does not have an interest in the proceeding that is contrary to that of the person under disability.

Acting as a litigation guardian should not be taken lightly. Some responsibilities include the following:

In Ontario, a minor under age 18 who is mentally competent may sue for under $500 as if he or she were of full age, without the assistance of a litigation guardian. The court must approve any settlement made by that individual.

A litigation guardian is also known as a *next friend*.

- ▶ Drafting pleadings
- ▶ Preparing court forms
- ▶ Negotiating a settlement
- ▶ Assembling evidence
- ▶ Interviewing witnesses
- ▶ Conducting the trial
- ▶ Attending at all court appearances
- ▶ Enforcing the terms of any settlement or judgment
- ▶ Retaining a lawyer if he or she feels that one is required

If the court perceives a litigation guardian to be biased, to be acting contrary to the interests of the person under disability, to be in a conflict of interest, or to be doing an inadequate job in handling the action, the court may remove or replace a litigation guardian, award costs against the litigation guardian personally, or both.

In addition, a litigation guardian is personally responsible for paying any costs of the action.

 **Example**

Winkler is 10 years old. His 18-year-old brother, Preston, robbed Winkler's piggy bank to the tune of $600. Mom, Laurena, is despondent. She has asked Preston to repay Winkler's losses but, after several requests, Preston still refuses.

Would the court approve of Laurena as a litigation guardian for Winkler? Would Laurena be in a conflict of interest? That question depends on how the judge sees it. If a judge found that the mother is in a conflict of interest by acting for one son who is suing another, then the judge may prefer that a more neutral party act as a litigation guardian.

Example

Sarah has been mentally disabled since birth. She is now 23 years old and works daily arranging flowers for Joshua, a florist. All was well until Joshua stopped paying Sarah for her work. Sarah could not, therefore, afford to pay her rent.

Bill, Sarah's landlord, has been keeping a watchful eye over Sarah since her parents died. He is sympathetic to Sarah's situation and does not want to take recourse against her for not paying her rent. Since Sarah has no living relatives capable of helping her, Bill offered to be her litigation guardian and take Joshua to court to recover her salary and compensate himself for her rental arrears.

Would the court approve of Bill as Sarah's litigation guardian? The court would look at all the circumstances of Bill and Sarah's relationship. Bill may be approved as a litigation guardian because of the close relationship and his history of helping her.

However, the court would also examine the reason for the lawsuit and any interest Bill might have in it. The court may consider Bill's involvement questionable. His interest is to get judgment for (settle for) enough money to pay the rent, and he may not be as concerned with the rest of the money Joshua owes to Sarah.

If the court decides that Bill is not a suitable individual to act as litigation guardian, the court may appoint another suitable person or the province's or territory's Public Guardian and Trustee.

❦ Example

Olga and her brother Boris lived in Boris's house for 20 years. Unfortunately, that seemed to end when Boris never returned from his wilderness trip. It has been years since the trip, and nobody knows whether Boris is alive or dead.

A week ago, a neighbourhood vandal named David broke into Boris's house. Olga chased him away. However, the vandal smashed an antique stained glass window in order to break in. Olga has asked David to repay her for the $1 500 it cost for her to replace the glass. Although David said he could not afford to pay, Olga is convinced he can pay and wants to sue him. However, it is Boris's house, so Olga would have to sue on his behalf. Since Boris is an absentee, Olga would like be the litigation guardian.

Would the court approve of Olga as Boris's litigation guardian? Olga has no interest contrary to that of Boris. Olga would not profit from the lawsuit since she simply wants to be reimbursed for the damage done to her brother's house.

🍁 Example

Freda is the proud mom of 16-year-old twins, Wilfred and Wilbur. One day, a bully named Jake beat up Wilbur. Wilfred tried to help his brother, but Jake punched Wilfred and broke his prescription eyeglasses. Jake also damaged Wilbur's leg brace. Freda is furious. She will be suing the school, the Board of Education, and the teachers in charge at recess time when this happened. She also wants to sue the bully, Jake, to recover the $200 it cost to replace Wilfred's eyeglasses and the $550 it cost to replace Wilbur's leg brace.

As discussed in section **2.2**, Freda will have to commence a single action rather than a separate action for each son. Wilfred could sue without a litigation guardian since he is pleading for less than $500 and is mentally competent. However, Wilbur's damages are greater than $500, so he requires a litigation guardian. But since Freda is also suing for $5 000 in punitive damages for the alleged negligence of the teachers, she will have to act as a litigation guardian for both sons.

Would the court approve of Freda as litigation guardian to Wilbur? Since Freda is the mother of both plaintiffs, likely no conflict of interest prevents her from acting on their behalf, nor would she have an interest contrary to that of her sons.

🍁 Example

Jesse is the grandmother and legal guardian of Jake, the 16-year-old bully, whose parents are in jail. The court would probably approve of her acting as litigation guardian. However, Jesse is very frail and requires dialysis. Her lawyer could not take on the role of counsel and be the litigation guardian. The judge may have no recourse but to appoint another suitable person or the Public Guardian and Trustee.

6.3 Commencing an action as litigation guardian

In order to commence a claim on behalf of a person under disability, the litigation guardian must file with the court a document consenting to act as a litigation guardian. You can obtain this pre-printed form from the court office. This form must be filed at the time the claim is issued or as soon as possible after having issued the claim. The litigation guardian then follows the same procedure as any other party to a lawsuit. In cases in which the court orders a person to act as a litigation guardian, no form is required.

6.4 Special powers of the court

The court has special powers over proceedings involving persons under disability. These special powers ensure that the rights of persons under disability are upheld. As a protective measure, the court

> must approve all settlements,

> may remove a litigation guardian at any time,

> may set aside a judgment brought against a person under disability (judgment at trial or default judgment),

> may set aside any step that has been taken to enforce the judgment (e.g., noting the defendant in default, default judgment),

> may require that money owed by or to a person under disability be paid into court or directly to that individual, and

> may award costs that the litigation guardian must pay personally.

Having established all of the above, you are now ready to commence a claim.

3
Preparing the Plaintiff's Claim

You will need to follow certain steps to commence an action (bring a claim). Each of these steps will be discussed in detail in this chapter:

(a) Obtain the claim form from the court office. You may be able to find the claim form on the Internet. Some provinces and territories have placed their forms there for convenient access and downloading. See the links to government Web sites posted on Self-Counsel Press's Web site at <http://www.self-counsel.com/canlaw/smallclaims/resources.html> for the Web site addresses of the various small claims court registries.

If you are a litigation guardian, also obtain the appropriate consent form.

(b) Prepare the claim.

If you are a litigation guardian, also prepare the appropriate consent form.

(c) Photocopy the claim for your records.

(d) Ask the court office to issue the claim. You will be required to pay a fee for this service.

If you are a litigation guardian, also file the consent form.

(e) Serve the claim on the defendant or defendants. If you named a partnership as a defendant (see chapter 4), you may have to obtain an additional court form to provide notice of the claim to each of its partners.

Serve each partner with the claim and notice form. If you do not do this, you will not be able to enforce a judgment against each partner personally.

(f) Obtain from the court office a form that will serve as your affidavit of service. Once prepared, this document will serve as evidence of having served the defendant or defendants with the claim.

(g) Prepare the affidavit of service and have it sworn.

(h) Photocopy the sworn affidavit for your records.

(i) File the affidavit of service with the court office.

The plaintiff's claim, defence, defendant's claim, counterclaim, crossclaim, and third party claim are referred to as *pleadings*. Pleadings are the most important documents the parties will produce.

The *plaintiff's claim* is the plaintiff's version of the dispute between the plaintiff and defendant. It does the following:

> Provides notice to the defendant or defendants and the court that an action has been started

> Names the parties and counsel, if any

> States the addresses of the parties to be used for service

> Pleads the amount for damages

> Pleads that prejudgment interest be awarded

> Provides sufficient details to the defendant and the court so they can be reasonably sure of the case at hand

> Provides the legal basis for the claim, that is, the cause of action

> Provides the sections of the legislation on which the plaintiff is relying

Generally, the court has the power to strike or amend a claim or dismiss or stay the action if the claim does any of the following:

> Discloses no reasonable cause of action

> Is scandalous, frivolous, or vexatious

Although the forms may differ, the principles in this chapter apply to the preparation of a defendant's claim, third party claim, counterclaim, or crossclaim (see chapter 4).

> May prejudice, embarrass, or delay the fair trial of the action

> Is otherwise an abuse of the court's process

1. The Plaintiff's Claim Form and Supporting Documents

Most court offices have pre-printed forms for the plaintiff's claim. In some areas, the pre-printed form must be used or court staff will not issue the claim. Check with your local courthouse staff about which form to use and about the fee they charge for issuing the claim.

Your claim form will include details of the plaintiff, the defendant or defendants, the amount of the claim, the type of claim, and the reasons for bringing the claim. Write all entries to the claim form and any attached documents in concise, non-technical language. As well, a claim must be well thought out and well organized, or the consequences can be disastrous. If you do not pay attention to detail, you may omit important facts or state facts inaccurately or out of sequence. Realize that both the defendant and the court will review the plaintiff's claim for any errors, inaccuracies, omissions, or exaggerations in preparation for trial.

To correct a critical error or omission, you would bring a motion for an order permitting you to amend the claim. As with any motion, the judge has complete discretion to grant or deny the request.

> Court office staff cannot assist you in preparing your claim or any other court document. Also, they cannot give legal advice. Only a lawyer can give legal advice.

1.1 The plaintiff

The person making the claim is called the *plaintiff*. The names of all plaintiffs should appear on the claim if more than one plaintiff is making the claim. If you are using a pre-printed form and run out of space on the form itself, fill in the names that will fit; then repeat those names and the names of the remaining plaintiffs on a separate sheet of paper. Label the separate sheet, "Complete List of Plaintiffs." Write on the form itself, "Complete List of Plaintiffs Is Attached," and then attach the separate sheet to your form.

Be sure to provide the full given name and surname of each plaintiff; initials and nicknames are insufficient. If the plaintiff goes by another name, identify this name as well. For example, "Ruth Anne Smith also known as Anne Smith" or "Ruth Anne Smith a.k.a. Anne Smith."

If the plaintiff is a corporation, identify the corporate name, and if the corporation is a numbered company, include this number. For example, name the plaintiff as "990099 Ontario Ltd. carrying on business as Tom's Towing Service," or "990099 Ontario Ltd. c.o.b. as Tom's Towing Service."

1.2 The defendant

The person being sued is called the *defendant*. The names of all defendants should appear on the claim if more than one person is being sued. Again, if you run out of space on the form itself, fill in the names that will fit; then repeat those names and the names of the remaining defendants on a separate sheet of paper. Label the separate sheet, "Complete List of Defendants." Write on the form itself, "Complete List of Defendants Is Attached," and then attach the separate sheet to your form.

You must name the defendants properly. Use the defendant's full name if he or she is an individual. If the defendant is a corporation, provide the exact name of the company. If you name a specific employee as a defendant, include the employee's name and position in the company. If the defendant is not incorporated (e.g., sole proprietorship or partnership), use the correct name of the business and name the proprietor or the partners in addition to the business name.

Use the correct name

Failure to correctly name a defendant may lead to defeat. You may be able to show all the requisite elements of your case and prove that you have suffered a loss, but, if you have failed to name or have misnamed a defendant, your losses are unlikely to be recovered. A defendant improperly named may bring a motion to dismiss the claim for that very reason.

After the claim is issued, you must serve each defendant named on the claim. Consequently, you must know the street address of each defendant. A post office box is sufficient only when the court needs to mail court documents. In the case of serving an employee or director of a company, you may serve such defendants at their place of business, but the place of business may not accept a claim on their behalf if it is uncertain whether those individuals are still with the company. In that case, it is best to serve such individuals at their personal residences.

1.3 Amount of claim

State the amount of the claim, excluding interest or costs. If relief other than money is requested, state specifically the relief you are seeking (e.g.,

Conducting name searches

A number of services are available that can assist you in your search for the defendant's address. Internet sites can provide information on defendants whose telephone numbers are published. See the links to the people and business search sites posted on Self-Counsel Press's Web site at <http://www.self-counsel.com/canlaw/smallclaims/resources.html>.

Government departments will do a name search for a fee. Private search agencies can also locate defendants, but be sure you ask about their fee in advance.

return of personal property). You should state this relief on a separate sheet of paper and refer to it on the form as a *schedule* (e.g., Schedule 'A,' 'B,' or 'C,' or whatever letter is appropriate). Using schedules will allow you to organize the claim without squeezing everything onto the form itself.

When claiming money, be sure that you understand the concept of damages explained in section **2.** later in this chapter.

1.4 Type of claim

Place a letter *X* in the box next to the type of claim that you are bringing: unpaid account, contract, motor vehicle accident, promissory note, services rendered, NSF cheque, damage to property, lease, or other.

1.5 Reasons for bringing the claim

You must state with reasonable certainty and detail what the claim concerns. Include the date, place, and nature of the occurrences on which the claim is based. The space allotted on this part of the form is seldom enough for most actions. If the space is sufficient, by all means, tell your story on the form itself. However, if you have a lengthy or complex claim, present it on separate sheets of paper marked as schedules.

2. Organizing Your Claim

Organize your pleadings so as to make them clear, neat, and orderly. Remember, if nobody understands what you are pleading, you are less likely to get everything you want and you may risk paying costs to the defendants for causing them to make unnecessary preparations. Organized pleadings will also allow you to reflect on your claim to ensure that you have recalled and included all critical details, issues, or remedies.

Consider dividing your claim into the following sections:

(a) Remedy sought

(b) Facts in chronological order (Schedule 'A')

(c) Documentary evidence (Schedule 'B')

(d) Excerpts from legislation (Schedule 'C')

Remember, though, that not every claim will require all sections; use whatever applies to your particular claim.

2.1 Remedy sought

Use the remedy sought section to state what you want to achieve if your claim is successful. You may wish to claim general, special, punitive damages, or any combination of these damages. You will also want to seek interest.

2.1.a General damages

General damages reinstate what you lost as a result of the defendant's conduct (and no more). (In Nova Scotia, costs for inconvenience and expense for attending at trial are referred to as *general damages*. Therefore, in that province, think about this section as just *damages* or the *amount claimed*.)

Some examples of general damages include the following:

▸ Reimbursement for repairs

▸ Repayment of a loan

▸ Payment of salary owed

▸ Payment of money owed under a contract

▸ Payment of money and cost to replace an NSF cheque

In the general damages section, you should also specify remedies such as the return of personal property. Be sure to list on a separate schedule to be attached to the claim which personal property is to be returned.

If you do not plead for the return of personal property, you will not be able to obtain judgment for the delivery of property or goods to you.

🍁 Example

Anita was locked out of her apartment when the landlord changed the lock on the entrance door following an order allowing him to evict her. Anita did not have an opportunity to retrieve her personal belongings from the apartment. The landlord refuses to speak with her, so she is forced to bring a claim.

Anita must specify in her claim that she is seeking a judgment ordering the landlord to deliver her personal belongings to her. She should list those items (e.g., clothes, shoes, dishes, tape recorder, VCR, television) on a separate sheet, attach it to the claim, and refer to it as Schedule 'B' (or other appropriate letter). Of course, she will need to prove later in the proceedings that she owned the listed items.

🍁 Example

Pam and Patrick wrote an activity book for children. They sent out dozens of copies to specialty bookstores. One of the bookstores has not paid them for the books they sold on their behalf. The store has also not returned unsold copies. Since they did not receive a response to their demand letter, they are bringing a claim. They must specify in their claim that they would like an order for the delivery of the unsold books and money for books sold.

2.1.b Special damages

Special damages are damages that you may incur as a result of the defendant's conduct. They can include the following:

➤ Loss of income (in the case of a personal injury or wrongful dismissal case)

➤ Loss of business opportunity

➤ Loss of enjoyment of life

➤ Loss of earning potential

➤ Loss of enjoyment of personal belongings

2.1.c Punitive damages

Punitive damages are damages over and above general and special damages. They are awarded only to punish the defendant and are awarded to deter the defendant from engaging in such behaviour in the future. The defendant must have acted in a serious, despicable way for the court to consider awarding punitive damages. Punitive damages may be awarded in cases in which the following occurred:

> The behaviour was clearly despicable.

> An adult has breached the trust of a child.

> An employer has acted grossly unfairly.

> The defendant has acted in bad faith.

> The defendant has committed a crime.

> The wrong done is socially unacceptable.

> The defendant is an advantage-taker.

2.1.d Interest

Prejudgment interest is the interest payable from the cause of action to the date of judgment. You must plead prejudgment interest or you will not likely receive it. Even if you plead it, the court will use its discretion to award it. The court will also determine the period for which prejudgment interest is appropriate.

 Example

If the claim for prejudgment interest is brought just inside the six-year limitation period for a contract, the judge may refuse to grant six-years' worth of prejudgment interest. The judge may exercise discretion and reduce the period in any number of ways:

> Prejudgment interest should apply from the time the first demand letter is sent to the defendant.

> The plaintiff should not be awarded interest for the entire prejudgment period because he or she waited deliberately before bringing the claim so as to make the defendant pay more in prejudgment interest.

> The plaintiff should not be awarded interest for the entire prejudgment period because the defendant was

not aware that damages flowed from his or her actions. In that case, a judge may decide to make prejudgment interest payable as of the time the defendant was likely to have found out (by hearing about it from a friend, for example).

If the rate of interest has not been pre-determined by the parties (e.g., in a contract), then the amount may be set in accordance with your provincial legislation or at a rate set by the judge. If the interest rate has been set by a contract, then you must indicate this in your claim. For example, the line should read, "Prejudgment interest at 24 percent per annum in accordance with an agreement between the parties."

You may also have the right to earn *postjudgment interest* on the amount of a judgment. Postjudgment interest is the interest on the amount awarded on judgment. The judge may, for whatever reason, refuse to award it, but that is rarely the case. It is almost always awarded unless evidence proves an extreme case of financial hardship on the part of the judgment debtor.

> Section 347 of the Criminal Code makes it a criminal offence for anyone to charge interest rates higher than 60 percent.

2.2 Facts in chronological order (Schedule 'A')

State the facts leading to the lawsuit in the order in which they occurred. You may wish to use separate headings for distinctly separate causes of action (e.g., if suing both in contract and in negligence).

2.3 Documentary evidence (Schedule 'B')

If your claim is based on a document, then attach a copy of the document to your claim. Examples of documents that should be included are a contract, a bad cheque, a lease agreement, or a promissory note.

Each document that you submit as evidence should be referred to as an *Exhibit*. For example:

> Exhibit 1: Contract

> Exhibit 2: Invoice

> Exhibit 3: Medical Report

Never attach an original document to a claim. Always bring the originals to the trial, however, if you have them. If you are unable to include a copy of the document, you must provide reasons within the claim to explain why this was not done (e.g., document was destroyed in a house fire, or document was submitted to Revenue Canada and is being requested).

If you know where the document can be found (e.g., with a government office, employer, hospital, or other institution), request it; then file a copy with the court and serve a copy on each party as soon as it arrives. Chapter 12 provides sample request letters.

In most provinces and territories, you must serve all documents you intend to use at trial at least 14 days before trial.

2.4 Excerpts from legislation (Schedule 'C')

You may wish to include photocopied sections of the legislation on which your claim is relying. You can get these from the law section of larger municipal libraries and often from the Internet (see the links to legislation and law-related Web sites posted on Self-Counsel Press's Web site at <http://www.self-counsel.com/canlaw/smallclaims/resources.html>. Each excerpt should be referred to as a numbered exhibit, continuing the numbering from where you left off numbering your Schedule 'B' exhibits. For example:

▶ Exhibit 4: Appropriate Sections of the Negligence Act

▶ Exhibit 5: Appropriate Sections of the Insurance Act

▶ Exhibit 6: Appropriate Sections of the Occupier's Liability Act

Attaching sheets to your claim

If you are attaching sheets to your claim as suggested, follow these steps:

▶ Write "See Attached Schedule" in the space on the form allotted for reasons.

▶ Label the first page of each schedule with the name of the schedule (e.g., Schedule 'A').

▶ Number your claim using continuous numbering throughout; that is, do not start numbering page one of Schedule 'B' as page one if it is page four of the claim.

▶ Do not count the form in your numbering; number only the attached sheets.

▶ Be sure to photocopy all schedules to be attached to the form.

▶ Attach the schedule or schedules to the form before presenting the claim to the court office.

The plaintiff must outline with sufficient certainty the nature of what is claimed and why it is claimed. It is important to think this out thoroughly and proofread it carefully, because the court will likely not be inclined to grant an award if it has not been specifically requested.

When you have completed your claim, read it over to ensure that it makes sense. Before you go any further, check your claim for accuracy, completeness, and effectiveness by working through Checklist 1 at the end of this chapter.

When you are satisfied with your work, you are ready to have a small claims court clerk issue the claim.

Sample claims are presented in chapter 12.

3. Issuing the Plaintiff's Claim

Before serving a claim on the defendant, you must first have it issued by the court office. To have a claim issued, take the following to the court office within the limitation period:

> The original copy of the claim

> One copy of the claim, including attachments, for each defendant

> One copy of the claim, including attachments, for yourself

> The fee for issuing the claim

Note: The fee may increase if you file a large number of claims.

The court clerk will issue the claim by dating, signing, and sealing the claim and assigning it a court file number. The court keeps the original copy in the court file but also signs a copy for each defendant.

In most jurisdictions, the smalls claims court office will accept only cash and certified cheques. Few court offices accept personal cheques, credit cards, and debit cards. To avoid surprises and risk missing a limitation period, take cash or a certified cheque.

4. Serving the Plaintiff's Claim

Service or *serving a claim* mean that a copy of the claim is delivered to the actual party named on the claim. In most provinces and territories, the plaintiff, not the court, is responsible for serving the claim. Read through chapter 13 before having your claim served.

If you know that the defendant is represented by a lawyer or agent, you must serve the lawyer or agent, not the defendant. If you are not sure whether the defendant is represented by a lawyer or agent, serve the defendant.

Once the claim is issued, the plaintiff must serve the claim within the appropriate time limit. The court may extend time for service at the request of the plaintiff before or after the time for service has passed. An extension is brought by motion. As with any motion, you must convince the court that you have a good reason for seeking an order to extend the time for service. See chapter 11 for the correct procedure for bringing a motion.

When a defendant has been served in accordance with the rules, you can say that service has been *effected*. The serving party should be prepared to provide proof that all defendants have been served with the claim.

Proof of service is most often provided in a document called an *affidavit of service*. The server swears in that affidavit that the defendant was served and outlines how that service was carried out. In some areas, proof may be provided orally at trial or in a document called a *certificate of service*. See chapter 12 for more information on service.

5. What Happens Next?

Issuing and serving the claim are the first in a series of activities. After you have completed these first two steps, a number of things might happen, many depending on the defendant's response or lack of response to the claim. Table 4 presents a summary of events that may occur next and tells you where to find information about them.

Yukon residents, note:

The court may order a discovery on motion if the court is satisfied that special circumstances make it necessary in the interests of justice.

A *discovery* is an examination at which the parties ask questions of each other about the lawsuit.

The purpose is to uncover information to facilitate settlement negotiations, narrow issues for trial, and to delve deeper into the allegations and defences made in the pleadings overall.

The presiding official has great discretion as to how the discovery is conducted and may make any order, including an order for the costs of the discovery.

TABLE 4
WHAT MAY HAPPEN AFTER ISSUING AND SERVING A CLAIM

IF	YOU SHOULD	AND CONSULT CHAPTER
The defendant files a defence past the time the rules allow	➤ Promptly assess whether you should bring a motion to have the defence struck	➤ 11
The defendant does not file a defence within the time allotted by the rules	➤ Promptly initiate default proceedings	➤ 3
The defendant admits liability for the entire claim and proposes terms of payment	➤ Dispute the terms within the time the rules allow, otherwise you will have to adhere to those terms	➤ 3
The defendant admits liability for the entire claim but does not propose terms of payment	➤ Request a payment hearing from the court	➤ 3
The defendant files a defence disputing only part of the claim but does not propose terms of payment	➤ Promptly review the defence ➤ Request a terms of payment hearing from the court	➤ 3
The defendant files a defence disputing the entire claim	➤ Promptly review the defence to determine which action to take ➤ Wait for a notice of settlement conference or assess whether you should request one yourself	➤ 3 and 7
The defendant proposes terms of payment (in admitting either partial or full liability) but does not pay as proposed	➤ Request judgment for the unpaid balance of the undisputed amount	➤ 11
You need to make changes to a document filed with the court	➤ Take steps immediately upon discovering that you need to make a change	➤ 5

TABLE 4 — Continued

IF	YOU SHOULD	AND CONSULT CHAPTER
You wish to strike all or part of the defence	➤ Assess whether you should bring a motion or application, considering a number of factors	➤ 5
You wish to withdraw your claim	➤ Assess whether you should withdraw the claim, considering a number of factors	➤ 5
You must appear on a motion or application brought by the defendant	➤ Respond to the motion or application	➤ 11
You must bring a motion	➤ Bring the motion	➤ 11
An unexpected event happens	➤ Deal with the event	➤ 5
You wish to negotiate a settlement or attend at a settlement conference	➤ Consider your terms, then try to settle	➤ 6 and 7
You wish to set the action down for trial	➤ Pay the fee and ask the court office to set the action down for trial	➤ 8

Northwest Territories residents, note:

If the amount claimed is greater than $1 000, the judge may, on application, order a discovery.

6. Default Proceedings

If the defendant fails to file a defence within the permitted time, you can initiate default proceedings. But you must wait until the waiting period lapses. The waiting period for commencing default proceedings may differ depending on the manner in which the claim was served. For example, if the claim was served by mail, the waiting period will be longer, to account for mailing time. Call the courthouse for information on the waiting period for your action.

6.1 Noting the defendant in default

If the defendant has not disputed your claim, then you should ask the court clerk to note the defendant in default and file a *notice of default judgment*. The clerk can do so only if you have filed your affidavit of service, and you have filed an affidavit swearing that you brought the action in the proper jurisdiction, in the case of a defendant who has been served outside of the court's jurisdiction.

In Ontario, the affidavit swearing that you brought the action in the proper jurisdiction is called an *affidavit establishing proper forum*.

If you do not file the affidavit swearing that you brought the action in the proper jurisdiction, the court may either deny your request or request that you attend before a judge to provide evidence that the claim was brought in the correct jurisdiction.

When the court notes the defendant in default, the court office will notify the defendant.

Put it in writing

Although the rules allow verbal requests for the defendant to be noted in default, for greater certainty, you may prefer to put it in writing. However, an attendance at the court office will allow you to both note the defendant in default and obtain a notice of default judgment.

Note: The noting in default may not apply to your jurisdiction.

The court has discretion as to whether to note the defendant in default. The following are some examples of cases in which the court has refused to note the defendant in default:

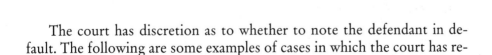

> The plaintiff has not filed an affidavit of service on a particular defendant with the court.

> The plaintiff has not filed an affidavit establishing proper forum with the court, thus preventing the court from verifying that the plaintiff brought the claim in the correct jurisdiction.

> The plaintiff presented the court with an NSF cheque when the court issued the claim and the court cannot proceed any further until the plaintiff pays the court and pays a service charge for processing the bad cheque.

> The defendant has contacted the court requesting that he or she not be noted in default, because filing a defence is not possible within the time permitted for a very good reason.

6.2 Default judgment

Once the court notes the defendant in default, you should try to obtain a default judgment. To obtain a default judgment, take the following steps:

(a) Obtain from the court office the correct form for requesting a (default) judgment.

(b) Prepare the form.

(c) Obtain and prepare the affidavit that is to accompany the form.

(d) Swear the affidavit in support of the request for (default) judgment. Do this by attending before a commissioner of oaths, who may be a lawyer or another person designated as a commissioner of oaths. You may swear the affidavit at the court office if a commissioner of oaths is present at the time you attend.

(e) Take a copy of your sworn affidavit for your records.

(f) Mail or take to the court office the form and affidavit, along with the fee.

(g) The court office may issue a default judgment if it is satisfied that the amount claimed is a debt or a liquidated (easily determined) demand in money, plus any interest requested in the claim.

(h) The court clerk will serve by mail notice of the default judgment on all parties named in the claim.

If more than one defendant is named in the plaintiff's claim, you may initiate default proceedings against any defendant who fails to file a defence. This is a fail-safe strategy that ensures you can collect on the judgment from any one of the defendants against whom judgment or default judgment is rendered. If you find yourself in this situation, obtain a default judgment only if you are quite sure that you will be able to enforce the total amount of the judgment against the defendant noted in default. Before you go any further, check your claim for accuracy, completeness, and effectiveness by working through Checklist 2 at the end of this chapter.

6.3 Damages assessment and adjudication hearing

Damages can be divided into two categories: liquidated and unliquidated.

6.3.a Liquidated damages

Liquidated damages refer to damages the amount of which the court can easily determine, thereby allowing the court to grant damages without further proof. Examples include the following:

> Damage resulting from a breach of contract in which the contract specifies what happens in the event of a breach (e.g., how much money will have to be paid in the event of a breach)

> Damages in the form of failing to pay an invoice, if that invoice makes it clear that the person invoiced is responsible for paying the amount requested

> Damages in the form of a debt in which the debt could be a loan or a credit card balance and when uncertainty does not veil the terms of the agreement

Generally speaking, if you are claiming liquidated damages and the defendant has defaulted, you may obtain default judgment without proving the damages at trial.

6.3.b Unliquidated damages

Unliquidated damages refer to damages the amount of which are not easily determined by the court, thereby requiring that evidence as to damages be brought before the court before damages can be granted. Examples include the following:

> Damage resulting from a breach of contract in which the contract does not specify what happens in the event of a breach

> Damage done by a service person (e.g., backhoe driver, dry cleaner, hairdresser, or tradesperson). In such cases, the court must be convinced that repairs were reasonable and that repair costs were applied only to remedy the damage done and not to add to the value of the object or property repaired (i.e., that repairs were not done to gain economic advantage)

> Damages in the form of an injury when medical proof and proof of medical expenses and loss of income are required

Claims for unliquidated damages must be proven because they are not obvious from the claim itself. In such cases, you should request a damages assessment hearing. The court clerk will advise you of a hearing date for this "mini trial" on the issue of damages. You should then read chapters 8 and 9 to learn how to prepare for and conduct your hearing.

In Nova Scotia, a damages assessment hearing is called an *adjudication hearing*.

The clerk does not notify the defendant of a damages assessment hearing. Defendants do not participate in these hearings because, by failing to file a defence, they have lost their rights to dispute any part of the claim.

Refer to chapter 11 for the correct procedure to follow in proving your damages.

7. Dealing with the Defence

A defendant who wishes to admit liability for all or part of the claim would be wise to settle the claim to avoid having judgment entered against him or her. However, a defendant might respond to the claim in other ways.

7.1 Defendant admits liability for a portion of the claim

When a defence is filed and the defendant admits responsibility for only part of the claim, the plaintiff may request default judgment on the portion for which liability is admitted.

❦ Example

In response to a claim for a broken bicycle and injuries to the plaintiff riding it, the defendant might admit to damaging the bicycle but deny that the plaintiff was injured in the process. In such a case, the defendant is admitting to only one of two allegations.

Obtaining a default judgment on the undefended portion simply settles that portion of the claim. The plaintiff may proceed to trial on the issues still in dispute.

7.2 Defendant admits liability for the entire claim

The defendant may file a defence in which he or she admits liability for the entire claim. Although this seldom happens, in this situation the defendant would be wise to settle the claim to avoid having judgment entered against him or her.

If the defendant is unable to pay the entire amount right away, he or she may propose terms of payment. For example, the defendant may offer to pay a certain amount of money into court each month.

Decide whether the payment terms are satisfactory and make your acceptance or refusal of those terms known to the defendant and the court. Refer to chapter 11 for guidance about how to proceed with terms of payment from this point onward.

7.3 Defendant disputes the entire claim

If the defendant disputes the entire claim, you are on your way to trial and other procedures may become necessary. The rest of this book will guide you through the remainder of your case.

8. Withdrawing the Claim

If you settle your action or decide that you no longer wish to pursue it, you may withdraw the claim in writing. The letter or form, if required, must be filed with the court. You should also send a copy to each party. Chapter 12 provides an example of a claim withdrawal letter.

9. After Judgment

If you have obtained default judgment or judgment following a damages assessment hearing, it is critical that you read chapter 10. That chapter will introduce you to various options for enforcing the judgment.

CHECKLIST 1
PREPARING THE PLAINTIFF'S CLAIM

- ❏ Is the claim clear?
  - ❏ Did you write in plain English?
  - ❏ Are events in the correct sequence?
  - ❏ Will your claim make sense to a reader who, like the judge, may never have met your client or have heard a case with that fact pattern before?
  - ❏ Does the claim present your story in a way that will be clear to a judge who has no knowledge of the facts or familiarity with the parties or their roles in the dispute?

- ❏ Is the claim accurate?
  - ❏ Did you check to ensure that you have not called the defendant by the plaintiff's name or the plaintiff by the defendant's name?
  - ❏ Did you check your spelling and grammar?

- ❏ Is the claim complete?
  - ❏ Have you identified all the parties?
  - ❏ Have you included all the relevant information?
  - ❏ Did you attach all supporting schedules and documents?
  - ❏ If you named a partnership as a defendant, did you prepare notice for each partner?

HAVING THE CLAIM ISSUED
- ❏ Was a remedy requested?
  - ❏ Did you include a request for prejudgment interest?
  - ❏ Did you include a request for general damages?
  - ❏ Did you include a request for special damages?
  - ❏ Did you include a request for punitive damages?
  - ❏ Did you request all available remedies (e.g., delivery of personal property)?
  - ❏ Did you include the correct dollar amounts?

- ❏ Did you present to the court office the following:
  - ❏ the original copy of the claim;
  - ❏ one copy of the claim, including attachments, for each defendant;
  - ❏ one copy of the claim, including attachments, for yourself; and
  - ❏ the fee for issuing the claim?

SERVING THE CLAIM
- ❏ Did you serve the claim on all defendants in the action in accordance with chapter 13?
- ❏ Did you complete an affidavit of service and have it sworn?
- ❏ Did you file the affidavit of service with the court office?

CHECKLIST 2
CHECKLIST FOR DEFAULT PROCEEDINGS

NOTING THE DEFENDANT IN DEFAULT

❏ If you served a plaintiff outside the jurisdiction in which you had the claim issued:
    ❏ Did you complete an affidavit establishing that you properly served the defendant?
    ❏ Did you file the affidavit with the court office?

❏ Did you make a written request to the court that the defendant be noted in default?

REQUESTING DEFAULT JUDGMENT

❏ Did you prepare a notice of default judgment?
    ❏ Did you make a photocopy of the default judgment for your records?

❏ Did you prepare and swear the affidavit supporting default judgment?
    ❏ Did you make a photocopy of the sworn affidavit for your records?

❏ Did you ask the court to issue default judgment by:
    ❏ filing the notice of default judgment;
    ❏ filing an affidavit supporting default judgment; and
    ❏ paying the appropriate fee?

DAMAGES ASSESSMENT HEARING

❏ Did you set the matter down for trial on the damages (damages assessment hearing) by:
    ❏ sending a written request to the court; and
    ❏ paying the appropriate fee?

❏ Did you prepare for the damages assessment hearing?
    ❏ Did you read the appropriate section of chapter 11?

AFTER JUDGMENT

❏ If you obtained default judgment or judgment following a damages assessment hearing, did you enforce the judgment, if necessary?
    ❏ Did you read chapter 10?

4
The Defence and Defence-Related Claims

So, you've been sued. It's not the end of the world. Even if you are at fault, you can find ways to save face and repair relationships between parties.

Your case is simple if all of the appropriate defendants are named in the plaintiff's claim and if you do not have a claim against any plaintiff or defendant. Each defendant named in the plaintiff's claim then simply files a defence on his or her own behalf. However, you may find yourself involved in a more complicated lawsuit that includes one or more defence-related claims.

1. Respond on Time

Before we turn to aspects of responding to a claim, you should be aware of how important it is to respond to a claim in a timely manner. Remember the following:

(a) You must file a defence within the appropriate time limit.

(b) You may also need to file a defence-related claim within the appropriate time limit: a counterclaim, crossclaim, third party claim, or defendant's claim.

(c) It takes time to determine whether the claim has been brought properly.

(d) It takes time to determine whether the claim provides enough information for you to respond to the allegations.

(e) It takes time to reflect on the allegations in the claim.

(f) It takes time and effort to gather evidence in support of your position.

(g) It takes time and effort to prepare your defence and file it with the court.

(h) It takes time and effort to file a counterclaim, crossclaim, or third party claim and have the court process it.

(i) All of this takes more time if a litigation guardian must be involved.

(j) If you fail to file a defence, you will be subjected to default proceedings, which could be costly and irreversible. If you are a litigation guardian, then you, personally, must pay costs.

(k) If you fail to file a counterclaim, crossclaim, or third party claim, you could wrongly end up taking full responsibility for something you may not have done.

This book refers to the counterclaim, crossclaim, and third party claim as *defence-related claims*. In Ontario, the rules give these pleadings the same name, the *defendant's claim*.

To get started, calculate your deadline for filing a defence using Table 5. Once you have established your filing deadline, take the steps that will lead you to filing a defence and, if necessary, issuing a defence-related claim. These steps are described in the next few sections.

A defence by any other name . . .

In Newfoundland, the defence is called a *response*.

In British Columbia and Yukon, the defence is called a *reply*.

In Alberta, New Brunswick, and Prince Edward Island, the defence is called a *dispute note*.

In Ontario and Nova Scotia, the defence is just a *defence*.

In Manitoba and Saskatchewan, the defence is presented orally at trial.

TABLE 5

PROVINCIAL AND TERRITORIAL DEADLINES FOR FILING A DEFENCE

PROVINCE OR TERRITORY	DEADLINE FOR FILING A DEFENCE
Northwest Territories	File a defence within 25 days of being served with the claim.
Yukon	File a reply within 20 days of being served with the claim.
British Columbia	File a defence within 14 days of being served with the notice of claim.
Alberta	File a dispute note within 20 days of being served with the civil claim.
Saskatchewan	The matter proceeds directly to trial following service of the claim.
Manitoba	The matter proceeds directly to trial following service of the claim. File a Notice of Intention to Appear within seven days of being served with the claim.
Ontario	File a defence within 20 days of being served with the plaintiff's claim.
New Brunswick	File a response within 30 days of being served with the claim.
Nova Scotia	File a defence within 10 days of being served with the claim.
Prince Edward Island	File a dispute note within 20 days of being served with the claim.
Newfoundland	File a response within 30 days of being served with the claim.

2. Are You a Person under Disability?

As a general rule, anyone can sue and be sued. However, the court has established special rules for any plaintiff or defendant who fits into the definition of *person under disability*. Refer to chapter 2 for details of the rules concerning persons under disability.

An action against a person under disability must be defended by a litigation guardian. In order to defend an action on behalf of a person under disability, the litigation guardian must file a consent with the court when the defence is filed. The litigation guardian should then follow the same procedures as all other parties to the lawsuit.

3. Reflecting on the Defence

If the plaintiff has done his or her job properly you will, by reading the claim, recognize all the essential ingredients for properly defending the claim. You will know who is suing you, what the party is claiming, and why. You will also know the location of the court office in which the claim was issued and when it was issued.

Although a time limit for filing your defence with the court may apply (see Table 5), it is important that you take time to reflect carefully on it. If this is the first time you have prepared a defence, we recommend that you plan your defence as suggested in this chapter. This exercise is useful even if you live in Manitoba or Saskatchewan and will only be presenting a defence orally at trial.

3.1 Gathering information about the claim

A careful examination of each paragraph of the claim will allow you to defend yourself against each allegation and agree or disagree with the facts as the plaintiff has set them out. You may also need to consider preparing a defence-related claim and you must not overlook this possibility.

Photocopy the plaintiff's claim and work from that copy, leaving the original intact. Mark your copy using the following codes:

- ❯ Place the letter *A* next to a statement that you wish to admit.
- ❯ Place the letter *D* next to a statement that you wish to deny.
- ❯ Place the letter *U* next to a statement about which you have no knowledge.

Some words you should know

A *statement* is a fact set out in the claim from the perspective of the plaintiff.

For example, "John Doe was at all material times an employee of the plaintiff" or "Jane Doe was the operator of the crane that the defendant owned."

An *allegation* is a statement that accuses the defendant of either doing or not doing something he or she should have done, or doing or not doing something he or she should not have done.

🍁 Example

> "The defendant suddenly and without warning struck the plaintiff on the face."

> "The defendant failed to comply with the terms of the agreement."

> "The defendant failed to exercise reasonable care in riding his bicycle."

Liability means responsibility for an action or lack of an action. If a defendant is found liable, that defendant is considered to have been responsible for the damages.

Damages refer to all negative consequences that an action or lack of action has caused. Damages also refers to the compensation sought or awarded for such negative consequences.

🍁 Example

> Actual physical damage to property

> Pain and suffering

> Financial losses

> Inconvenience and expense

3.2 Categorizing the information

Before you can begin writing your defence, you should categorize the statements of fact and allegations made in the plaintiff's claim. This exercise will allow a precise analysis of the claim and ensure that you do not miss anything crucial. Try the following recommended procedure.

3.2.a Organize the statements of fact

Organize the statements of fact, one per line, into a chart as follows:

Column 1   Summarize the statement of fact and indicate the paragraph of the claim in which each fact appears

Column 2   If the statement is correct, write a letter *Y* for *Yes*; otherwise, write a letter *N* for *No*

| | Column 3 | If column 2 contains an *N*, state your version of that statement of fact |
| | Column 4 | If you provided a different version of a statement in column 3 and you can prove that your version occurred, write a letter *Y* in column 4, otherwise, write a letter *N* |

1 STATEMENT OF FACT IN PLAINTIFF'S CLAIM	2 IS IT CORRECT?	3 INCORRECT STATEMENT; DEFENDANT'S VERSION IS . . .	4 CAN DEFENDANT PROVE IT?
Fact 1, Paragraph X in claim:	Y		Y
Fact 2, Paragraph X in claim:	N		N
Fact 3: (and so on . . .)			

3.2.b Organize the allegations of liability

Organize the allegations of liability into a chart as follows, one per line:

	Column 1	Summarize the allegation
	Column 2	If you are willing to admit liability for the allegation, write a letter *Y* for *Yes*; otherwise, write a letter *N* for *No*
	Column 3	If column 2 contains a letter *N*, state why you refuse to admit liability by choosing a reason from Table 6
	Column 4	If you stated a reason in column 3 and you can prove that you should not be liable, write a letter *Y* in column 4; otherwise, write a letter *N*

1 ALLEGATION OF LIABILITY	2 ADMIT LIABILITY?	3 DO NOT ADMIT LIABILITY BECAUSE . . .	4 CAN DEFENDANT PROVE IT?
Allegation 1, Paragraph X in claim:	Y		Y
Allegation 2, Paragraph X in claim:	N		?
Allegation 3: (and so on . . .)			

3.2.c Organize the allegations of damages

Organize the allegations of damages, one per line, into a chart as follows:

Column 1   Summarize the alleged damages

Column 2   If you are willing to admit that damages occurred as alleged, write a letter Y; otherwise, write a letter N

Column 3   If column 2 contains a letter N, state why you disagree by choosing a reason from Table 7

Column 4   If you stated a reason in column 3 and you can prove that you should not be liable, write a letter Y in column 4; otherwise, write a letter N

1 ALLEGATION OF DAMAGES IN PLAINTIFF'S CLAIM	2 DAMAGES EXIST AS ALLEGED?	3 DAMAGES DO NOT EXIST AS ALLEGED BECAUSE...	4 CAN DEFENDANT PROVE IT?
Allegation 1:	Y		Y
Allegation 2:	N		?
Allegation 3: (and so on . . .)			

TABLE 6
REASONS YOU MAY NOT ADMIT LIABILITY

REASON YOU DO NOT ADMIT LIABILITY	EXAMPLES
1. There is fault on the part of the plaintiff.	► The plaintiff could have prevented this act by doing certain acts (specify) or not doing certain acts (specify).
2. There is an alternative explanation for the alleged damages.	► I did not do the alleged act. ► It was an accident beyond my control. ► It was an act of God (e.g., earthquake). ► There was no contract or agreement. ► That was not my understanding of that term in the contract.
3. The plaintiff owes me money or has my things. **PREPARE A COUNTERCLAIM (DEFENDANT'S CLAIM IN ONTARIO) IN ADDITION TO A DEFENCE.**	► The plaintiff owes me money so I held the goods back. ► The plaintiff did not return my deposit. ► The plaintiff owes me more money than I owe.
4. Somebody else is responsible for the damages. **PREPARE A CROSSCLAIM OR THIRD PARTY CLAM (DEFENDANT'S CLAIM IN ONTARIO) IN ADDITION TO A DEFENCE.**	► Someone else was overseeing the actions that I was doing. ► Someone else was ordering me to act or not act in a certain way. ► Someone else had been doing a certain act (specify) that caused the damages. ► Someone else did something that caused me to do a certain act (specify) to the plaintiff.

TABLE 7

REASONS YOU DO NOT AGREE WITH DAMAGES

REASON YOU DO NOT AGREE WITH DAMAGES	EXAMPLES
1. I did commit the alleged act, but this action did not cause the plaintiff's damages.	▶ My bumper did make contact with the plaintiff's fence but it did not cause the damages alleged.
2. The damages were *de minimus* (so minor that this claim is frivolous).	▶ The damages are so small that there is no virtually no damage at all. ▶ The damage was minimal, but the plaintiff recovered his or her losses through mitigation.
3. The plaintiff failed to mitigate damages.	▶ The plaintiff has not done anything to reduce his or her damages.
4. Other reasons . . .	

3.3 Recognizing procedural problems in the plaintiff's claim

Look for potential procedural problems in the claim by working through the following questions.

3.3.a Was the claim properly prepared?

If the small claims court rules require that a claim be prepared using a particular form, and the plaintiff has not used that form, challenge the validity of the claim. Note that the court has discretion to accept the claim under a particular set of circumstances.

3.3.b Was the claim properly issued?

If the claim has not been properly issued or the court did not issue it at all, ask the court to dismiss it. You may be required to bring a motion or application to do this, or you may be able to dismiss an improper claim outright.

3.3.c Was the claim brought in the appropriate court?

Territorial jurisdiction refers to the court office or area that has jurisdiction to hear the action.

The general practice is to bring the claim wherever the plaintiff deems appropriate, unless the rules provide otherwise. The territory or jurisdiction in which the claim should be brought is where the trial will be held.

If you are not content with the plaintiff's choice of jurisdiction, you may request a jurisdictional hearing or a motion or application for a court order for a change of venue.

Note: The court may order that the action be tried in another jurisdiction if it is satisfied that the balance of convenience substantially favours holding the trial at that place. In determining the balance of convenience, the judge will evaluate a number of factors:

▸ The locale where most of the witnesses live

▸ The area in which the plaintiff and defendant live

▸ Whether evidence or witnesses can be relocated with relative ease, especially if access is an issue for witnesses or parties

▸ Other factors brought to the attention of the judge

Arguments for both sides must be persuasive, requiring a review of the law in this area. Often, however, common sense prevails.

Table 8 displays rules for choosing territorial jurisdiction.

3.3.d Was the claim brought within the appropriate limitation period?

A claim must be brought within the limitation period that applies to the province or territory where the cause of action arose. If it is not brought within that time, you may bring a motion or application to have the claim dismissed.

You should also deal with a missed limitation period in the defence. The defence should include a statement such as, "The claim was commenced outside the limitation period in accordance with the Limitations Act (*and/or any other relevant legislation*) and should be dismissed."

The court may, in extremely rare circumstances, grant an extension of the limitation period on the plaintiff's motion or application. However, a

TABLE 8
CHOOSING A TERRITORIAL JURISDICTION

PROVINCIAL OR TERRITORIAL JURISDICTION	

Northwest Territories	▶ where a sitting of the Territorial Court is held, nearest to the place where:
	  • the cause of action arose; or
	  • the defendant or any of the defendants reside
	▶ unless a different place of trial is requested in the defence, the trial will be held at the place named in the claim

Yukon	▶ the rules are silent on jurisdiction — check local practice with the court office
British Columbia	▶ where the defendant resides or carries on business; or ▶ where the cause of action arose
Alberta	▶ where, in the opinion of the clerk, the defendant or one of the co-defendants resides or carried on business at the time the claim was issued; or ▶ where the cause of action arose

Saskatchewan	▶ the most equitable location in the opinion of the judge based on the following factors, in the following order of priority:
	  • any agreement between the parties about location of trial
	  • the place where the claim arose
	  • the place where the defendant resides
	  • the place where the plaintiff resides

Manitoba	▶ where the hearing is before a court officer, at the administrative centre of the court that is nearest the place where:
	  • the defendant resides or carries on business; or
	  • the cause of action arose
	▶ where the hearing is before a judge, at the judicial centre of the court that is nearest to the place where:
	  • the defendant resides or carries on business; or
	  • the cause of action arose
	▶ at another location at the agreement of the parties, the judge or the court office, as the case may be

TABLE 8 — Continued

PROVINCIAL OR TERRITORIAL JURISDICTION	
Ontario	➤ in the place where: • the cause of action arose; or • the defendant, or any one of the defendants, resides or carries on business
New Brunswick	➤ in the judicial district in which the claim is filed or in a more convenient location
Nova Scotia	➤ in the county in which: • the defendant or one of several defendants lives or carries on business; or • the cause of action arose
Prince Edward Island	➤ the rules are silent on jurisdiction — check local practice with the court office
Newfoundland	➤ the rules are silent on jurisdiction — check local practice with the court office

compelling reason must be given before such an order will be made. Ignorance of a limitation period is not a compelling reason and will not sway the court unless it would be a grave injustice for a claim not to be allowed.

3.3.e Was the claim brought within the appropriate notice period?

A notice period may apply to your case if a statute requires the plaintiff to notify the defendant that an action will be commenced. This is the case if the defendant is a government body or its employees, servants, and agents. It is also the case when the claim is based on legislation that requires notice to be given to the defendant before an action is commenced.

If the plaintiff fails to provide notice within the time allowed, the claim is *statute-barred;* that is, the claim cannot be legally brought even though the limitation period has not expired.

Other requirements may be made as well. Check the legislation that applies to your particular lawsuit to see if you have a defence relating to a missed notice period.

The court may, in extremely rare circumstances, grant an extension of the notice period or waive notice on motion or application. However, a compelling reason must be given before such an order will be made. Ignorance of the notice period is not a reason that will sway the court unless it would be a grave injustice for a claim not to be allowed.

3.3.f Was the claim served within the appropriate time limit?

The plaintiff must serve the issued claim on each defendant (or the defendant's lawyer, if one is involved) within the time period the rules specify.

The court may extend time for service at the request of the plaintiff before or after the time for service has passed if the plaintiff brings a motion or application requesting such an order. The defendant may also bring a motion or application to have the claim dismissed because it was not served within the proper time limits. However, the court may exercise discretion to extend the time for service or renew the claim.

3.3.g Is the cause of action reasonable?

Cause of action means the reason for bringing the claim. The reason for bringing a claim must be legally acceptable or the claim may be dismissed. These reasons are legally acceptable either because they are legislated or because they exist as causes of action in the common law (judge-made law).

In addition, *cause of action* refers to the whole cause of action, not portions of it. If the plaintiff is claiming damages for several items arising out of the same act of wrongdoing, the items cannot be split among separate claims.

Some legislation provides for ways to resolve disputes without first resorting to the courts. If such avenues are available to the plaintiff, he or she cannot bring a claim in the courts unless all avenues of appeal under that legislation have been attempted. Each province and territory will have its own set of special legislation. Some broad examples include statutes dealing with the following issues:

> ❯ Labour and employment
> ❯ Social welfare
> ❯ Human rights
> ❯ Workers' compensation

> Health and safety

> Auto insurance

Also, if the contract contains an arbitration or mediation clause, then the parties must first try resolving their contractual dispute through those channels.

3.3.h Are the appropriate parties named?

Are you named as a partner of a firm or as a sole proprietor of a business but are not one? If you were sued as a partner in a firm and admit that you were a partner in the firm at the material time (at the time of the events referenced in the claim), then you must file a defence in the name of the partnership, not separately.

If you were sued as a partner in a firm and deny that you were a partner in the firm at the material time, then you should file a defence separately from the other alleged partners or partnership.

If you are the sole proprietor of a business and deny that you were the sole proprietor of the business at the material time, then you should file a defence separately from the business itself.

3.3.i If you are a partner in a limited partnership in Ontario, were you served with a notice to alleged partner along with the claim?

In the case of a partnership in a firm, you will generally be served with a claim naming the firm. In Ontario, a notice to you as partner in a partnership must accompany the claim if the plaintiff intends to enforce a court order or judgment against a partner personally.

If you are a partner in a firm and do not receive a notice accompanying the claim, the plaintiff will not be able to enforce a court order or judgment against you personally. In that situation, you can have enforcement proceedings set aside by bringing a motion.

3.3.j Is the claim frivolous, scandalous, vexatious, or an abuse of the court's process?

Generally, if a claim cannot succeed by any stretch of the imagination, you could plead in your defence that the claim is frivolous, scandalous, or vexatious.

3.3.k Does the claim contain errors, inaccuracies, omissions, or exaggerations?

Errors, inconsistencies, exaggerations, and things that the plaintiff left out of the claim will all be useful when drafting the defence as well as when presenting your case at trial. Create a list of such problems.

Now that you are well organized, you should be able to prepare the defence (and defence-related claims) without much more effort.

4. Preparing the Defence

Of course, you may choose not to file a defence at all. Not filing a defence is standard procedure in Manitoba and Saskatchewan, where your defence is given orally at the trial. While not filing a defence may save you a filing fee and preparation time, it may also mean that —

➤ default (quick) judgment may be entered against you, which is difficult to reverse on motion or application, and

➤ you may not be in a position to negotiate terms of payment that suit your needs.

Four different approaches for preparing a defence, depending on your analyses made earlier in this chapter, are outlined and discussed here.

Approach A	You agree that you owe the amounts claimed but need to work out the terms of payment.	See section **5** Terms of Payment
Approach B	You dispute a portion of the claim.	See section **6** Disputing a Portion of the Claim
Approach C	You dispute some or all of the claim and attribute those to another person.	See section **7** Defence-related Claims
Approach D	You dispute the entire claim.	See section **8** Disputing the Entire Claim

5.   Terms of Payment

If you agree that you owe the amounts claimed but need to resolve the terms of payment, you may propose to pay a certain amount each month. You must be reasonable in what you are proposing to pay. If you are not, you may be required to attend a hearing at which a court official will make an order for payment that could be higher than what you proposed to pay. See chapter 11 for more information about terms of payment hearings.

6.   Disputing a Portion of the Claim

If you are disputing a portion of the claim, you should clearly lay out those facts and allegations that you dispute. Then, admit to the portion of the claim for which you are responsible and propose reasonable terms of payment.

7.   Defence-related Claims

You may bring one or more of three defence-related claims in addition to a defence. You would do this if you dispute some or all of the claim and attribute responsibility for those parts to another person. The three types of defence-related claims are:

> *Counterclaim*. You claim that the plaintiff owes you something.

> *Third Party Claim*. You claim that someone else is responsible.

> *Crossclaim*. You have a claim against another defendant.

Defence-related claims may generally be served on the defendants to those claims and the parties in the main action at any time before the trial of the main action. Usually, though, they are served at the time that you file the defence.

Ontario residents, note: All three defence-related claims are simply known as the *defendant's claim*.

The counterclaim, third party claim, and crossclaim serve the following purposes:

> Provide notice to the parties to the claim and the court that an action has been started

> Name the parties and counsel, if any

> State the addresses of the parties to be used for service

> Plead the amount for damages

- Plead that prejudgment interest be awarded
- Provide sufficient details to the defendant and the court so they can be reasonably sure of the case at hand
- Provide the legal basis for the claim (i.e., the cause of action)
- Provide the sections of the legislation on which the claimant is relying

7.1 The plaintiff owes you (counterclaim)

You, the defendant named in the plaintiff's claim, may have a claim against the plaintiff. If this is the case, you not only need to file a defence, but also a defendant's claim.

Note: This is different from claiming that the plaintiff contributed to his or her misfortune (contributory negligence), a claim that can be made right in the defence.

Counterclaims are not limited to the same set of events covered in the plaintiff's claim. Other events unrelated to the plaintiff's claim may be the source of a counterclaim. However, a counterclaim is invalid if it involves a previous court action that was dismissed or in which judgment was entered, because those events have already been decided in a court of law.

The concept of *res judicata* means that you cannot use events as the basis for your current action if they have already been decided in a court of law.

✹ Example

Marla was recently fired from her job as a waitress at Spaced Out Café. She filed a claim alleging that her employer did not pay her the appropriate amount of vacation pay, amounting to $500. Kurt, her former boss, was served with a copy of the plaintiff's claim. Within the 20-day deadline, Kurt filed a defence. He also prepared a defendant's claim (counterclaim) naming Marla as a defendant. Kurt alleged that Marla did not return her uniform in accordance with her employment contract. Kurt claimed that the special spacesuit waiting staff wear is worth $525. Therefore, he claimed that Marla owed him $25.

✹ Example

Anthony hired Dirk's Fine Pavers Inc. to pave his driveway. Alexander paid Dirk the deposit to cover the materials but refused to pay the remaining $700 for labour. Dirk sued Anthony. Anthony prepared a defence admitting that he did not pay the balance. He also prepared a defendant's claim (counterclaim) alleging that Dirk's Fine Pavers Inc. owed him $300 for repairs made to damage Dirk caused. Apparently, Dirk was drunk while operating the equipment and spread tar over a large area of the interlocking-brick patio next to Anthony's driveway. Therefore, Anthony admitted to owing Dirk only $400.

7.2   Someone else is liable (third party claim)

When other people or corporations are implicated in a dispute but are not named in the claim, you may add such individuals as parties to the lawsuit. These added persons are known as *third parties*. In this situation, the new claim is called a *third party claim* and the original claim is referred to as the *main action*.

 **Example**

> Kylie was walking on the sidewalk when suddenly and without warning a cyclist struck her. Kylie filed a claim against the cyclist, Sergio. Sergio, the defendant, quickly filed a defence. He also issued a third party claim naming Morris as a defendant. In his defendant's claim, Sergio blamed Morris for the accident because Morris rollerbladed in front of Sergio, causing him to swerve his bicycle into Kylie. Sergio, therefore, believes that Morris should be liable for Kylie's damages.

🍁 **Example**

> Eleanor launched a lawsuit against her mechanic, Alf, who installed a new motor in her car. The motor only lasted two days before it failed, leaving Eleanor stranded in the middle of nowhere and costing her both towing and taxi charges. Eleanor took Alf to court for defective work. When Alf was served with a copy of the plaintiff's claim, he filed a defence. He also filed a defendant's claim (third party claim), naming the manufacturer of the automobile part as a defendant. Alf strongly felt that the defect was not due to

the quality of work but due to the manufacturer's negligence in assembling the various parts.

When a third party claim has been filed, one trial will involve plaintiffs and defendants named in both the main action and the third party action unless the court orders otherwise. Sometimes, it is not possible to have one trial for both the main action and the third party action. In such cases, the court may order separate trials or direct that the third party claim proceed as a separate action. The court may do this if it is of the view that the third party claim may complicate or delay the trial of the main action; or a single trial would prejudice a party at trial.

7.3 Claiming against another defendant (crossclaim)

In some situations you may wish to make a claim against one or more of the defendants named in the plaintiff's claim or a defence-related claim. In this case you would bring a crossclaim.

 **Example**

Marg took an expensive designer suit to the town's dry cleaning service. When she went to pick up the suit, the dry cleaning staff told her it had discoloured badly. The dry cleaner denied that his staff were negligent and suggested two alternative explanations for the ruined suit. One possibility is that the chemical manufacturer may not have mixed the chemicals in proper proportions or that the label on the suit may have provided an inaccurate percentage of wool and viscose, causing the staff to use the inappropriate blend of chemicals for cleaning. Marg sued the dry cleaner, the chemical manufacturer, the designer, the clothing manufacturer that sewed the label onto the garment, and the textile company that labelled the fabrics sent to the designer. Jag, the dry cleaner, filed a defence and issued a defendant's claim (counterclaim), alleging that the plaintiff did not pay him his dry cleaning fee of $15.

The designer, chemical manufacturer, the sewing company, and the textile company each filed a defence. They also each filed a defendant's claim (crossclaim) alleging wrongdoing to each other.

Defence-related claims are similar to the plaintiff's claim because they are used to make claims of wrongdoing and request compensation. Be sure to read chapter 3 to gain insights into preparing a claim.

8. Disputing the Entire Claim

If you are disputing an entire claim, you will need to prepare and file a defence.

8.1 Preparing the defence

The defence, defendant's claim, and plaintiff's claim are referred to as *pleadings*.

The defence is the defendant's version of the dispute between the plaintiff and defendant. It serves the following purposes:

> Reply to the allegations set out in the plaintiff's claim

> Reply to the claim for damages

> Provide the sections of the legislation on which you are relying

If you do not pay attention to detail, you may leave out important details or state facts inaccurately or out of sequence. To correct a critical error or omission, you would bring a motion or application for an order permitting you to amend the defence. As with any such request, the judge has discretion to grant or deny it. In addition, the plaintiff and the court will review the defence for any errors, inaccuracies, omissions, or exaggerations in preparation for trial.

The court may strike or amend a claim or dismiss or stay the action if the claim —

> discloses no reasonable cause of action,

> is scandalous, frivolous, or vexatious,

> may prejudice, embarrass, or delay the fair trial of the action, or

> is otherwise an abuse of the court's process.

Prepare the defence with the utmost care to enhance your chances for successfully dismissing the claim.

8.2 The form and supporting documents

Most provinces and territories require that the defence be prepared on a pre-printed form and that a court fee be paid. Sample 28 in chapter 12 shows one such form from the Ontario office. Contact your local court office to obtain a copy of the form for your province or territory.

The remainder of this section leads you through the process of preparing the form and any documents that need to be attached. It also shows you how to organize your pleadings. Do not gain a sense of false confidence from the simplicity of pre-printed forms. A defence that is poorly thought out and poorly organized can have disastrous consequences.

Although not every defence will require all of the following sections, consider organizing it as follows, using whatever is applicable to your particular case.

8.2.a Your defence (Schedule 'A')

In this section of your defence you should identify which parts of the claim are in dispute and state your defence as follows:

(a) Identify the paragraphs of the claim that the defendant admits.

(b) Identify the paragraphs of the claim that the defendant denies.

(c) Identify the paragraphs of which the defendant has no knowledge.

(d) Plead that the claim is statute-barred (if applicable to your case).

(e) State the defendant's version of events for each allegation that the defendant denies.

(f) Provide a defence for each allegation that the defendant denies.

(g) State that the plaintiff failed to mitigate damages (if this applies to your case).

(h) Plead any legislation that the defendant is relying on.

(i) Plead any costs that the defendant wishes to recover.

8.2.b Documentary evidence (Schedule 'B')

If your defence is based on a document, attach a copy of the document to your defence. Examples of documents that should be included are a contract, a bad cheque, a lease agreement, or a promissory note, if the plaintiff has not already included these as part of the claim. Documentary evidence is specifically required by the rules of Ontario, Saskatchewan, Northwest Territories, and Yukon.

Each document that you submit as evidence should be referred to as an *Exhibit*. For example:

- Exhibit 1: Contract
- Exhibit 2: Invoice
- Exhibit 3: Medical Report

Never attach an original document to the defence. Always bring the originals to the trial, however, if you have them. If you are unable to include a copy of the document, you must explain within the defence why this was not done (e.g., document was destroyed in a house fire, or document was submitted to the Canada Customs and Revenue Agency and is being requested). If you know where the document can be found (e.g., with a government office, an employer, hospital, or other institution), request it; then file a copy with the court and serve a copy on each party as soon as it arrives. Chapter 12 provides sample request letters.

8.2.c Excerpts from legislation (Schedule 'C')

You may wish to include photocopied sections of the legislation on which your defence is relying. Each excerpt should be referred to as a numbered exhibit, continuing the numbering from where you left off numbering your Schedule 'B' exhibits. For example:

- Exhibit 4: Appropriate Sections of the Negligence Act
- Exhibit 5: Appropriate Section of the Insurance Act
- Exhibit 6: Appropriate Sections of the Occupier's Liability Act

You should, through your defence, admit facts that are true, take responsibility for allegations that you do not wish to dispute, and dispute the facts and allegations that are unfounded.

You should also plead in your defence any procedural problems with the claim, including any or all of the following:

- The claim discloses no reasonable cause of action.
- The claim is statute-barred because it was brought outside the limitation period.
- The claim is statute-barred for failing to comply with a notice period.

▸ The claim is statute-barred because the statute provides for a dispute resolution mechanism that must be exhausted before the claim is brought.

▸ The claim fails to disclose sufficient particulars.

▸ The claim is frivolous, scandalous, or vexatious.

When you have completed the defence, read it over to make sure it makes sense. Check it for accuracy, completeness, and effectiveness by working through Checklist 3 at the end of this chapter. When you are satisfied with your work, you are ready to file the defence with the court office.

9. Filing the Defence

After preparing your defence, you must file it with the court office where the claim was issued. Before the defence can be filed, you must take or mail the following documents to the court office:

▸ The original copy of the defence for the court office

▸ One copy of the defence, including attachments, for each plaintiff

In most provinces and territories, the court clerk will serve the defence on each plaintiff by mail or by fax.
However, in Nova Scotia and Yukon, the defendant is responsible for serving the defence.

- One copy of the defence, including attachments, for each defendant
- One copy of the defence, including attachments, for yourself
- The fee for filing the defence, if required

10. What Happens Next?

Once the defence is filed with the court and the plaintiff has been served, a number of things might happen. Table 9 presents a summary of events that may occur next and tells you where to find information about them.

> **Northwest Territories residents, note:**
>
> If the amount claimed is greater than $1 000, the judge may, on application, order a discovery.
>
> **Yukon residents, note:**
>
> The court may order a discovery on motion if the court is satisfied that special circumstances make it necessary in the interests of justice.
>
> A discovery is an examination at which the parties ask questions of each other about the lawsuit.
>
> The purpose is to uncover information to facilitate settlement negotiations, narrow issues for trial, and to delve deeper into the allegations and defences made in the pleadings overall.
>
> The presiding official has great discretion as to how the discovery is conducted and may make any order, including an order for the costs of the discovery.

11. Default Proceedings

If you fail to file a defence by the deadline, the plaintiff can initiate default proceedings.

The waiting period for commencing default proceedings may differ depending on the manner in which the claim was served. For example, if the claim was served by mail or applies to a defendant outside the province or territory in which the claim is brought, the waiting period is longer.

TABLE 9

WHAT MAY HAPPEN AFTER ISSUING AND SERVING A DEFENCE

IF	THIS MAY HAPPEN	AND
You need to make changes to a document filed with the court	► Take steps immediately upon discovering that you need to make a change	► Read chapter 5 (Dealing with Changes)
The defendant filed a defence past the time allowed by the rules or has not filed a defence at all	► Call the court office and ask if the defendant has been noted in default or if default judgment was entered against the defendant. If not, immediately file a defence. If you have been noted in default, bring a motion or application to have it or any default judgment set aside	► Read chapter 11 (Other Appearances); more specifically, read the section on motions and applications
You admit liability for the entire claim and propose terms of payment	► Immediately start making payments to the plaintiff in accordance with proposed terms ► If the plaintiff has a litigation guardian, the money must be paid into court, unless the court orders otherwise	► Read chapter 11 (Other Appearances)
You admit liability for the entire claim but do not propose terms of payment	► You may need to respond to the plaintiff's request for a payment hearing from the court. You could also request a payment hearing if you are unable to make substantial payments	► Read chapter 11 (Other Appearances)
You file a defence disputing the entire claim	► Wait for a notice of pre-trial (settlement) conference or assess whether you should request one yourself ► The plaintiff or defendant may file an amended claim or amended defence	► Read chapter 7 (The Settlement Conference) ► Read chapter 5 (Dealing with Changes)

TABLE 9 — Continued

IF	THIS MAY HAPPEN	AND
You propose terms of payment (in admitting either partial or full liability) but do not pay as proposed	▶ Expect the court clerk to sign judgment for the unpaid balance of the undisputed amount if the plaintiff makes such a request ▶ You may bring a motion or application to set aside the order if there are sufficient and compelling reasons why the payments could not be made	▶ Read chapter 11 (Other Appearances); more specifically, read the section on motions and applications
You wish to have the court strike all or part of the claim	▶ Assess whether you should bring a motion, considering a number of factors	▶ Read chapter 5 (Dealing with Changes)
You must appear on a motion or application brought by the plaintiff	▶ Respond to the motion or application	▶ Read chapter 11 (Other Appearances)
An unexpected event happens	▶ Deal with the event	▶ Read chapter 5 (Dealing with Changes)
You wish to negotiate a settlement	▶ Try to settle	▶ Read chapter 6 (Trying to Settle)

Refer to Table 10 to determine what steps a plaintiff may take if you fail to file a defence by the deadline.

Once you have been noted in default or default judgment has been obtained against you, you can no longer file a defence or take any other step in the proceeding unless a judge otherwise permits.

If you are in default, the judge will likely order a damages assessment trial. The purpose of a damages assessment trial is to permit the plaintiff to prove his or her unliquidated damages to the court. This proceeding is described fully in chapters 2 and 10. If you fail to file a defence, you are not entitled to be notified of the damages assessment trial nor participate in it.

In Manitoba and Saskatchewan, the defendant need not file a defence, but if he or she fails to show up for the trial, he or she would be in default and a damages trial would be held.

TABLE 10
WHAT TO DO WHEN THE DEFENDANT IS IN DEFAULT

PROVINCE OR TERRITORY	WHAT THE PLAINTIFF MUST DO WHEN THE DEFENDANT IS IN DEFAULT
Northwest Territories	Steps to take if no defence is filed within 25 days of serving the claim: (a) File proof of service of the claim with the court. (b) Ask the court to note the defendant in default. (c) The clerk may sign default judgment for debts, liquidated damages, or the recovery of goods. (d) The plaintiff will proceed to trial for an unliquidated demand in money.
Yukon	Steps to take if no reply is filed within 20 days of serving the claim: (a) File proof of service with the court. (b) Request in writing that the court sign default judgment. (c) The clerk may sign default judgment for debts, liquidated damages, or the recovery of goods. (d) The plaintiff will proceed to trial for an unliquidated demand in money.
British Columbia	Steps to take if no reply is filed within 14 days of serving the notice of claim: (a) File proof of service of the notice of claim with the court. (b) Request in writing that the court make a default order requiring the defendant to pay the amount plus costs. (c) Request a hearing from the court if your claim is not for a debt.
Alberta	Steps to take if no dispute note is filed within 20 days of serving the civil claim: (a) File proof of service of the civil claim with the court. (b) Request in writing that the court enter default judgment. (c) The plaintiff will proceed to trial when the claim is not the result of a contract with the defendant.

TABLE 10 — Continued

PROVINCE OR TERRITORY	WHAT THE PLAINTIFF MUST DO WHEN THE DEFENDANT IS IN DEFAULT
Ontario	Steps to take if no defence is filed within 20 days of serving the plaintiff's claim: (a) Request in writing that the clerk note the defendant in default. (b) If your claim is for liquidated damages, prepare a default judgment and ask the clerk to sign it. (c) If you claim is for unliquidated damages, request in writing that the matter be set down for a damages assessment trial.
New Brunswick	Steps to take if no response is filed within 30 days of serving the claim: (a) The clerk will enter default judgment for liquidated damages. (b) The clerk will enter an interim judgment for unliquidated damages, and damages assessment trial will follow.
Nova Scotia	Steps to take if no defence is filed within 10 days in response to the claim: (a) Request in writing that the court award a quick judgment.
Prince Edward Island	Steps to take if no dispute note is filed within 20 days of serving the claim: (a) File with the court a written request for judgment. (b) If the plaintiff's claim is for a debt or damages and the claim discloses a cause of action, the registrar shall enter judgment. (c) If the claim is entirely or partly for damages, the registrar may add a further endorsement to the Notice of Claim stating that the judgment entered with respect to damage is interlocutory (temporary) and arrange for a damages assessment trial.
Newfoundland	Steps to take if no response is filed within 30 days of serving the claim: (a) Request in writing that the court award default judgment.
Saskatchewan	The rules do not provide for default proceedings. The matter proceeds directly to trial following service of the claim.
Manitoba	The matter proceeds directly to trial following service of the claim. If the defendant does not appear at the hearing, the judge or deputy registrar may sign a Certificate of Decision on Default.

12. Setting Aside a Default Judgment

If you are a defendant who has been noted in default or against whom default judgment was entered, you may still have hope to have these default proceedings reversed. Any party in default may bring a motion requesting the court to set aside the noting of default or entry of default judgment.

The judge may grant a request on *such terms as are just*. In other words, if the judge is convinced that the party bringing the motion was in default for a good reason, he or she may grant such an order but attach conditions to it. Conditions may be how long the defendant will have to file a defence or any other terms the court deems (considers) just. The judge may also award the plaintiff costs for the inconvenience resulting from the default.

If you can get the other parties to consent in writing, the court clerk may even set aside the noting of default or the entry of default judgment without requiring a motion.

CHECKLIST 3
CHECKLIST FOR PREPARING A DEFENCE

❏ **Is your defence clear?**
  ❏ Did you write in plain English?
  ❏ Are events in the correct sequence?
  ❏ Will your defence make sense to a reader who, like the judge, may never before have met the defendant or have heard a case with that fact pattern?
  ❏ Does the defence present your story in a way that will be clear to a judge who has no knowledge of the facts or familiarity with the parties or their roles in the dispute?

❏ **Is your defence accurate?**
  ❏ Did you check to ensure that you have not called the defendant by the plaintiff's name or the plaintiff by the defendant's name?
  ❏ Did you check your spelling and grammar?

❏ **Is your defence complete?**
  ❏ Have you identified all the parties?
  ❏ Have you included all the relevant information?
  ❏ Did you attach all supporting schedules and documents?

❏ **Did you plead available procedural defences (if applicable to your case)?**
  ❏ Did you plead that the claim is statute-barred by virtue of:
    ❏ being brought outside the limitation period?
    ❏ being brought outside the notice period?
    ❏ being brought when other statutory avenues were not exhausted?
  ❏ Did you dispute the claim for general damages?
  ❏ Did you dispute the claim for special damages?
  ❏ Did you dispute the request for punitive damages?
  ❏ Did you dispute the claim for prejudgment interest?
  ❏ Did you plead all the legislation upon which you are relying?

❏ **CRITICAL: DID YOU FILE YOUR DEFENCE WITH THE COURT ON TIME?**

❏ **Did you file your defence by taking to the court office the following:**
  ❏ the original copy of the defence?
  ❏ one copy of the defence, including attachments, for each plaintiff?
  ❏ one copy of the defence, including attachments, for each defendant?
  ❏ one copy of the defence, including attachments, for yourself?
  ❏ the fee, if required?

❏ **If you are also filing a defence-related claim, refer to Checklist 2.**

5
Dealing with Changes

Any court action may be complicated by changes. These may be changes that —

- ▶ you wish to make,
- ▶ another party wishes to make, or
- ▶ the court wishes to make.

For example, you may wish to change the trial date or location. Or, you may wish to change the contents of your claim, defence, or other court documents.

Bear in mind that changes affect the parties, the court, and the proceedings. Therefore, try to deal with them in the least expensive, least disruptive manner to keep inconvenience, expense, and delay at a minimum for everyone involved in your case.

Requesting a change or responding to a request for change in the proceedings is a decision that requires some thought. The following questions may help you decide whether or not you wish to request a change or challenge a change being requested:

- ▶ Is the change critical in that it would seriously affect the proceedings? Or is it minor?
- ▶ Is the request for a change made with reasonable notice to the parties and the court?
- ▶ How might the change affect the parties?

- How might the change affect the court?
- Is the request for a change reasonable?
- How should the change be made? At what cost? At what effort?
- Is the change likely to produce other changes?
- Is a party likely to oppose the change?
- How close to trial is the potential change?
- What consequences are likely to result from the change?
- How costly is the change to the parties?
- How might you respond to the change that is requested or made?
- What happens if you don't respond to a change that is requested or made?
- How likely is it that your request will be granted?

Changes can often be made if all parties agree to allow the change; that is, on the consent of all parties. It is always a good idea to try to get the written consent of the other party.

Once you have decided that you wish to make a change, consult the small claims court rules to see if the change is possible and how the change should be made. The rules provide the court with broad authority to grant or refuse requests for changes to the proceedings. Table 11 outlines the rules of general discretion for each province and territory.

Some sections of small claims legislation or small claims court rules provide the court with wide latitude in granting or denying requests or making orders. You might refer to these rules when bringing a motion or application to request a change or when trying to convince the court that the change the other party is requesting should not be granted.

1. Dealing with Changes to Court Documents

An amendment is a change to a court document. It is possible in most cases to amend court documents even if they have already been served on the parties and filed with the court.

Spelling and grammar errors in court documents are minor and need not be corrected unless they distort the meaning of the pleadings.

Many changes to the proceedings require court approval, which is often sought by way of a motion or application. Read chapter 11 for insights into bringing motions and applications.

TABLE 11
RULES OF GENERAL DISCRETION

PROVINCE OR TERRITORY	SECTIONS OF SMALL CLAIMS COURT ACTS, REGULATIONS, OR COURT RULES
British Columbia	**Section 2(2)** provides that the court may make any order or give any direction it thinks necessary to achieve the purpose of the small claims court legislation and rules.
Manitoba	No general rules of discretion are outlined in the small claims court rules.
New Brunswick	No general rules of discretion are outlined in the small claims court rules.
Newfoundland	**Rule 12(4)** allows the judge to impose a condition or give a direction the judge considers fair. **Rule 12(11)** permits the judge to extend or shorten a time limit referred to in the rules on terms the judge considers fair. **Rule 12(12)** provides that a judge may make any order or give any direction he or she considers fair for a party who has violated one of the small claims court rules.
Northwest Territories	No general rules of discretion are outlined in the small claims court rules.
Nova Scotia	**Section 14** provides that the court will permit all necessary amendments or grant other relief at any stage in the proceeding, upon proper terms, to secure the just determination of the matters in dispute between the parties.
Ontario	**Rule 1.03** allows the court to treat the rules liberally to secure the just, most expeditious, and least expensive determination of every proceeding in the lawsuit. **Rule 2.01** allows the court to grant all necessary amendments or other requests for changes so as to secure the just determination of the issues in dispute. **Rule 2.02** allows the court to dispense with the compliance of any rule at any time if necessary in the interest of justice. **Rule 3.02(1)** allows the court to lengthen or shorten any time period in the rules, on such terms as are just.
Prince Edward Island	No general rules of discretion are outlined in the small claims court rules.

TABLE 11 — Continued

PROVINCE OR TERRITORY	SECTIONS OF SMALL CLAIMS COURT ACTS, REGULATIONS, OR COURT RULES
Saskatchewan	**Section 71(1)** permits the court to grant all necessary amendments or other relief, on such terms as are just, to secure the just determination of the matters in dispute. **Section 72(2)** allows the court to waive compliance with any part of the regulations at any time if it is in the interest of justice. **Section 72(2)** permits the court to lengthen or shorten any time prescribed by the small claims court regulations for an order, on such terms as are just.
Yukon	**Rule 1(2)** allows the court to make any order that is just. **Rule 1(4)** allows the court to impose such terms and directions as are just. **Rule 71(1)** allows the court to grant all necessary amendments or other relief, on such terms as are just, to secure the just determination of the matters in dispute. **Rule 71(2)** allows the court to waive compliance with any rule at any time when it is necessary in the interest of justice. **Rule 72(2)** permits the court to lengthen or shorten any time prescribed for an order, on such terms as are just.

However, you should amend your claim or defence if it requires a change that is likely to affect the outcome of your lawsuit. If, for example, you wish to add or delete a party or allegation, then amend your pleadings. If you wish to withdraw a claim, defence-related claim, or defence, then write to the court office advising them of this.

1.1 Amending pleadings

Amendments to pleadings can be made without a motion in most cases. Amended documents should be served on all parties, even those in default, and filed with the court. Beware, though, that if pleadings are amended too close to trial, a motion or application may be required to allow the amendment. The other parties may have to amend their pleadings in response, leaving them pressed for time. Often, amendments made too close to trial can result in adjournment of the trial.

Take the following steps to amend your claim or defence:

(a) Photocopy the claim or defence and work with that photocopy.

(b) Make the necessary changes. In British Columbia, you must also initial changes.

(c) Underline all added words and numbers.

(d) Put a strike (~~strike~~) through all words and numbers that should be removed.

(e) Insert words by placing an insert character (^) between the two words where the added words should be inserted. <u>Underline</u> the added words.

(f) Photocopy the amended claim or defence so that you have enough copies for all parties, as well as one for the court and one for your records.

(g) File the amended copy with the court.

(h) Serve all parties with an amended copy.

Making amendments to pleadings

In British Columbia and in Yukon, you will require a judge's permission if you wish to reactivate the same pleading.

In Ontario, amendments must be made at least 30 days before trial or you must bring a motion for permission to make an amendment.

In Newfoundland, British Columbia, and Yukon, amendments to pleadings may be made at any time before the settlement conference. After that, you will require the permission of a judge, which can be sought by bringing a motion (or application).

1.2 Amending affidavits

An affidavit is a sworn document. Therefore, it is critical to verify that the contents of an affidavit are correct before serving it on a party and filing it with the court. If you realize after swearing an affidavit that you made a mistake, however, you could take several steps to make the correction.

Minor errors such as typing, spelling, or grammar need not be changed since they are not critical to the outcome of the proceedings.

Sometimes, you may discover information useful to your case after your sworn affidavit is served on a party and filed with the court.

To correct an error or add information, take the following steps:

(a) Prepare a supplementary affidavit, as described in section **1.3** below.

(b) Swear before a lawyer or commissioner of oaths that the contents of the supplementary affidavit are true.

(c) Serve the supplementary affidavit on the parties.

(d) File the supplementary affidavit with the court.

If you are the party who receives a supplementary affidavit, you have the opportunity to prepare a responding supplementary affidavit if you disagree with the contents of the supplementary affidavit. The steps are the same whether you are correcting or adding information or responding to those changes.

1.3 Supplementary affidavits

The basics of preparing affidavits (see chapter 12) apply to supplementary affidavits with a few small differences.

You need not and should not repeat all the paragraphs of the original affidavit that you are trying to add to or correct. If you are correcting the original affidavit, state —

(a) the paragraph that contains the error,

(b) the reason you made the error,

(c) the correct version of the facts, and

(d) that all other paragraphs of the original affidavit are correct as sworn.

If you are adding to the original affidavit, state —

(a) the facts that have come to your attention since the original affidavit was sworn,

(b) the date or approximate date you discovered the additional facts, and

(c) that all other paragraphs of the original affidavit are correct as sworn.

In both cases, remember that you then need to swear before a lawyer or commissioner of oaths that the contents of the supplementary affidavit are true.

1.4 Changing other documents

If you need to change any other documents, make the necessary changes and serve each party with the amended document. Promptly file a copy with the court office.

Also, if you are amending a court document, you will have to serve the document on all parties and on any new party that is added to a claim. Depending on the court location you are in, this may be done before or after filing the amended document with the court. This means spending money on photocopying the amended documents and paying for postage.

2. Making Changes to Procedures

2.1 Changing the date of a proceeding

Adjourning a proceeding, or changing its date, should be done with caution for a couple of reasons. If a party or the court is inconvenienced by an adjournment, if the request is brought close to or on the day of the proceeding, or if the request is made to the court without notice to the parties, then the court may order you to pay costs for inconvenience.

There are two ways to request an adjournment of a proceeding such as a pre-trial (settlement) conference, motion, trial, or judgment debtor examination:

(a) *Write a letter to the trial scheduling clerk or motions clerk, or simply address it to the court office.* Request an adjournment in this way if any of the following circumstances apply to your case:

(i) You have the consent of the other parties and are requesting the change before the appearance. Try to get the consent of the parties before requesting an adjournment. It is best to get this consent in writing and attach it to your letter to the court.

(ii) You do not have the consent of the other parties and you are requesting the change before the appearance. The clerk will only approve of an adjournment if you have a very good reason for not attending. For example, you may have surgery scheduled for that date or the date may fall on a religious holiday.

(b) *Bring a motion or application.* Request an adjournment by motion or application if another party refuses to consent or advises you that they will oppose your request for an adjournment. Confirm the party's intention in writing and attach it to your motion materials.

Generally, it is common courtesy to consent to the first request for an adjournment, unless the request for an adjournment is, in your view, an abuse of process.

Note: If the request for an adjournment is an abuse of process, the court may adjourn a trial and award one party to pay another party's costs for any inconvenience and expense resulting from the adjournment.

2.2 Changing the location of a trial

There are two ways to request a transfer of your trial to another jurisdiction:

(a) *Write a letter to the trial scheduling clerk.* Request a transfer this way if you have the consent of the other parties. It is best to get this consent in writing and attach it to your letter to the court.

(b) *Bring a motion requesting a change of venue.* The hearing of this motion is called a *jurisdictional hearing.* You would bring a motion requesting a change of venue when one of the other parties does not agree with and intends to oppose your suggestion of changing the location of the trial. See chapter 11 for more information about bringing a motion.

3. Responding to Changes

3.1 Responding to procedural changes

You should probably not challenge a procedural change if any of the following circumstances apply to your case:

- ❯ The request is reasonable.
- ❯ A delay in the proceedings would not prejudice your case.
- ❯ The court would likely grant the procedural change anyway.

3.2 Responding to amended documents

If you received an amended pleading and it affects your own pleading, amend your documents to respond to the changes the opposing party made. File amended documents with the court and serve them on all parties, where required.

3.3 Responding to motions or applications

A court will make an order on motion or application if it is permitted by the court rules, if it is a reasonable and necessary request, and after considering whether the request is on consent from the other parties or if the other parties are opposing it.

You should oppose a motion or application only if the order being sought will hurt your case. If a party is seeking a change by motion or application, the court could order that party to pay costs to the other parties if the motion or application is frivolous or brought late enough in the proceedings so as to inconvenience the other parties. If you oppose a motion or application to which you ought to consent, the court may order you to pay costs to the moving party (the party bringing the motion or application).

4. Dealing with Missing Key Evidence

If key evidence or witnesses disappear before trial, you should explain this in a letter to the court and request an adjournment of the trial. You should try to get the consent of all parties. However, if any party opposes your request for an adjournment, bring a motion to seek an order staying the proceedings until the key evidence or witness is located. Similarly, if you cannot locate evidence that a judge ordered must be found before the action can proceed, write a letter to the court when you have located it so that proceedings may be continued.

5. What to Do When a Witness Fails to Show up for Trial

Sometimes witnesses fail to show up for trial. At other times, a witness arrives at trial but refuses to remain in attendance or to comply with the court's demands. In such cases, the judge may complete a bench warrant or a warrant for arrest of defaulting witness. This means that the witness may be arrested anywhere in your province or territory if that witness was served with a subpoena or summons to witness before trial. Police officers arresting the summonsed witness will bring the witness promptly before the court if the witness can be found.

A witness may be held in custody until his or her presence is no longer required. The judge will order the release of the witness on such terms as are just and may even order the witness to pay costs for his or her disappearance.

6. Dealing with a Request for Separate Trials

When an action involves a defendant's claim, the trial on the merits of the defendant's claim is tried together with the merits of the plaintiff's claim (which is the main action). However, any party may request by motion that separate trials be held for the main action and the defendant's claim.

Separate trials may be allowed when the defendant's claim may unduly complicate or delay the trial of the action or cause undue prejudice to a party. In fact, in many provinces and territories, the rules of the court specifically allow the claims to proceed as separate actions.

7. Transferring to the Higher Court

Any party may request that the action be transferred from the small claims court to a higher court in that province or territory. Some reasons you might transfer out of small claims court include the following:

> *Monetary jurisdiction.* If you discover after issuing a claim for damages for personal injury that your injuries are more severe than you thought or that new injuries result from the same cause of action, then your claim may exceed the monetary jurisdiction of the small claims court and ought to be transferred (unless, of course, you wish to waive the amount in excess of the small claims court's monetary limit).

> *Cause of action (subject matter).* If you have commenced an action for a matter that cannot be dealt with in the small claims court (e.g., construction lien, family matter), then you must abandon (withdraw) your claim and bring it in the court of proper jurisdiction. Take care not to miss a limitation period, though.

> *Remedy.* If you are seeking a remedy (such as an injunction or judicial review of a government decision), then you cannot seek such a remedy in the small claims court and should seek to transfer your

file to the higher court where such a remedy can be awarded at the hearing of the matter.

The procedure for bringing a motion in a higher court is beyond the scope of this book, and you should consult a lawyer in such cases.

Briefly, such a motion must be brought according to the rules of the higher court, a different set of rules that are more complicated than those of the small claims court. It will cost you money to bring the motion, plus the costs of preparation and service on all parties.

Some courts only hear motions to transfer to a higher court once a year; others hear them more often. Be prepared for some time to pass before your motion is heard. If it is urgent that your motion be heard as soon as possible, ask the court office staff if it is possible to arrange a quicker hearing.

8. Transferring from the Higher Court

Any party may request that the action be transferred from the higher court to the small claims court. Such a request should be brought well before trial, if possible. You must do this by bringing a motion or application. This topic is beyond the scope of this book but court staff in your jurisdiction will likely provide you with guidance.

9. Combining Actions Started in Different Courts

Sometimes two related actions are brought in different courts: one in small claims court and one in the higher court. In the interests of the cost of trying both actions and inconveniencing witnesses who must testify in both trials, the court may join the actions. Any party may request by motion or application that the actions be joined and tried in the higher court or the small claims court, depending on the monetary jurisdiction issues.

10. Changes in Representation

If you were unrepresented by counsel or an agent when you initiated the action or became involved in it and later retained counsel or an agent to act on your behalf, you should advise the court of this change in representation. Do so in a letter to the court, and send a copy to all parties, advising them of your representative's address, telephone number, and fax number. Do this promptly so that your representative is kept informed of the proceedings.

Likewise, if you were represented at the outset of the action and later decided to proceed without representation, write a letter to the court advising them of the change. Do this immediately to ensure that you are notified of upcoming proceedings.

11. Address, Telephone, and Fax Changes

If your address, telephone number, or fax number changes during a lawsuit, write a letter to the court, and send a copy to all parties, advising them of your new address, telephone number, and fax number. Do so without delay, or you may miss out on key developments.

6
Trying to Settle

Whether you are representing yourself or acting as an agent for the plaintiff or defendant, you will search for the most satisfactory way of resolving a dispute. Sometimes, the only way of doing that is to let a lawsuit proceed to trial. A trial provides the parties an opportunity to have their day in court, during which they can recount on the record their versions of the events and have an impartial party, the judge, determine the result of the lawsuit.

Keep in mind that a trial is almost always couched in uncertainty because you cannot be sure of the verdict until the judge delivers it. You may be confident that you will win at trial, but a number of factors may affect the result:

▸ The judge may rule that you have not provided sufficient evidence to prove your side of the story.

▸ The judge may accept the story of the other party even though you insist that the story is correct as you (and your witnesses) testified.

▸ The judge may rule that the law supports one party due to the version of facts presented and may decide for that party.

▸ The judge may rule that the law provides relief for your version of the facts but may award the other side because it is more fair or equitable based on the facts the judge heard from each side.

1. Why Settle?

You should always try discussing settlement at least once before trial. Some of the benefits of negotiating a settlement include the following:

(a) Settling means the dispute has been resolved and the case is over. Settling is likely to save time, money, and effort for all parties.

(b) The parties should, for future relations, remain on decent terms. This is especially important in small communities where one of the parties is the only person or business in the area who provides a particular service or product. It is also important when relatives, friends, neighbours, co-workers, employers, or employees are on opposing sides.

(c) You may not have a strong case, so a trial may go either way. Perhaps your case relies heavily on credibility, as in cases in which the judge must decide which party is telling the truth. An example of such a case is when the dispute is over an oral agreement. Another example is when most or all of the evidence comes from oral testimony.

(d) The settlement (pre-trial) conference judge or referee or the trial judge may send you out of the courtroom to discuss settlement, if you haven't already tried to do that. A judge may refuse to hear your case unless you have attempted settlement negotiations.

(e) If you fail to accept a reasonable settlement offer and proceed to trial and lose, you may be ordered to pay costs to the other party.

2. When Should You Consider Settlement?

You may settle the matter with the other parties at any time before the judge's verdict. You may make an offer at various stages:

(a) *Before the pre-trial (settlement) conference or trial.* If it is your opinion that the case should be settled, you may wish to approach the other side as soon as possible. If you are an agent representing a plaintiff or defendant, leaving this until the last minute will not impress your client or the judge. It may also annoy the other parties who have put time, effort, and expense into preparing for trial. This may affect both the possibility of settlement and the terms, including the day from which interest may be calculated if awarded.

(b) *When another party proposes a settlement*. Read the terms of the offer carefully, and pay special attention to any expiry date or deadline for responding to the offer. Missing a deadline may cause you a lot of grief (e.g., you may be ordered to pay costs). Use a tickler sheet (described in chapter 8) to assist you in preventing that from happening.

(c) *At the pre-trial (settlement) conference or mediation or afterwards*. The official presiding over the settlement conference or mediation will likely inform you as to the strength of your case or may, in fact, urge the parties to settle the matter. If you have not considered settlement at this point, ask for a brief recess, think about the terms you would be content with, and then approach the other parties.

Read chapter 7 for a better understanding of the pre-trial (settlement) conference. It is an important part of the legal process.

(d) *At trial*. If things are going badly for one party, he or she may decide to make an offer to settle. An offer can be made by requesting the judge to call a recess; then the parties can step outside the courtroom and try to negotiate a settlement. If an offer is made, the other party may choose to accept it or reject it and continue with the trial. If the other party accepts the offer, return to court and inform the judge that the parties have settled the matter. Get the terms of the settlement in writing as soon as possible thereafter, and have both parties sign the document. This document, discussed in section **6.5**, is referred to as *minutes of settlement*. It should be filed with the court.

3. Parties under Disability

Special rules apply to parties under disability (see chapter 2). Any settlement of a claim involving a party under disability requires court approval. Therefore, if you are a litigation guardian, you may negotiate a settlement on behalf of a party under disability but it is not final unless a judge approves it.

4. Evaluating Your Case

If you are plaintiff or defendant who wishes to represent yourself in small claims court, the following guidelines may help you evaluate your case. To save time and stay organized, you might approach this by creating a chart such as the one in Table 12. This method of analysis is merely an example; there are certainly a number of other ways you might do this analysis yourself.

Mediation is hot!

A mediation is conducted by a neutral third party who facilitates open discussion between the parties. It can work only if the parties agree to participate in the mediation.

Ask your local court office if mediation is available in your area, if there is a cost for the service, and what the procedure is for signing up.

Mediating a case has a number of advantages. One obvious benefit is that the parties discuss the case in an informal setting, allowing the parties to have input into any settlement reached. If left to a judge, the case would be beyond the parties' control. Since mediation is not as adversarial and public as a courtroom, more privacy is available, and the parties may be able to preserve their relationship.

If the case settles during mediation, the mediator may assist the parties in shaping the terms of settlement. Another advantage is that the mediator will often prepare the settlement document (minutes of settlement, release, or both) for the parties to sign. The cost of mediation, if any, may be worked into the settlement agreement.

In Yukon, you may elect to have your case decided by mediation rather than by trial. If you have elected mediation and it does not resolve your case, you would attend at a pre-trial conference as the next step in the proceeding.

4.1 Determine your goal

Your ultimate goal in suing or trying to settle may or may not be the same as the remedy being sought in the plaintiff's or defendant's claims. Often, in trying to settle, you may be content with an apology from the other party. The question to ask is, "What do you want at the end of the day?" Are you seeking money, an apology, return of goods, performance of a service, or maintaining a positive relationship with the other side? Often, it is a question of which remedy is of greater priority.

Using Table 12 to analyze your case will be a good supplement to a "gut feel" about how you think you might fare at the end of the day.

TABLE 12

EVALUATING YOUR CASE

FACT	EVIDENCE FROM			SUPPORTED BY LAW OR EQUITY			STRENGTH OF CASE		
(Oldest to most recent)	Document	Photo or Object	Witness	Legislation	Case Law	Equity	Weak	Unsure or 50/50	Strong

Consulting with a lawyer

Only a lawyer can provide a professional evaluation of a case by applying the law to the facts of the particular case. If your case seems complicated or you do not wish to take the risk of proceeding on your own, consider retaining a lawyer, even if it is only to clarify parts of the law relating to your case.

A lawyer referral service is likely offered by the Law Society in your province or territory. This service usually offers a brief free consultation with a lawyer. Check the telephone directory to locate the service in your area.

To get the most out of the brief consultation session, prepare a summary sheet of the facts in your case and bring a photocopy of the relevant documents or other evidence such as photographs. These will help the lawyer guide you, if that is possible in such a brief period of time. Sometimes, extending the consultation period is worth the money.

4.2 Gather the facts

Facts are the details about the events that occurred. The facts may be material or immaterial facts. Material facts are those that will help prove your case. For example, the fact that the parties signed an agreement is material to a breach of contract action. The date that the agreement was formed as well as the witnesses present are also material facts, but the clothes the parties wore when they signed the agreement are immaterial.

If you are using Table 12 to evaluate your case, list each material fact in chronological order (from the oldest to the most recent of events pertaining to the action), one per line.

4.3 Gather the evidence that supports the facts

Evidence refers to documents, photographs, objects, and testimony of the parties, witnesses, and expert witnesses that prove that the facts occurred as alleged. Evidence may be either relevant evidence or irrelevant evidence. See chapter 8 for a discussion of evidence.

Use Table 12 to summarize the evidence you have and to indicate the strength of that evidence in proving your case:

➤ For *documents* that are, in your opinion, strong evidence of the fact to be proven, place a capital letter D in the appropriate box. For documents that are weak evidence, place a small letter d in the box.

> For *photographs* that are, in your opinion, strong evidence of the fact to be proven, place a capital letter *P* in the appropriate box. For photographs that are weak evidence, place a small letter *p* in the box.

> For *objects* that are, in your opinion, strong evidence of the fact to be proven, place a capital letter *O* in the appropriate box. For objects that are weak evidence, place a small letter *o* in the box.

> For *witnesses* who can, in your opinion, provide strong evidence of the fact to be proven, place a capital letter *W* in the appropriate box. For witnesses who can provide only weak evidence, place a small letter *w* in the box. (Witness preparation is a key component of getting the most out of your witness. Chapter 8 discusses how you should prepare your witnesses.)

4.4 Determine the applicable law

When determining the law that applies to your particular set of facts, you will need to consider legislation, common law, and equity.

The Self-Counsel Press Web site lists the Web sites for various provinces and territories, where you may find relevant *legislation* as well as other legal resources. Check <http://www.self-counsel.com/canlaw /smallclaims/resources.html>.

The *common law* is comprised of decisions in court cases. Previous decisions are applied to present-day cases when the facts are similar, a point of law is similar, or both the facts and the law are similar. It is often tricky to figure out just how a common law decision may apply to your case for a variety of reasons:

> Judges make decisions by taking into consideration a complex set of facts, applying the law that was in effect at the relevant time, and coming to a just decision in the circumstances.

> It is often not possible to find a precedent case with facts exactly like your own. Therefore, the judge must often use discretion in deciding whether a precedent case applies to the present set of facts.

> The law is constantly evolving due to a changing society and its changing perceptions of justice. Therefore, what was once a valid precedent case may no longer be desirable. In such a case, the judge presiding over your trial will have to make a law by setting another precedent.

> Finding, reading, and interpreting common law cases is a skill that judges and lawyers learn in law school and through experience gained by working in the legal profession. A lawyer will be able to make an educated decision as to whether a precedent case applies to a set of facts that have yet to appear before the court.

Equity deals with principles of fairness outlined in common law cases. While the law may support a particular party's set of facts, the judge may decide to rule in favour of the other party or in favour of both parties on separate issues if the judge believes that such a decision would be fair.

4.5 Weigh the strengths and weaknesses of your case

There is no formula for assessing whether the evidence and law are likely to support the facts of your case and lead you toward your goal of obtaining the relief you are seeking. Often your "gut feeling" will determine whether or not you will settle or litigate. Nonetheless, you should at least try to guess (based on a careful reflection of the points outlined in this chapter) whether or not you would be successful at trial. Table 12 will help you organize your information so that your analysis will consider as many aspects as possible.

4.6 Be objective

Try to put aside your anger, resentment, vengeance, and other emotions. The more objectively you can evaluate the case, the more likely you will reach a decision that will benefit you. Imagine being the judge. Ask yourself, "What would the judge think about this case?"

Also be objective when assessing the strengths and weaknesses of your witnesses. A witness who presents your case poorly on the stand can sometimes do more damage to your case than by not presenting at all.

4.7 Make the decision

Only you can decide if your case is strong enough to withstand trial or if you should settle. Your lawyer or agent can only form an educated opinion and advise you as to your chances of winning a lawsuit or, if loss is inevitable, the estimated amount of damages you may be awarded if you are successful. Table 13 provides a list of questions to ponder in making your decision.

Take a look at Sample 1, which evaluates a lawsuit launched over a breach of contract from both the plaintiff's and the defendant's points of view.

TABLE 13
SHOULD YOU SETTLE?

	THE PLAINTIFF SHOULD ASK:	THE DEFENDANT SHOULD ASK:
Could you settle?	What amount would cover your losses and expenses? What amount would satisfy you? What terms would satisfy you?	What amount would you be capable of paying? What payment schedule would you be able to adhere to? What terms would satisfy you?
Would you settle?	Is the defendant a party who would likely honour the terms of a settlement agreement (e.g., make payments, if required)? Does the defendant have a history of bouncing cheques, cheating, moving to avoid paying a debt, or other undesirable behaviour? Does the defendant have a reputation for taking advantage of plaintiffs such as yourself? What do you think your chances are for winning the case? Is the defendant a party who might consider a reasonable settlement proposal? Would the expense, time, and effort of allowing a matter to proceed to trial be worth it?	Do you think you will be found partially or fully liable as alleged in the statement of claim? Would the plaintiff honour the terms of a settlement agreement (e.g., honour a promise not to pursue the matter further, if required)? Does the plaintiff have a reputation for taking advantage of defendants such as yourself? What do you think your chances are for winning the case? Is the plaintiff a party who might consider a reasonable proposal?
What would you settle for?	What terms are non-negotiable? What terms are negotiable?	What terms are non-negotiable? What terms are negotiable?

Note: Additional facts may be factors in determining whether settlement negotiations are successful.

5.   The Offer to Settle

5.1 Making the offer

An offer to settle may be made verbally, unless the rules of the court specifically require an offer to be in writing. However, oral offers can be risky for several reasons:

(a)   The other party may deny that an offer was ever made.

(b)   The other party may have a different understanding of the terms of the offer.

(c)   You may have difficulty obtaining costs if there is no written proof of the offer.

So, play it safe and put the offer in writing, if not initially, then as soon as possible after the verbal offer was made.

> The earlier you settle, the better for all the players in the process.

5.2 Serving the offer

An offer must be served on the other party. This means that you must bring the offer to the attention of the other side by serving the party or parties with the offer.

Note: Refer to the service rules in chapter 13.

> In British Columbia, serve an offer to settle within 30 days of the completion of the settlement conference.

5.3 Withdrawing the offer

On some occasions it may become necessary or desirable to withdraw an offer served on the other party. For example, new evidence may have surfaced changing the way you feel about the case. It could be that the other party is being unreasonable or is refusing to negotiate.

Sometimes, the other party takes too long to respond to an offer when a generous expiry date or no expiry date is provided. A deadline or expiry date is a highly recommended part of the offer. Including an expiry date may assist you in gauging the co-operation or interest level of the other side for settlement.

You may withdraw the offer at any time before the trial ends. However, this must be done in writing and served on the other party. In other

EVALUATING A LAWSUIT

EVALUATING THE STORY OF THE PLAINTIFF

FACT	EVIDENCE FROM			SUPPORTED BY LAW OR EQUITY			STRENGTH OF CASE		
(Oldest to most recent)	Document	Photo or Object	Witness	Legislation	Case Law	Equity	Weak	Unsure or 50/50	Strong
January 2: Defendant agreed to pay me $5 000, half as deposit and the remaining half upon performance of service	D contract, deposit cheque		W plaintiff						
January 15: Work in progress and almost completed when deposit cheque was returned for insufficient funds (NSF cheque)	D NSF cheque notice		W plaintiff						
January 18: Continued with work and asked defendant to replace the cheque with a certified cheque or money order — said he would — seemed concerned and trustworthy		P	W my staff						
January 20: Completed work — defendant not around at the time			W my staff						
February 15: No word from defendant so sent demand letter for payment of full amount	D letter		W my staff						
March 1: Sent second demand letter threatening law suit if no payment terms arranged	D letter		W my staff						
April 1: Issued and served a claim on defendant	D claim								

Additional facts:

Although there was no animosity between the parties initially, the plaintiff is annoyed because he waited so long before hearing from the defendant. He figured that the defendant was evading him so that he would not have to pay for the work. He felt that returning his call would surely result in telephone tag. This plaintiff met two such defendants in other actions. He settled both only to find out that this is a frequent problem in running his small business. He is tired of settling for less than the full amount, plus interest and costs incurred in collecting the money owed. He is concerned that this defendant might be hoping for a settlement for less than the amount of the claim so that he, too, could take advantage of the fact that the plaintiff, a businessperson, does not have time to spend preparing for and attending at court. He has had to write off debts like this before for lack of time to prepare and attend at court.

EVALUATING THE STORY OF THE DEFENDANT

FACT	EVIDENCE FROM			SUPPORTED BY LAW OR EQUITY			STRENGTH OF CASE		
(oldest to most recent)	Document	Photo or Object	Witness	Legislation	Case Law	Equity	Weak	Unsure or 50/50	Strong
January 2: Defendant agreed to pay plaintiff $5 000, half as deposit and the remaining half upon performance of service	D contract, deposit cheque		W my neigh-bour						
January 18: Plaintiff told me about the NSF, said he would continue with work and asked for a replacement certified cheque or money order — I agree to produce it but was concerned and puzzled as to why a good cheque would have bounced — called bank to ask for an explanantion — bank said they would look into it	D NSF cheque notice	P	W my staff						
January 19: I got a call and had to leave for Australia on an emergency family matter — no time and too distressed to call plaintiff	D letter		W my staff						
March 1: Returned home from trip — reviewed mail collected in my absence — saw demand letter — heard answering message from bank — called bank — their mistake in processing cheque			W, W (spouse, neigh-bour)						
March 5: Received second demand letter — called bank for confirmation letter re: their mistake			W bank manager						

FACT	EVIDENCE FROM			SUPPORTED BY LAW OR EQUITY			STRENGTH OF CASE		
(Oldest to most recent)	Document	Photo or Object	Witness	Legislation	Case Law	Equity	Weak	Unsure or 50/50	Strong
March 9: Received confirmation letter from bank manager — left message for plaintiff who did not get my return call April 1: Served with claim — immediately filed defence			W self						

Additional facts:

The defendant was more than willing to pay the full amount. However, since he feels the returned cheque is not his fault, he does not wish to pay interest or costs for the proceedings. He is willing to settle for the amount of the contract alone.

Here are some hypothetical results of the lawsuit in these samples:

Hypothetical Result No. 1

As in most scenarios, there is room for negotiation. It is easy to see how the parties might settle this matter without proceeding to trial. The defendant makes an offer to pay for the work without interest or costs. The plaintiff agrees, providing that the money is received in the form of a certified cheque or money order. The defendant agrees to these terms.

Hypothetical Result No. 2

The judge hears the stories of the plaintiff and defendant and decides that it would be most fair if the plaintiff got his money without interest and costs. Note that such a decision would have made it better to settle than to take the case to trial.

Hypothetical Result No. 3

The judge hears the stories of the plaintiff and defendant and finds that the defendant should pay for the work and interest on the overdue amount, but makes the interest payable on the day that the defendant discovered that the bank was at fault. The judge feels that the defendant should have immediately paid the amount to avert a law suit. However, the defendant offered to pay the amount of the claim plus interest from the beginning. Therefore, the judge did not award costs to either party since she feels that the plaintiff should have accepted this reasonable offer.

words, write a letter to the other party stipulating that the offer is withdrawn effective immediately or as of a particular date. You do not need to provide a reason why an offer is being withdrawn.

6. Responding to the Offer

If you have been served with an offer to settle a case, you can accept the offer, make a counter offer, accept the offer with conditions of payment, or reject the offer.

6.1 Accepting the offer

You cannot accept an offer after the trial. The verdict is final. There are no opportunities for settlement once the judge has made a decision. If you need to buy time to consider settling, ask for recess or an adjournment before the trial. Granting an adjournment is at the judge's discretion, but if you can get the other party to agree to an adjournment for the purpose of negotiating a settlement, the judge will more likely be willing to grant it. It is to your advantage to settle earlier because you may be able to avoid paying additional cost penalties.

6.2 Making a counter offer

If you are pleased with the offer generally but would like to accept it on slightly different terms, you may make a counter offer. A counter offer is simply another offer that changes conditions made in the original offer. It is best done in writing to ensure that there is a record of the terms you accepted. Once you serve the counter offer on a party, the party can accept it, counter it, or reject the counter offer outright.

6.3 Accepting the offer with conditions of payment

If the defendant offers to pay the plaintiff money, the plaintiff may accept that offer on the condition that the defendant pays the money into court. Such a condition or settlement requirement is often useful when the defendant must abide by a payment plan. If such a condition is included in the settlement agreement, the offer is accepted when the defendant makes the payment into court and notifies the plaintiff that the money has been paid into court.

In British Columbia, a third party who accepts an offer to settle must pay the settlement funds into court. Unless all parties agree, only a judge may order that the money be removed from the court.

However, if the defendant has agreed to this condition but has failed to make the payment into court, the plaintiff may choose one of the following two options:

(a) The plaintiff may make a motion or application to the court for an order enforcing the offer as accepted.

(b) The plaintiff can proceed to trial as if the offer had never been made.

Note: Settlement offers cannot be used in court until after the verdict, at which time the costs are at issue and the judge should be made aware of the offer to settle.

To pay money into court, take the following steps:

(a) Obtain the appropriate funds.

(b) Obtain a requisition from the court office.

(c) Fill out the requisition.

(d) Take the requisition and the payment to the court office.

(e) Obtain a receipt and file it away in a safe place.

The court generally mails the payment to the judgment creditor. However, many jurisdictions have a requisition system in which the judgment creditor must request from the court payment of the monies paid into court. This generally entails filling out a requisition form available at the court office.

6.4 The manner of settlement

Sometimes things happen at the eleventh hour. Consequently, accepting an offer to settle may be in the form of a verbal agreement just outside the courtroom during recess. If that happens, go back into the courtroom and tell the judge the terms of the settlement. This way the settlement will be on the record and will allow the other party to confirm the settlement before the judge. You can then ask the judge to award the appropriate costs, unless they are included in the settlement terms.

If the other party has prepared the minutes of settlement, read it very carefully. Make sure that you understand it and agree with all the terms before you sign.

Unless settlement is on the court record, it is finalized when all parties sign *minutes of settlement*. This document simply lists all of the terms of the settlement. Minutes of settlement are usually prepared after the parties reach a settlement agreement. Any party may prepare this document but all parties should sign it in the presence of at least one witness.

If you settle the case during a pre-trial conference, then the pre-trial judge or referee may make an order that states the terms of settlement. For example, the defendant may agree to have judgment entered against him or her but may not be able to pay right away. In this case, both sides must establish payment terms.

The following may then occur:

(a) A judge may ask the parties to discuss the terms on their own or may facilitate their discussions.

(b) A judge may also refer the matter to a referee who can discuss payment options at a special appointment set up by the court based on how the pre-trial judge or referee endorses (or notes) the record.

(c) If the pre-trial judge or referee does not put the terms on the record and the two sides do not sign it to make it binding, you may have to put the settlement terms in writing. This would be accomplished through the minutes of settlement.

When a judge makes a note in your court file, the judge is *endorsing the record*.

6.5 Drafting minutes of settlement

The minutes of settlement are the written record of the terms of settlement and the consequences of not adhering to those terms. The following should be included in the minutes of settlement:

(a) Official claim number

(b) Date of the settlement

(c) Plaintiff's name

(d) Defendant's name

(e) Money to be paid to the judgment creditor, including payment method (payment into court, cash, cheque), payment schedule, and interest rates

(f) Other terms to which the parties have agreed, in great detail if necessary

(g) Signatures of all individuals party to the agreement

(h) Signature and name of a witness

(i) Clause that this action settles the matter and precludes further action on this matter

(j) Enforcement clause stipulating what happens if terms are not complied with

(k) Other terms and clauses as you deem necessary

Sample 2 and Sample 3 show minutes of settlement.

6.6 Drafting the offer to settle and the release

A *release* is a written record that outlines the terms of settlement and specifies that the defendant is released from further payments or court actions for the same events on which the action was based. While minutes of settlement typically result from lengthy negotiations with numerous terms, a release is often a very simple document.

If you are making a written offer to settle, attach a release to be signed, witnessed, and returned to you before payment. Sample 4 shows an offer to settle and accompanying release.

6.7 Rejecting the offer

A party does not have to accept an offer even if it is reasonable, and does not have to give a reason for rejecting an offer. However, you may wish to note your rejection of the offer in writing and serve that notice on the offeror.

If you are rejecting an offer, do so in a professional manner. Behaving in an impolite or arrogant manner may discourage future settlement negotiations, intensify the dispute, and harm future relations between the parties.

Above all, be aware of the possible cost consequences or penalties of rejecting an offer.

7. When Settlement Seems Impossible

If you settled your case, congratulations! If not, you may wish to consider a settlement conference.

If your case did not settle during a settlement (pre-trial) conference, continue on to the relevant portions of chapter 7.

If the action does not settle and there is no pre-trial (settlement) conference, you will have to proceed to trial.

If you mediated your case in Yukon and it did not settle, you will proceed to a pre-trial conference.

SAMPLE 2
MINUTES OF SETTLEMENT

MINUTES OF SETTLEMENT

Finedining v. Moving Company Limited

The plaintiff and defendant agree to settle the above action on the following terms:

1. The defendant shall pay to the plaintiff $1 065.00 (one thousand and sixty five dollars and zero cents) in full and final satisfaction of the above claim within 10 days.

2. The plaintiff and defendant shall sign a release which shall release each other from any further action or claim arising out of this claim.

Signed this 22nd day of June 200–:

Anne Finedining
_____
Anne Finedining

Jody Dodyson
_____
Director, Moving Company Limited

I.M. Witness
104 Nice Street
Toronto, ON M5P 4M4
_____
Signature and Address of Witness

U.R. Witness
14353 Queen Street
Toronto, ON   M5M 5M5
_____
Signature and Address of Witness

SAMPLE 3
MINUTES OF SETTLEMENT INVOLVING PAYMENT INTO COURT

Freddy Farmer sprays fruit trees for people. He generally does this for free in return for some of the fruit. One day, he went to spray the trees belonging to his friend, Ollie South. The ground was moist from the spring runoff. Freddy just wasn't thinking and ploughed through Ollie's nicely landscaped backyard to get to the fruit trees. In the process, Freddy demolished a large section of sod. Ollie was furious when Freddy refused to take responsibility for his action. Ollie took Freddy to court.

After a pre-trial conference, the two decided to settle amicably to preserve their working relationship. However, Freddy could pay for the damage only in installments. They drafted the following minutes of settlement.

Court File No. T1111/99

MINUTES OF SETTLEMENT

South v. Farmer

The plaintiff and defendant agree to settle the above action on the following terms:

1. The defendant shall pay to the plaintiff $700.00 (seven hundred dollars and zero cents) in full and final satisfaction of the above claim.

2. The payment shall consist of seven payments of $100.00 to be paid into court on the 15th of every month commencing on March 15, 200–.

3. The plaintiff and defendant shall, upon receiving the final payment, sign a release which shall release each other from any further action or claim arising out of this claim.

Signed this 10th day of April 200–:

Freddy Farmer	*Oliver South*
Freddy Farmer	Oliver South
I.M. Witness	*U.R. Witness*
101 Farm Street	110 Farm Street
Chiliwack, BC V2R 5H5	Chiliwack, BC V3R 6H6
Signature and Address of Witness	Signature and Address of Witness

---

SAMPLE 4
OFFER TO SETTLE AND RELEASE

Suppose the plaintiff was suing for damages to an expensive oak dining table as a result of its delivery by the defendant's moving company. The defendant proposed to settle and chose to use a release as a written record of that straightforward settlement. The defendant sent a letter of offer and enclosed the release.

January 25, 200–
Moving Company Limited
14353 Queen Street
Toronto, ON M5M 5M5

Dear Ms. Finedining:

Re: *Finedining v. Moving Company Limited*, Court File No. T9999/99

We propose to settle the above action on the following terms:

1. The defendant, Moving Company Limited, shall pay to the plaintiff the all-inclusive amount of $1 065.00 which includes:

    (a) $1 015.00 for damages to the oak dining-room table alleged to have been damaged while the defendant was moving it from one residence to another on November 11, 200–; and

    (b) $50.00 for filing the plaintiff's claim.

2. This offer is conditional upon the plaintiff signing and returning to the defendant the enclosed release.

This offer is valid until 4:30 p.m. on February 19, 200–.

Sincerely yours,

MOVING COMPANY LIMITED

Jody Dodyson

Jody Dodyson
President

Enclosure

SAMPLE 4 — Continued

RELEASE

Finedining v. Moving Company Limited

The plaintiff, Anne Finedining, of 100 Nice Street, Toronto, Ontario, agrees to accept the amount of $1 065.00 (one thousand and sixty five dollars and zero cents) as full satisfaction for the above action in exchange for a full release of the defendant, its agents and employees, from any liability whatsoever for the incident that occurred on or about November 11, 200–, during which the plaintiff sustained damage to her oak dining-room table.

Signed this 10th day of February 200–:

Anne Finedining	*Jody Dodyson*
Anne Finedining	Director, Moving Company Limited
I.M. Witness	*U.R. Witness*
104 Nice Street	14353 Queen Street
Toronto, ON M5P 4M4	Toronto, ON M5M 5M5
Signature and Address of Witness	Signature and Address of Witness

Cost Consequences of Rejecting an Offer

Under the British Columbia Rules

Defendant Does Not Accept Plaintiff's Offer

If the defendant rejects the plaintiff's offer, the trial judge may award the plaintiff a penalty if the plaintiff is awarded an amount that is the same as or less than the plaintiff's offer (including interests and costs).

Plaintiff Does Not Accept Defendant's Offer

If the plaintiff rejects the defendant's offer, the trial judge may award the defendant a penalty if the defendant is awarded an amount that is the same or less than the defendant's offer (including interests and costs).

Under the Ontario Rules

Defendant Does Not Accept Plaintiff's Offer

If the plaintiff makes an offer within seven days of the trial that the plaintiff does not accept and the offer has not expired or been withdrawn, the court may award the plaintiff up to twice the costs of the action if the plaintiff wins, providing that the plaintiff obtains a judgment at least as or more favourable than that of the terms of the offer to settle.

Plaintiff Does Not Accept Defendant's Offer

If a defendant makes an offer within seven days of the trial and the plaintiff does not accept that offer and the offer has neither expired nor been withdrawn, then the court may award the plaintiff up to twice the costs of the action if the plaintiff wins, providing the plaintiff obtains a judgment at least as or more favourable than that of the terms of the offer to settle.

Under the Northwest Territories Rules

Defendant Does Not Accept Plaintiff's Offer

If the defendant does not accept the plaintiff's offer and the plaintiff obtains a judgment equal to or more favourable than the terms of the offer, the court may award the plaintiff up to double the costs of the action.

Plaintiff Does Not Accept Defendant's Offer

If the plaintiff does not accept the defendant's offer and the plaintiff is not awarded more than the terms of the offer, the court may award the defendant the costs of his or her action from the date the offer was made.

7
The Settlement Conference

The settlement conference is a meeting that takes place after the pleadings have been filed with the court and before a trial is scheduled. The conference is an informal discussion between the parties and their lawyers or agents and a conference official (a judge, deputy judge, or referee). It differs from mediation in that a court official is involved and, once it is arranged, it forms part of the claims process.

1. The Purpose of a Settlement Conference

The goal of a settlement conference is to settle the action without having to go to trial. As discussed in chapter 6, there are a number of good reasons to attempt to reach a settlement agreement before going to trial.

A claim or defence may contain many issues, but, depending how clear the pleadings are, they may not all be in dispute. For example, a simple breach of contract case will typically involve at least the following issues:

- Was there a contract?
- Was there a breach of contract?
- What damages arose from the breach?
- Did the plaintiff mitigate (take measures to minimize) his or her damages?

A settlement conference can also be called a *pre-trial conference*.

Only the rules of British Columbia, Prince Edward Island, Ontario, Yukon, and Newfoundland provide for settlement (pre-trial) conferences. A pilot project for settlement conferences is underway in Saskatchewan.

A settlement conference allows parties to narrow those issues in a claim or defence that are in dispute. This can benefit your case in the following ways:

(a) It may assist you in settling the matter.

(b) If you cannot settle the matter, only those issues that are still in dispute after the settlement conference will be addressed at trial. If the issues are narrowed down before trial, the trial will be shorter and less costly for the parties.

(c) The conference official will tell the parties what issues and evidence they should focus on to support their case. This could be a recommendation to a party to admit certain facts, to call an expert witness, or to obtain evidence. Merely attending at the settlement conference fulfills this purpose as it causes the parties to review their facts, evidence, and objectives before the trial.

(d) The conference judge or referee will have an idea of how much court time the trial will require, thereby assisting the court in scheduling matters for trial.

(e) A settlement conference can also bring a quick end to the action if the conference official strikes a claim or defence.

(f) The conference official may order that evidence or names of witnesses be served on the parties before trial. Contracts, leases, insurance policies, receipts, and other documents on which your claim is based must be attached to the claim itself when it is issued and served on the defendant. However, often parties become aware of other documents and items after the action has commenced. These may be damage estimates, medical reports, police reports, and so on. There could also be physical evidence or the name of a witness. The settlement conference official will tell the parties that, if they have not already, they should disclose to each other all such evidence they intend to call at trial.

2. Requesting a Settlement Conference

Generally, a settlement conference is not mandatory unless a judge orders it or unless a particular jurisdiction makes it mandatory. Therefore, if you wish to have a settlement conference and it is not automatically scheduled, you must request one of the court.

More than one settlement conference may be convened in certain circumstances. If you feel that an additional conference would facilitate

Ask your local court office about its practice of conducting settlement conferences. Settlement conferences are mandatory in British Columbia, Prince Edward Island, and Newfoundland.

settlement, request one and state the reason for the second request. The court has the discretion to grant or deny your request.

In Yukon, if a third party files a reply after the settlement conference, another settlement conference will be held unless otherwise ordered by the court.

 ## Example

A judge at a previous settlement conference ended that conference because crucial evidence was missing. She endorsed (wrote on) the court record that another settlement conference may be granted at the request of the party who locates the missing evidence.

 ## Example

If a judge thinks that too many settlement conferences were convened, the first settlement conference was not productive, or the parties were not adequately prepared, then he or she may order that no further settlement conferences are permissible on that file.

3. Attendance at a Settlement Conference

Once a party receives notice of a settlement conference, he or she must attend, either represented by a lawyer or agent or self-represented. In some jurisdictions, trial dates are set at settlement conferences so it is in every party's best interest to attend. Witnesses, however, do not attend at settlement conferences.

Who must attend a settlement conference?

In Ontario, the parties themselves need not attend a pre-trial conference, unless they are unrepresented. However, any person attending on behalf of the parties should have instructions to settle the claim on behalf of those whom they represent.

In Newfoundland, the parties themselves must attend a settlement conference, even if they are represented by an agent or by counsel.

In British Columbia, special rules for attendance apply at a settlement conference if the claim arises out of a motor vehicle accident.

Do not take the settlement conference lightly. If a party who has been notified does not show up at the settlement conference, the court may do any of the following:

> Adjourn the settlement conference to another date

> Dismiss an action in whole or in part if the plaintiff does not attend

> Grant judgment against a particular defendant if that party fails to attend

If it is impossible for a particular party to attend, request an adjournment in one of the following ways:

(a) Try to get the written consent of the other parties to adjourn and agree to a date two or three months away. You can then notify court office staff, who will arrange a new date at that time.

(b) If you cannot get the consent of the other parties to adjourn, write to the court and explain why you cannot attend. Examples of reasons the court may accept as legitimate include sickness, family emergencies, religious holidays, and counsel scheduling conflicts. Be sure to send a copy to the other parties and include some preferred dates.

(c) If you do not notify the court office of an adjournment or request an adjournment of the court, you or another representative must attend the hearing to provide the reason you cannot continue with the conference as scheduled.

Keep in mind that the longer you wait to get an adjournment, the more likely you will inconvenience the others involved in this process. You will also lose credibility if you wait too long to request an adjournment when circumstances show that you could have done so much earlier. Also, remember that a settlement conference judge may award costs against a party if the judge feels that he or she has deliberately delayed the matter or inconvenienced another party or court when it was within his or her power to request an adjournment in a timely manner.

4. Preparing for the Settlement Conference

You must be thoroughly prepared for the settlement conference or the court may order you to pay the costs of the other parties.

While preparation for a settlement conference is considerably less involved than preparation for trial, it is not wise to take too many shortcuts. Furthermore, proper preparation for a settlement conference will reduce the time it will take you to prepare for trial should trial be necessary. Take the following steps to prepare:

(a) Review the case thoroughly at least a week before the conference.

(b) Identify the facts and issues that are in dispute.

(c) Review the law in this area.

(d) If settlement is a prospect, prepare a list of settlement terms and conditions (refer to chapter 6 for a detailed review of this topic).

(e) If settlement is not a prospect, decide how many witnesses you expect to be calling at trial. The conference official may ask you for this information.

Take the following items to the settlement conference:

▸ Plaintiff's claim

▸ Defence claim, defendant's claim, or both

▸ Documentary evidence (contracts, leases)

▸ List of documentary evidence

▸ Statement of facts

▸ List of issues to be resolved

▸ Case law you are relying on (one copy) (optional)

▸ Offer to settle

▸ Other court forms filed for this case

▸ Copies for all parties and conference official of any documentary evidence not yet produced to them

▸ A list of witnesses you expect to be calling at trial if the matter proceeds to trial

▸ Daytimer to ensure that trial date does not conflict with existing responsibilities

▸ A calculator

5.   Conference Procedure

The procedure for settlement conferences is far from rigid. They are simply informal discussions. While the exchange of comments may vary the order and substance of the discussion, the events will generally unfold as follows:

(a)   When your case is called, the parties should first introduce themselves to the conference official and to each other, if they have not already met.

(b)   The conference official will ask the parties if they have discussed settlement. If the answer is "No" and no offers have been considered, the official may send the parties out to discuss the matter, or may adjourn the conference. Most often, however, the official will simply continue with the settlement conference in the hope that the narrowing of issues, the disclosure of evidence, and the mutual assessment of the parties as witnesses at trial will result in settlement.

(c)   The conference official will ask the plaintiff to state the issues in dispute and present his or her position on those issues.

(d)   The conference official will ask the defendant or defendants to state the issues in dispute and present his or her position on those issues.

(e)   The conference official will discuss the strength of each party's case.

(f)   The conference official may ask the parties to consider settlement based on the discussions at the settlement conference.

(g)   The conference official may endorse (write on) the record that the matter has settled, that the settlement conference has been adjourned (postponed) to a date in the future, or that the case is to proceed to trial.

(h)   If the conference official is a judge or deputy judge, he or she may make any order he or she sees fit. If the official is a court-appointed referee, he or she may recommend that a judge make an order.

(i)   When the conference has concluded, the parties should obtain a photocopy of the endorsement before leaving. Ask the official for a copy. The only time you need not request a copy is if the matter is proceeding to trial and no other orders have been made.

5.1 Role of the parties

Each party plays an important role at the conference. For that reason every party should be well prepared and able to present his or her position with confidence but not arrogance. Attempt to act respectfully with the conference official and with the parties present and to discuss openly and honestly the issues in the case.

5.2 Role of the conference official

The conference official could be a judge, a deputy judge, or another individual appointed by the court and typically called a *referee* or *prothonotary*.

The role of the conference official is to —

(a) preside over the settlement conference,

(b) assess the strengths and weaknesses of a claim,

(c) assess the strengths and weaknesses of a defence,

(d) attempt to bring about settlement,

(e) make any orders as he or she sees fit, and

(f) prepare a memorandum summarizing the issues still in dispute, the issues to which the parties now agree, relevant evidence, and information about the number of witnesses expected to testify at trial. Such a memorandum is prepared at the discretion of the conference official and is usually written when the parties are expected to proceed to trial.

A judge or designated official may recommend how the issues should be formulated and how the issues can be simplified. He or she may also suggest which claims or defences should be eliminated because they are not supported by evidence, and which facts or documents should be admitted without further proof.

5.3 Orders

A judge or other individual appointed by the court will likely have the authority to make a number of orders. Some examples include the following:

> Order amending pleadings

> Order striking out a claim or a defence

> Order referring a matter to a payment hearing

> Order for costs

The conference official typically has discretion to make any other order related to the conduct of the case. Examples are orders that —

> the plaintiff file a medical report with the court;

> the plaintiff or defendant serve all parties with certain evidence and file such evidence with the court;

> a party requires a litigation guardian; and

> will facilitate the proof of evidence or the management of a trial.

5.4 Costs

The official presiding over the settlement conference has the discretion to award costs in special circumstances. Consider requesting costs in the following circumstances:

> A party attends so inadequately prepared as to frustrate the purposes of the settlement conference.

> A party who was notified of the settlement conference fails to attend.

Always ask that *costs be made payable forthwith* (without delay). If the judge refuses to make that order, then request that *costs be made payable following the disposition of the matter* (following settlement or trial).

If costs are awarded against you, pay the party who received the cost award directly unless the court orders otherwise. It is best to pay by a method that will give you proof of payment. Examples include payment by cheque, money order, or having the party sign an acknowledgment.

The following is an example of an acknowledgment.

❦ Example

I, Joe Shmoe, plaintiff in action C-90909 commenced in the Charlottetown Small Claims Court, acknowledge that on June 1, 200-, I received the sum of $50.00 cash from the defendant, Jane Shmane, as payment of the costs awarded by Deputy Judge Peteroff at the settlement conference held on May 31, 200–.

A prothonotary in Prince Edward Island has the same powers as a judge for settlement conferences.

6. After the Settlement Conference

6.1 If the action settles during the conference

If the action settles during the settlement conference, the parties should prepare and sign minutes of settlement if the judge has not endorsed the record as to the terms of settlement. See chapter 6 for more information on the minutes of settlement. Remember that the minutes of settlement are a binding agreement; all parties must abide with the terms of the settlement.

6.2 If the action does not settle during the conference

If the action does not settle during the conference, both parties must keep confidential the information exchanged at the settlement conference, unless the parties consent to the use of certain information.

🍁 Example

> Suppose the defendant admits during the settlement conference that he or she breached a contractual term. You cannot use this information at trial, unless the defendant agrees. You would then have to prove liability at trial. If liability is admitted, then you will tell the judge at the outset of the trial. This is called *admitting liability on the record*. You would then have to prove only the remaining issues.

If no settlement is reached, the matter will proceed to trial. Check with the conference official or court office as to what steps, if any, are necessary to arrange for a trial date. In some jurisdictions, the trial date is set during the settlement conference making further steps unnecessary. In other jurisdictions, the court takes care of it, either on its own or at the request of one of the parties.

If the matter is set down for trial, be sure to read chapters 8 and 9. Most of all, consider making another attempt to settle the action before trial.

If you settled, congratulations! If not, keep reading.

8
Preparing for Trial

1. Setting the Matter Down for Trial

If a pre-trial conference does not result in settlement, the action must be set down for trial. In some jurisdictions this is the plaintiff's responsibility. Elsewhere, the court clerk mails a notice of trial to the parties without any request on their part. This is very much a function of local practice, so check the procedure with your court office.

It is in the plaintiff's interest to have the action move along. The defendant could bring a motion to dismiss the action for delay so it is a good idea for the plaintiff to set the matter down for trial if the court does not normally do this without first receiving a request from one of the parties.

To set the matter down for trial you should write a letter to the court requesting that the action be set down for trial and then pay the fee for this service, if required.

Chapter 12 provides guidance on writing this type of letter. When the clerk fixes a date for trial and serves a notice of trial on the parties, note the trial date in your diary or calendar.

> Proper preparation for trial involves understanding trial procedure, advocacy, and evidence. These topics are covered in chapter 9.

2. Organizing the Case

Preparing for trial is a time-consuming task. However, careful preparation is almost always less costly than hasty, thoughtless preparation. If you prepare gradually and well enough before trial, you may even be able to settle the lawsuit.

Regardless of whether you are a plaintiff or defendant, here are some tips for preparing thoroughly and efficiently.

2.1 Keep a decent filing system for your case

You should start a filing system for your case from the outset. Organize the file into distinct sections in a file folder or binder, using clearly labelled tabs or sticky notes. Once you have done that, file information as soon as it comes in. In this way, information will be at your fingertips whenever you need to refer to it, such as when one of the parties calls or when you need to review evidence. If you need to respond to a motion, you will be able to meet the deadline much more easily with an organized file. Refer to Sample 5 for a tickler sheet of your file's contents.

The following sections for your filing system are recommended:

▸ *Summary of Proceedings*. Fill in the tickler sheet in Sample 5 to summarize the case and its developments.

▸ *Pleadings*. The pleadings are the plaintiff's claim, defendant's claim, and the defence.

▸ *Correspondence*. Letters between you and the parties should be kept in date order, with the oldest at the bottom and the most recent correspondence on top.

▸ *Other Documents Arising out of the Proceedings*. Motion materials, affidavits, court orders, court notices, offers to settle, and so on, should be kept in date order with the oldest at the bottom and the most recent document on top.

▸ *Evidence*. Documents, receipts, photographs, and other items to be used as evidence to support your case should be separated into two sections:

  ▸ *Liability*. The liability section should include evidence as to whether the defendant is liable for the alleged action or lack of action leading to the damages (i.e., evidence as to proof of fault).

  ▸ *Damages*. The damages section should include evidence as to the damages or harm done as a result of the alleged wrong (i.e., receipts, repair estimates, photographs, etc.), as well as evidence as to whether the plaintiff mitigated (acted to reduce) his or her damages.

SAMPLE 5
TICKLER SHEET

Cause of Action: Date: _____   Location: _____

Type of Action: _____   Notice Period: _____   Limitation Period: _____

TICKLER	PROCESS	DATE	TO PARTY
BEFORE THE LAWSUIT	Demand Letter Sent		
PLAINTIFF'S CLAIM	Issued Within Limitation Period		
	Claim Served		
	Claim Served		
	Affidavit of Service Filed		
DEFENCE	Defence Filed		
	Defence Filed		
	Defence Received		
DEFENCE-RELATED CLAIM	Defendant's Claim, Third Party Claim, Counterclaim, Crossclaim Issued		
	Claim Served		
	Claim Served		
	Affidavit of Service Filed		
SETTLEMENT	Settlement Conference Requested After Defence Filed		
	Settlement Conference		
	Offer Sent		
	Offer Sent		
	Offer Accepted		
	Offer Accepted		
	Action Set Down for Trial		
TRIAL	Trial		
	Witnesses Summonsed		
	Documents Disclosed		

> *Notes*. The notes section should include notes you keep on the case throughout the various proceedings. Be sure to sign and date each note.

> *Costs*. The costs section includes receipts documenting expenses such as service of documents, photocopying charges, letters documenting salary loss as a result of attendance at trial, and so on.

2.2 Update your summary of proceedings sheet as events unfold

If you keep your summary of proceedings up-to-date, it will provide you with a quick glance of the proceedings, their dates or anticipated dates, and a quick telephone list of parties.

2.3 Start preparing at least one month before trial

If you do not start preparing your case early, you may run into some difficulties: key witnesses may have moved away or gone on vacation, documents you need as evidence may be hard to obtain on short notice, or you may overlook facts or documents in a rushed preparation.

Develop a trial strategy at least one month before trial.

2.4 Create a trial binder

It is best to set up a trial binder at the outset of the action. You should not leave this task any longer than two weeks before trial.

A well-organized trial binder will be an invaluable tool at trial. It will assist you in entering evidence and will minimize fumbling for documents during trial. It will also help you review the case in an organized way.

A common approach involves obtaining a three-ring binder and tabbed section dividers or sticky notes or whatever it takes to separate materials into various sections.

Arrange the binder into the following sections, and fill them in as you work through the next two chapters:

(a)   Opening statement

(b)   Examination-in-chief

(c)   Cross-examination

(d)   Closing arguments

(e)   Pleadings

(f)   Other court documents

(g)   Evidence

(h)   Theory of the case

(i)   Authorities (legislation, case law, etc.)

(j)   Notes

The next task is to establish a trial strategy or theory of the case.

3.   Developing a Trial Strategy

The trial strategy is often referred to as the *theory of the case*. Think of the theory of the case as a road map. You can only decide the route you will travel if you know where you want to end up. So, know what you want to achieve at the end of the trial, then determine how you will achieve it.

Having a clear trial strategy will help you present your case in a clear manner, focused only on what is important for the judge to hear, understand, and believe. You, as advocate, will be more relaxed because you have properly prepared your case and will have increased your likelihood of winning. A clear trial strategy also enables you to determine the witnesses, documents, and other evidence you will require at trial, and helps you to recognize and object to the other side's attempts to introduce irrelevant evidence.

3.1   Identifying the issues

Before moving on, it is important to understand the word *issue*. An issue in a lawsuit is a point in question. Each allegation is an issue. Each question pointing to a breach of a common law or statutory duty is an issue. A simple breach of contract case, for example, will typically involve at least the following issues:

▶ Was there a contract?

▶ Was there a breach of contract?

▶ What damages arose from the breach?

▶ Did the plaintiff mitigate (act to minimize) his or her damages?

A simple negligence action involves proof of at least the following issues:

1.   Was there a duty or an obligation requiring the defendant to abide by certain standards of conduct?

2. Did the defendant fail to perform the duty or honour the obligation?

3. Was there causation (i.e., the act or failure to act caused the damages)?

4. Was there actual loss or damages?

You will need to review the pleadings and identify all the issues. If you have attended at a pre-trial conference, you should be familiar with which issues are in dispute and will be the focus of the trial.

In order to develop a trial strategy (theory of the case), the plaintiff and defendant or their representatives should answer all of the following questions for each major issue:

PLAINTIFF'S CASE	DEFENDANT'S CASE
1. What is the plaintiff suing for?	1. What is the defendant being sued for?
2. What result does the plaintiff want?	2. What result does the defendant want?
3. What must the plaintiff prove to win?	3. What must the defendant prove to win?

3.2 Evaluating the issues

You should think about each issue from your own perspective and try to imagine the perspective of the other parties. By answering the same questions as if you were the other party, you will help yourself guess and assess the strategies the other side might use. In this way, it will be less likely that the case your opponent presents will catch you off guard. Once you have worked through these questions, you should be able to state your theory of the case in a few short sentences. Sample 6 shows how you could develop your trial strategy, while Sample 7 shows some examples of the plaintiff's and defendant's theory of case.

Once you have outlined your strategy, stick to it. If you deviate from your strategy, you run the risk of covering evidence that will have no bearing on the judge's decision and waste the valuable time of the court, the parties, and the witnesses. Furthermore, sticking to your strategy will help prevent disruptions in the flow of evidence because your opponent and the judge will not have to object to evidence you are presenting.

SAMPLE 6
DEVELOPING A TRIAL STRATEGY

The plaintiff is bringing a claim against a former tenant for failure to pay rental arrears. The plaintiff asks three questions from the view of each party (each plaintiff and each defendant).

Theory of the Case for Plaintiffs

QUESTION	ANSWER
What is the plaintiff suing for?	Arrears in rent (a breach of contract)
What result does the plaintiff want?	Judgment that the defendant owes the arrears and must pay the plaintiff
What must the plaintiff prove to win?	The plaintiff's case will have to prove all of the following three elements: 1. That the plaintiff and defendant had an oral or written (lease) agreement for rental accommodations 2. That the terms of the agreement were that the defendant had to pay certain amounts on certain days for a certain period of time 3. That the defendant breached the agreement by not paying certain amounts on the required day or days

The plaintiff's theory of the case is:

The defendant breached the rental agreement by failing to pay rent as required by the agreement.

Note that the answers are a great starting point for determining what evidence you will need to present in court.

Theory of the Case for Defendants

QUESTION	ANSWER
What is the defendant being sued for?	Arrears in rent (a breach of contract)
What result does the defendant want?	Judgment that the defendant does not owe the arrears and should not pay them

SAMPLE 6 — Continued

QUESTION		ANSWER
What must the defendant prove to win?	A. No rental agreement existed OR	The plaintiff and defendant did not have an oral or written (lease) agreement for rental accommodations For example, suppose two people have moved in together or live as common-law spouses, and when one of them leaves, the other, having relied on his or her money to pay the rent, deems there to have been a rental agreement
	B. Agreement existed but not on terms plaintiff alleges OR	The terms of the agreement relating to when and what the defendant had to pay is not the same as the plaintiff's claim alleges For example, the plaintiff agreed to accept gardening services in lieu of rent
	C. Agreement existed and defendant paid accordingly OR	The defendant did not breach the agreement but paid in accordance with his or her understanding of the agreement
	D. Agreement existed but defendant did not pay because the plaintiff violated the agreement OR	The plaintiff breached the agreement by failing to provide rental accommodations according to the agreement (no heat, water, parking spot, peace and quiet, or other conditions)
	E. Agreement existed but defendant did not pay because of mitigating circumstances	The terms of the agreement were the same, but the defendant was willing but unable to pay because of mitigating circumstances such as: ▶ the defendant was laid off or had excessive medical bills; or ▶ the defendant made partial payments to the best of his or her ability, but the plaintiff rejected this proposal

Note: The list of defences provided is by no means exhaustive as each case is based on different facts.

The defendant's theory of the case is (using Defence B above):

The defendant did not breach the agreement as alleged since the plaintiff agreed to accept the defendant's gardening services in lieu of rent money.

SAMPLE 7
TRIAL STRATEGIES

THEORY OF THE CASE FOR PLAINTIFFS	THEORY OF THE CASE FOR DEFENDANTS
▶ The defendant entered into a lease with the plaintiff, failed to abide by its terms, and now the plaintiff is trying to recover arrears.	▶ The defendant entered into a lease with the plaintiff, but the defendant should not pay since the plaintiff failed to provide living accommodations in accordance with the terms of the agreement.
▶ The defendant vandalized the plaintiff's backyard and should pay for repairs and landscaping work for which the plaintiff had to pay.	▶ The defendant was not convicted of this crime and claims this is a case of mistaken identity.
▶ The plaintiff renovated the defendant's kitchen but has not received money since the 50 percent deposit was made and is trying to recover it from the defendant.	▶ The defendant does not owe money to the plaintiff since the work was not of the expected quality.
▶ The defendant fired the plaintiff who must now recover the termination pay not paid although rightfully owed to the plaintiff.	▶ The defendant does not owe termination pay because the plaintiff was terminated for cause.
▶ The defendant failed to clear the steps to his residence thereby causing the plaintiff to slip and fall.	▶ The plaintiff slipped and fell because she lost her balance trying to juggle groceries as well as a baby stroller.

Now that you have your trial strategy, the next task is to organize your evidence.

4. Organizing Evidence

Starting early to organize your evidence means your chances of reviewing the evidence with witnesses will not be under time constraints. In addition, you will have ample time to obtain additional evidence that you may need. If you are relying on an institution to provide you with receipts or documents, you will need two or three months to compile it all. Starting as early as you can may prevent the need for adjournments.

Organize your evidence at least three to four weeks before trial.

Read through chapter 9 for more information on the types of evidence you may produce.

The plaintiff must prove his or her case on the *balance of probabilities*. This means the plaintiff must provide proof that it is more likely than not that the events surrounding an issue took place in the way the plaintiff's evidence shows, rather than the way the defendant's evidence shows. The defendant's evidence should convince the judge that the defendant's version of events is more likely to have taken place than the plaintiff's version. The judge will make a decision by following the evidence both sides present, considering the evidence presented, assessing the credibility of parties and witnesses, and listening to the closing arguments.

To plan the evidence you will present at trial, refer to your trial strategy. You must present evidence for each element that you have to prove. This proof may be through oral testimony of witnesses, agreements, letters, business records, receipts, invoices, photographs, and other documents, or through articles (e.g., damaged goods).

For each issue, the plaintiff and defendant should answer, "What type of evidence must I introduce to prove that element?" Take a look at Sample 8, which outlines the evidence needed by the plaintiff and by the defendant in order to prove each case.

Place copies of documentary and photographic evidence in your trial binder. If you are missing evidence, make a note of what you will need to obtain. Then, without further delay, find that evidence. You may need to write to the bank to request bank statements or other documentation. These requests take time (and usually have a fee associated with them), so make your requests without delay.

If your evidence includes photographs, place them in an envelope and then insert the envelope in your trial binder. Develop film evidence without delay.

5. Preparing Witnesses

You should prepare your witnesses within two or three weeks of trial.

Once you have your trial strategy and your evidence organized, you will want to meet with your witnesses, each separately. Before committing witnesses to appear at trial, review your case to assess the witnesses who will be most useful. Limiting the number of witnesses will preserve valuable court time and reduce the costs of the lawsuit. At your meetings with your witnesses you should do the following:

> ▸ Prepare each witness for the events that will unfold on the day of trial.

EVIDENCE NEEDED TO PROVE A CASE

Evidence needed for the plaintiff to prove his or her case

WHAT MUST THE PLAINTIFF PROVE TO WIN?	WHAT EVIDENCE CAN BE USED?
1. That the plaintiff and defendant had a verbal or written agreement for rental accommodations	Written agreement: lease or other written agreement Verbal agreement: ▶ testimony of the plaintiff ▶ testimony of witness who saw the defendant sign the lease or was present when the plaintiff and defendant formed their verbal agreement
2. What the terms of the agreement were (when and what the defendant had to pay)	Written agreement: lease setting out rent amount and payment intervals Verbal agreement: testimony of the plaintiff as to when the rent was to have been paid and the amount
3. That the defendant breached the agreement by not paying the required amount	▶ testimony of the plaintiff ▶ testimony of the plaintiff that rent was not paid as required ▶ testimony of the plaintiff that the defendant did not pay after all ▶ defendant's account summary (if available) showing outstanding rent

Evidence needed for the defendant to prove his or her case

WHAT MUST THE DEFENDANT PROVE TO WIN?		WHAT EVIDENCE CAN BE USED?
A. No rental agreement existed OR	The plaintiff and defendant did not have an oral or written (lease) agreement for rental accommodations	For example, testimony of defendant The testimony of defendant or written agreement demonstrating that the terms were not the same as those alleged in the plaintiff's claim
B. Agreement existed but not on terms plaintiff alleges OR	The terms of the agreement relating to when and what the defendant had to pay is not the same as the plaintiff's claim alleges or	For example, terms not clearly set out in agreement
C. Agreement existed and defendant paid accordingly OR	The defendant did not breach the agreement but paid in accordance with his or her understanding of the agreement	For example, the plaintiff unilaterally increased rent or did so without prior notice and the defendant paid the rent according to the agreement
D. Agreement existed but defendant did not pay because the plaintiff violated the agreement OR	The plaintiff breached the agreement by failing to provide rental accommodations according to the agreement	For example, testimony of defendant and a witness that the plaintiff breached some term of the rental agreement (no heat, water, parking spot, or other conditions)
E. Agreement existed but defendant did not pay because of mitigating circumstances	That the terms of the agreement were as alleged but the defendant was unable to pay because of mitigating circumstances such as: • the defendant was laid off or had excessive medical bills • the defendant made partial payments to the best of his or her ability but the plaintiff rejected this proposal	For example, testimony of the defendant as to the mitigating circumstances plus: • proof of difficult circumstances in the form of a lay-off notice, a doctor's certificate • proposal as to amount defendant was willing to pay

- ▸ Explain the trial procedure.

- ▸ Explain the method of questioning you will use with each witness (such an *examination-in-chief* is explained in the advocacy section of chapter 9).

- ▸ Explain the method of questioning the opposing side will use on each witness (such a *cross-examination* is explained in the advocacy section of chapter 9).

- ▸ Refresh each witness's memory about the events they will be required to testify. Be careful not to make suggestions as to what witnesses should say.

- ▸ You can even consider providing a sheet for each witness summarizing his or her evidence. You must, however, inform them that such a sheet is a rough outline, not a rigid program. Stress that questions and answers should not be memorized and that testimony must be natural.

- ▸ Let each witness know that preparation for trial is an acceptable practice and that, while you cannot coach them as to what testimony they should give, you are there to go over their stories and familiarize them with the trial process.

- ▸ Determine whether an interpreter will be necessary for the trial. If so, arrange for one well ahead of time. You can call the Ministry of the Attorney General in your province or territory, who may keep a registry of freelance court interpreters.

By properly preparing your witnesses well in advance of the trial, you will call on more relaxed witnesses who can improve your chances of success at trial. Furthermore, meeting with them beforehand allows you to assess the witnesses as to their presentation and credibility and allows you to reflect on the strategy and evidence to be used.

It is not always possible to find an ideal witness but, in preparing your witness, you can guide the witness as to the dress and conduct that is appropriate for court.

Every witness will require some preparation. Some experienced witnesses such as police officers and doctors require minimal preparation. In such cases, verify that the witnesses have participated in trials in the past. If they have, all you will need is a brief review of the evidence they will be presenting.

What makes an ideal witness?

An ideal witness is someone who —

- has first-hand knowledge of the event he or she is testifying about,
- can give the facts accurately, and presents well by —
  - dressing for court, not for a picnic, dance, or tavern,
  - respecting the court and not being argumentative,
  - remaining calm, not emotional about the circumstances,
  - listening well and not interrupting,
  - speaking clearly, and
  - making good eye contact.

In contrast, a person who has seldom or never been a witness in a trial will require a lot more preparation. You will have to explain things like court procedure, court conduct, how one should dress for court, and where the court is located. You may find it helps to fill in information and give witnesses copies of the witness information sheet shown in Sample 9.

All witnesses must be told when and where to show up. You should also forewarn a witness as a matter of precaution that he or she may be served with a summons.

If you go to court without properly preparing your witnesses, you run the risk of having something go awry. Take the time to prepare and you won't regret it.

6. Summonsing Witnesses

Some witnesses are willing and able to testify in court; others are not. While you may feel confident that certain witnesses will attend on request, it could be disastrous if a key witness fails to attend. You must use your discretion as to whether or not you wish to request the court to issue a summons.

A summons to witness (also known as a *subpoena*) is a court document that —

(a) orders a witness to give evidence in court at the stated date, time, and place,

Try to serve the summons to witness or subpoena within three weeks of trial.

SAMPLE 9
WITNESS INFORMATION SHEET

To: _____ Date: _____
      [name of witness]   [month, day, year]

Your attendance will be required at trial in the matter of:

_____   v.   _____
[name of plaintiff], Plaintiff(s)   [name of defendant], Defendant(s)

You will be testifying for ❏ The Plaintiff(s)   ❏ The Defendant(s).

❏ Expect to receive a Summons to Witness (Subpoena).
    Show it to your employer when asking for the day off.

❏ Thank you for agreeing to attend without a Summons to Witness.

Arrive on this date	
Arrive at this time	Please arrive 30 minutes early.
Arrive at this location	_____Court located at_____ [name of town or city] [name of town or city]
Please bring with you these items	1. Holy Book (if other than the Bible) that may be used to swear you in as a witness. You may also be affirmed. 2. All documentary or physical evidence related to the above action that is within your possession.
Please wear business attire	Definitely no denim, hats, gloves, rollerblades, and so on. Dress conservatively, as you would for a business meeting.
Please Note	If you have been summonsed and do not attend the trial, the judge may issue a warrant for your arrest. Witnesses who attend but do not co-operate with the trial process may be found in contempt of court and may serve a jail sentence. It is a criminal offence to lie while testifying under oath. Listen to the entire question asked of you at trial; then answer loudly enough for the judge and court reporter to hear you.

Please ensure that the party serving your Summons to Witness (Subpoena) has your current telephone number so that you may be notified in the event that the trial is rescheduled.

If you have any questions about the trial, please call _____
                                                              [your name]

at_____.   **THANK YOU.**
      [telephone number]

Witness Information Sheet sent by: _____
                                              [your name]

via ❏ Fax   ❏ Regular Mail   ❏ Registered Mail   ❏ Courier   ❏ Personal Delivery

(b) orders the witness to remain in court until attendance is no longer required,

(c) orders the witness to produce at trial any documents or things listed on the summons,

(d) orders the witness to produce at trial all other documents relating to the action if it is within the witness's custody, possession, or control,

(e) warns the witness that the court will issue a warrant for the arrest of any witness who does not attend, and

(f) is proof that court attendance is required and that absence from work for that reason is mandatory and justified.

As a precaution, you may wish to serve each of your witnesses with a summons to witness. Bear in mind, though, that the cost can be considerable. The court has the power to order a party to pay a witness compensation for inconvenience and expense if the judge is satisfied that a party has abused the power to summons a witness.

If a summons to witness has been served and a witness who has evidence that is material to the action does not attend in court or has left the trial without completing his or her testimony or without the judge's permission, the court may direct the police to apprehend a witness and bring him or her promptly to the court.

The apprehended witness may be —

▶ detained in custody until he or she is no longer required by the court,

▶ released on such terms as are just, or

▶ ordered to pay costs arising from his or her failure to attend in court or remain in attendance.

The following steps will enable you to summons a witness:

(a) Complete a summons to witness or subpoena for each witness.

(b) Take the completed summons or subpoena to the court office.

(c) Give the court office the appropriate witness fee for each witness. You must provide separate amounts for each summons. If you have two witnesses, you cannot write one cheque for both fees, but a separate cheque for each. A higher fee applies to summons witnesses who live outside of the jurisdiction. (This is the first type of fee required for issuing the summons.)

(d) The court office staff will check to ensure that proper funds have been paid and will place the funds in an envelope and staple it to the summons or subpoena.

(e) Pay the appropriate fee for issuing the summons. If you have more than one summons, you do not have to pay this fee separately. (This is the second type of fee required for issuing the summons.)

(f) Court office staff will sign and seal the summons or, in other words, issue it.

(g) You must now personally serve the summons to witness to the person named on the summons. You can do this yourself or have a process server or someone else do it.

Process servers

A process server is a person or corporation that takes care of serving court documents to parties and witnesses involved in lawsuits. A fee is paid for each document served. If the process server travels a great distance, he or she may also bill for mileage travelled.

If you have trouble serving the witness, read chapter 13 for alternatives the court may grant.

(h) Notify all parties that you have served one or more witnesses with a summons. This notice should be made in writing.

(i) The person who served the witness must provide proof of service by way of an affidavit or certificate of service. The proof should be that he or she served the witness named in the summons or subpoena, and paid the appropriate attendance fee.

> The affidavit should be sworn before a commissioner of oaths. Keep the affidavit or certificate of service in your file binder. The trial judge may ask to see it should he or she require proof that you summonsed a witness who did not attend.

In Nova Scotia, an affidavit or certificate of service is presented orally at trial.

7. Preparing Yourself as Advocate

To properly prepare yourself for presenting the case to the court, read all of chapter 9 on trial procedure, whether you are representing yourself or someone else. Take time to learn the trial procedure to the best of your ability, starting as soon as it seems likely that the case will proceed to trial.

8.   Planning your Presentation

Prepare your presentation at least one week before trial.

Thoroughly review your strategy and supporting evidence at least one week before trial. Begin by reading through your file binder.

Then do the following with the help of chapter 9:

(a)   Write your opening statement.

(b)   Determine the order of witnesses.

(c)   Write out questions for examination-in-chief.

(d)   Write out questions for cross-examination.

(e)   Write your closing argument.

Use your imagination to rehearse the trial. Make changes to your questions, opening statement, and closing argument, if required. Place these in the appropriate sections of your trial binder.

When planning the order of witnesses, consider that you should present the evidence in a clear and logical manner. It is best to present the evidence in chronological order: from beginning to end. Attempt to balance the order of witnesses with their needs. For example, a witness may prefer to attend in the afternoon because he or she is working the night shift and would be virtually incoherent early in the morning.

Present your best two witnesses or your witnesses with the most favourable testimony for your case first and last for most impact. Present your worst witnesses or the witnesses with testimony damaging to your case somewhere in the middle of the order.

Planning the order of witnesses is no small feat when your case involves complex facts and numerous witnesses. If there is only one witness, it is probably best to have the plaintiff (or defendant) testify first, then have the witness testify for that party.

Once your preparation is complete, you will only need to finalize details a day or two before the trial.

9.   Finalizing Details

Try to get a good night's sleep the night before the trial. If you don't, you run the risk of not following the evidence and missing some key opportunities to test statements made by opposing witnesses.

On the day before trial, make three copies of all authorities (legislation, case law, etc.) you intend to rely on in court and insert them into the appropriate section of your trial binder. Mark the cover of your own copy so that you don't give a marked up or highlighted copy to the judge or to the other parties.

Remember to leave telephone or fax messages for witnesses, reminding them of their court appearance and where you will meet them.

Review your case early in the day or, preferably, when you are not too tired to absorb details. Then organize your briefcase to contain all the items you will need to take to court. We suggest taking the following:

- Trial binder
- Articles and documentary evidence not in the trial binder
- Offer to Settle
- The whole file or, at least, the correspondence section
- Pens and highlighters
- Diary, in case of adjournment
- A calculator

Review Checklist 4 to ensure that you do not overlook anything.

CHECKLIST 4
PREPARING FOR TRIAL

TIME BEFORE TRIAL	
a.s.a.p.	❑ **Has the matter been set down for trial?**
a.s.a.p.	❑ **Did you read chapter 9 on trial procedure in its entirety?**
a.s.a.p.	❑ **Did you organize the file?**
a.s.a.p.	❑ Did you update your tickler sheet (Sample 5) ❑ Did you organize the trial binder?
4 weeks	❑ **Did you develop a trial strategy?**
3 to 4 weeks	❑ **Did you organize the evidence?**
3 weeks	❑ **Did you summons or subpoena witnesses?**

2 to 3 weeks	❑ **Did you prepare the witnesses for trial?**
	   ❑ Did you meet with each witness?
	   ❑ Did you explain the trial procedure?
	   ❑ Did you explain the examination-in-chief and cross-examination?
	   ❑ Did you arrange for an interpreter, if necessary?

a.s.a.p.	❑ **Did you prepare yourself as advocate by reading the advocacy section in chapter 9?**

1 week	❑ **Did you plan your presentation?**
	   ❑ Did you prepare an opening statement?
	   ❑ Did you prepare questions for examination-in-chief?
	   ❑ Did you prepare questions for cross-examination?
	   ❑ Did you plan the order of witnesses?
	   ❑ Did you prepare your closing arguments?

1 or 2 days	❑ **Did you finalize trial details?**
	   ❑ Did you make three copies of all authorities (legislation and case law)?
	   ❑ Did you make three copies of all documentary evidence?
	   ❑ Did you remind witnesses of the trial and where to meet you?
	   ❑ Did you review your case?
	   ❑ Did you organize your briefcase to contain:
	      ❑ trial binder?
	      ❑ articles and documentary evidence not in the trial binder?
	      ❑ client instructions to settle, if possible?
	      ❑ offer to settle?
	      ❑ the whole file or, at least, the correspondence section?
	      ❑ a couple of pens and highlighters?
	      ❑ diary, in case of adjournment?
	      ❑ a calculator?

Notes:
   (a) time before trial = at least this much time before trial
   (b) a.s.a.p. = as soon as possible

9
Trial Procedure

At last the trial date is upon you. It's a day filled with excitement. Yet the day of trial can also be filled with confusion and anxiety if you aren't familiar with the trial process. You must meet with your opposition, be an advocate, listen carefully, and respond to any number of events that may occur on your day of trial. It can be draining, but there is nothing like preparation to reduce the strain. This chapter will prepare you by teaching you the skills you should have to properly present (or advocate) your case.

1. The Day of Trial

To ensure that the day of your trial unfolds smoothly, be sure to arrive at court early. If you do not show up by the time your trial starts, the matter may be resolved without your involvement. You will also start off on the wrong foot with the judge, who will lose respect for you if you cannot show up in time for your own trial.

If you are in a rush before the trial, you and your fellow participants will be nervous. Your witnesses may wonder about your whereabouts and, perhaps, panic if you do not arrive on time. They will not be effective witnesses if they have already had a harrowing start to the day.

Furthermore, even if you show up just a few minutes late, you will not have an opportunity to speak to the clerk or the other parties. You may also miss opportunities to settle the matter before trial.

Of course, sometimes compelling reasons may make you late for trial. The court is understanding about most situations but, if you must be late, call the court office that morning and inform them that you will be arriving to proceed with trial but will be late. In this way, the court clerk can schedule you for the latter part of the list. Attempt to avoid lateness at all costs, however.

Remember, the courtroom is no place for children, unless they are parties or witnesses. Leave your children with a caregiver on the day of trial, and be sure that your child care arrangements cover the entire business day.

1.1 The courtroom and its players

A number of people may participate in a trial depending on the nature of the trial, the number of parties and whether they are represented, and the availability of court resources. Sometimes a clerk and a reporter are present during trials. At other times, only one of the two will be present. A third court officer may be present in some cases. This officer could be a court assistant or simply a court office employee who is observing the proceedings. The number of officials may differ even within a particular province or territory. Refer to Table 1 for an overview of likely trial participants.

Note: All parties must attend at trial unless that trial date has been adjourned ahead of time. The judge may remove the action from the trial list if none of the parties attend on the day of trial.

If the plaintiff fails to attend, the court may dismiss the claim and allow the defendant to prove the defendant's claim (if any).

If the defendant fails to show up, the court may strike the defence and any defence-related claims and the plaintiff may proceed to prove his or her claim.

Figures 1 and 2 show where the participants are seated when they do attend. The witness stand may be positioned on either side of the judge.

Note: The gates shown in Figure 1 may not be found in your particular courtroom.

Being familiar with the layout of the courtroom will help you attend to tasks before court begins, that is, before court is in session.

1.2 Before court is in session

You need to be aware of or take care of a number of things before court is in session.

FIGURE 1
WHERE TO SIT IN THE COURTROOM
(One plaintiff and one defendant, both self-represented)

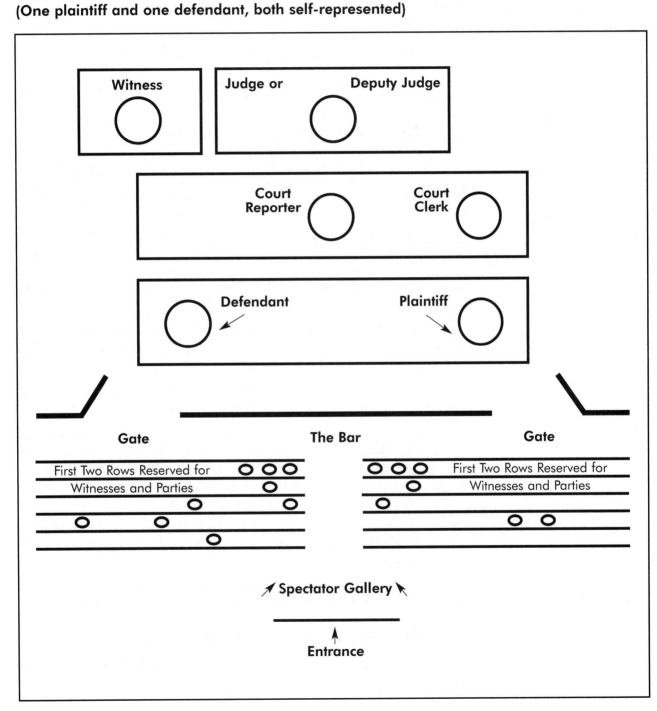

FIGURE 2
WHERE TO SIT IN THE COURTROOM
(Two plaintiffs and two defendants, both represented by counsel)

D1 = Defendant #1, D2 = Defendant #2
RD1 = representative of Defendant #1
RD2 = representative of Defendant #2

P1 = Plaintiff #1, P2 = Plaintiff #2
RP = Plaintiffs' representative

First, you should check the docket (or trial list). The docket is kept outside each courtroom door. Sometimes, a docket for all rooms in a particular courtroom is kept in the hallway entering into each courtroom or it is posted on the court office door. Find your case name on the list. Write down the judge's name and make a note of the number next to your case. This will help you estimate how much time will pass before your case is heard. Realize that this is only a rough estimate, however, because a number of things could happen that are out of the parties' control. For example:

> The judge will first hear from parties on the list who would like to adjourn trials for that day. Then, if your case is listed first, it will most likely be heard first. However, it is up to the judge to decide if he or she wants to hear another case before your case.

> If your case appears further down on the docket, you may be heard later in the day or even on another day, because some trials take longer than estimated.

> If your case is further on the list, it may be heard sooner than you expect because one or more cases ahead of yours may settle before their trials begin or there may be requests for adjournments.

> Let your client and witnesses know where on the list your case appears as well as the courtroom in which the trial will be held. Tell them not to wander from the courtroom waiting area; they should stray no farther than the washrooms.

Once court is in session, the judge will likely indicate if any cases on the docket cannot be heard that day. As the cases progress, one by one, the judge will get a better idea if the entire list will be accommodated that day. If the judge is convinced that the cases will not all be heard, he or she may tell certain parties to return in the afternoon, the next day, or at another date. In that case, the participants may leave and return as the judge orders.

Try to identify the opposing parties you may not have met or ask your client (if you are an agent) to do this. If you know who the other parties are, you could —

- ▶ approach the other side to try to negotiate a settlement,
- ▶ exchange with the parties any legislation and case law you intend to use, or
- ▶ ask the other side which witnesses are present to testify.

Enter the courtroom early and tell the clerk your name and that you are the plaintiff or defendant, as the case may be. Let the clerk know if you will be using a court interpreter and the name of the interpreter. If the parties have agreed to adjourn the trial, tell the clerk that your intentions are to adjourn and the reason for it.

You should be seated at least five minutes before trial. *Parties* should sit in the spectator gallery and should only cross the bar to speak with the court clerk or when their case is called.

Witnesses should be seated in the first two rows, if space permits. When your case is called, the judge may order that witnesses be excluded from the courtroom. Witnesses should then leave and sit outside the courtroom until the clerk calls their names. Once a witness has testified, he or she may remain in the courtroom.

Spectators (people coming along to watch but not testify) should sit behind the first two rows of the spectator gallery.

1.3 When court is in session

When court is in session, a number of things may occur before your case is heard:

(a) Parties may ask for an adjournment.

(b) The judge may send parties out to discuss settlement, if they have not already had such discussions or if their settlement discussions were progressing well outside the courtroom and the parties would like to continue them.

(c)   The judge may hear a plaintiff-only trial arising from default proceedings and during which the plaintiff need only prove his or her damages.

(d)   The judge may hear a motion (or application) on another matter.

The judge will first deal with cases in which parties are requesting adjournments or other matters that can be disposed of quickly. Then, the judge will deal with cases set for trial.

2.   Trial Procedure

Figure 3 illustrates the order of events at trial.

Note: Parties may request a recess or adjournment throughout the flow of events, but the judge has discretion as to whether or not to grant them.

3.   Advocacy

If you are a plaintiff, you must prove your claim on a balance of probabilities. This means that you must convince the judge that the facts you presented are more likely to have occurred than the facts the defendant presented. If you are a defendant, you will have to show that your version of the facts is more likely to have occurred than the plaintiff's version of the facts. Whether you are the plaintiff or defendant, sound advocacy techniques are vital in order for you to get your story out effectively. Effective advocacy is a combination of the following:

> *Preparation*. Know the facts of the case about which you are advocating. Reflect carefully on your case. Plan your approach thoroughly. Prepare for trial properly. Let chapter 8 be your guide.

> *Knowledge*. Be familiar with the necessary rules of the small claims court. Be familiar with the rules of evidence.

> *Ability to keep track*. Listen carefully and make notes on the main points that witnesses say.

> *Presentation*. Dress in business attire (i.e., no denim, corduroy, or clothes made out of shimmering fabrics, and no excessive jewellery). Your appearance should be conservative, if possible.

> Speak loudly, clearly, and make eye contact with the judge. Know how to enter evidence and question witnesses.

FIGURE 3
ORDER OF EVENTS AT TRIAL

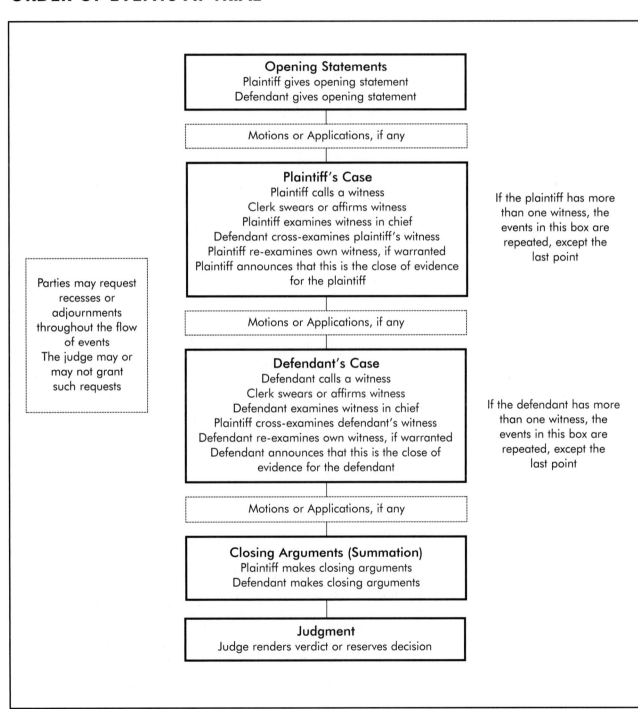

> *Confidence*. While experience will naturally increase your confidence, thorough preparation will reduce your anxiety and enhance your confidence.

> *Style*. You may wish to attend at court and observe the styles of other parties. Decide what works and what doesn't and, if you feel comfortable doing so, adopt some aspects of the presentation styles of others.

Treat all participants with courtesy and respect.

> *Experience*. Every time you make an appearance in court, your presentation will improve. Practise your opening and closing statements so that you are familiar with them, and you will feel more confident in the courtroom.

3.1 Conduct in the courtroom

There are certain ways to conduct yourself in court. Read through Checklist 5 to determine appropriate courtroom behaviour, both for spectators and for the parties in dispute.

Remember to keep confidential the information exchanged at a settlement conference unless the parties consent to the use of certain information. If, for example, the defendant has made an admission, you cannot bring this to the court's attention without first obtaining the defendant's permission. If you get permission, you may then tell the judge in your opening statement that the defendant has admitted liability for all or some of the allegations made in the claim. You would then have to prove at trial only the contested allegations.

3.2 Advocacy skills

Whether you are advocating on your own behalf or on behalf of a client or friend, you will need skills to make your presentation effective, interesting, and most of all persuasive.

Good advocacy skills are important, because a case presented in an organized, chronological fashion will help the judge to understand the facts. Furthermore, a case presented in as professional manner as possible will mean fewer distractions and a smooth flow of evidence, thereby allowing the judge to better follow the trial.

Use Checklist 6 to work on your advocacy skills.

CHECKLIST 5
APPROPRIATE COURTROOM CONDUCT

General Courtroom Conduct

WHEN COURT IS IN SESSION (JUDGE OR DEPUTY JUDGE IS SEATED ON THE BENCH) THERE ARE:	
THINGS YOU SHOULD DO **AND**	**THINGS YOU SHOULD NOT DO**
☑ When walking in or out of the courtroom and when walking in and out of the bar, bow to the judge or deputy judge only.	☒ Do not chew gum or eat or drink anything inside the courtroom.
☑ When the judge enters the courtroom at the start of a session or after a recess, bow to the judge.	☒ Do not speak, or even whisper, to anyone unless you are within the bar and it is your turn to speak.
☑ Seat yourself with the least possible interruption to others.	☒ Do not play with keys or the coins in your pockets.
☑ When the judge speaks to you, stand up and respond, then sit down again.	☒ Sit quietly and read your notes while you are seated in the spectator gallery.
☑ When the court clerk says, "All rise," stand up and remain standing until you are told to be seated.	☒ Do not open loud zippers or snaps on briefcases — do that before you enter the courtroom.
☑ Address the judge as "Your Honour."	☒ Do not interrupt anyone who is speaking.
☑ Address the Deputy Judge as "Sir" or "Madam" or "Your Worship," or "Your Honour," if you are not certain the person is a judge or deputy judge.	☒ Do not walk in and out of the courtroom unless it is absolutely necessary — it is very disruptive.

Courtroom Conduct for Parties Themselves

WHEN COURT IS IN SESSION AND, IN ADDITION TO THE ABOVE GUIDELINES, THERE ARE:	
THINGS YOU SHOULD DO **AND**	**THINGS YOU SHOULD NOT DO**
☑ Ask for recess if you need time to speak with any of the parties or representatives.	☒ Do not talk or whisper to a fellow plaintiff or defendant while someone else is speaking.
☑ Ask for recess if you need to leave the courtroom while your case is being heard.	☒ Do not walk into the gallery or out of the courtroom when your case is being heard.
☑ Address opposing parties, witnesses, and clients as "Mr." or "Ms."	☒ Do not act in a rude, insulting, or humiliating manner toward any party or any representative.
☑ Refer to opposing parties, witnesses, interpreters, paralegals, and clients as "Mr." or "Ms." whe speaking about them before the judge.	☒ Do not pass notes to your co-plaintiff, co-defendant, or anyone else in a manner that is distracting or disrespectful.
☑ Refer to opposing counsel, paralegals, or student representatives as "My friend" when speaking about them before the judge.	☒ Do not comment on another person's personal, religious, political beliefs, nor about their race, ethnic origin, sexual orientation, or physical appearance. Always behave professionally.

CHECKLIST 6
EFFECTIVE ADVOCACY SKILLS

EFFECTS TO ACHIEVE	SKILLS TO WORK ON
Effective Presentation	➤ Speak slowly. The judge takes notes. The court reporter either takes notes or repeats everything you say into a dictation mask. The court reporter's notes may end up in the form of transcripts, which are official court trial notes. Be mindful of the judge. If the judge is writing, slow down or even stop talking until the judge looks up or tells you to continue. ➤ Speak loudly. The microphones you see in court do not amplify your voice; they record what you say for the purpose of preparing transcripts. However, that does not help you be heard during the trial. ➤ If the judge cannot hear you, he or she will ask you to slow down or speak up. Such requests may unnerve you or interrupt your train of thought. ➤ Do not mumble. To prevent mumbling, lift your head when you speak. Place your notes on the podium or, if there is no podium, hold them up high in order to force your head up. This way you will not mumble into your notes. You cannot persuade a judge who cannot hear you. ➤ Avoid repeating words at the beginning or end of a sentence. For example, avoid using: "okay," "alright," "now," "well," "so," "um," and "eh."
Clarity	➤ Prepare, prepare, and overprepare your case before the trial. The more organized you are, the more clear your case will be to the court. ➤ Read your notes carefully several times. The more you read them, the more you will notice unnecessary words that can be removed or replaced with cleaner, shorter sentences.
Credibility	➤ Never mislead the court, no matter how bad the outcome might be for you. ➤ Never behave disrespectfully toward anyone in the courtroom. Do not shout, show anger, or call anyone by a derogatory name.
Persuasiveness	➤ Use simple well-organized arguments, emphasizing only that which is truly important to emphasize. ➤ Make periodic eye contact with the judge. If the judge looks confused or is too absorbed in his or her note taking, stop talking until he or she looks up and makes eye contact with you. ➤ When questioning a witness, make eye contact with the witness.
Accurate Note-Taking	➤ Do not try to write down every word unless you are a very fast, neat writer. Write down key phrases. Above all, listen carefully. Do not fumble with your notes while a witness is on the stand. ➤ You will need to take good notes so that you can keep track of what witnesses are saying. Your notes will help you question your witnesses, cross-examine your opponent's witnesses, and think of things to add to your closing argument, if there are any surprise statements from witnesses.

3.3 Opening statements

The opening statement is your opening performance. These are the first words you will say before an open court.

Unlike trials in the higher courts, opening statements in small claims court are not lengthy or dramatic as there is no jury to impress. The small claims court judge may even dispense with opening statements in cases in which the pleadings clearly indicate what the trial is about. However, unless the judge asks you not to give an opening statement, go ahead and make one that is short and simple.

An opening statement should contain the following:

- An introduction of the parties (if you haven't done that earlier)
- A brief statement of the issues
- A brief statement of facts about which both parties agree
- A brief statement of admissions made by the parties (e.g., the defendant has admitted liability or two defendants have taken equal responsibility for liability)

A variety of opening statements are presented in Sample 10. Read them to get a good idea of how varied they can be, depending on the type of case, the number of defendants, whether the parties are represented, and other factors.

3.4 Questioning witnesses

Evidence is generally entered through witnesses unless all parties agree to enter documents such as business records, expert reports, accident reports, and medical records as evidence without further proof.

Entering documents as evidence without further proof

By entering documents as evidence without further proof, the evidence is being entered without having a witness prove the existence, creation, or authorship of the documents. Instead of summonsing a medical doctor, for example, the parties may consent to have the doctor's report entered into evidence without the necessity for having the doctor testify. Of course, this means you will have no opportunity to cross-examine the doctor about the report. The provincial or territorial legislation governing evidence will determine whether it is possible to enter certain documents into evidence and will provide guidelines for serving the other party with reports.

SAMPLE 10
OPENING STATEMENTS

OPENING STATEMENTS OF THE PLAINTIFF	OPENING STATEMENTS OF THE DEFENDANT
Good morning, Your Honour. My name is Jane Buck; that's B-U-C-K, initial J. I am the plaintiff. The defendant, Mr. Sable, is present. This case is about rental arrears owed to the plaintiff. The alleged arrears resulted when the defendant repeatedly failed to pay his rent in accordance with the rental agreement. The defendant has since moved out of the plaintiff's apartment building. The only issue is whether the defendant owes me rental arrears of $2 000. Thank you, Your Honour.	Good morning, Your Honour. My name is Roger Sable; that's S-A-B-L-E, initial R. I intend to show that there are no arrears as alleged. Rather, the arrears are part of an illegal rent increase and I, therefore, owe no money at all. Thank you, Your Honour.
Good morning, Your Honour. My name is Ella Bella; that's B-E-L-L-A, initial E, the plaintiff in this matter. Mr. Ernie Villa, director of the defendant, Fix Nix Inc., is here on behalf of that corporation. This is an action for damages resulting from imrproperly performed repairs on the plaintiff's lawn tractor. The plaintiff alleges that the blade was not securely bolted to the frame of the tractor, thereby causing it to fly off and injure me. Thank you, Your Honour.	Good morning, Your Honour. My name is Ernie Villa; that's V-I-L-L-A, initial E, director of the defendant, Fix Nix Inc. The defendant denies any wrongdoing in repairing Ms. Bella's lawn tractor. The evidence will show that there was a manufacturer's default in the bolts used. Your Honour, may I bring a motion to amend the pleadings, to add a defendant, Wild Parts Ltd., manufacturer of the bolt? An adjournment would not be necessary as this is being done on consent of Wild Parts Ltd., whose representatives are ready to proceed with the trial today.
Good morning, Your Honour. My name is Monty Sell; that's S-E-L-L, initial M. I am the plaintiff. My friend, Ms. Roulette, represents the defendant, Mary Lou Boo, and my friend, Mr. Farnik, represents the defendant, Jake Forsake. This case deals with a fist fight. We are here to determine two issues: first, whether Ms. Boo is liable to the plaintiff for assaulting me; and second, to what degree is Mr. Forsake responsible for damages resulting from the fight. Thank you, Your Honour.	Good morning, Your Honour. My name is Desiree Roulette; that's R-O-U-L-E-T-T-E, initial D. I am counsel for the defendant, Ms. Boo. Ms. Boo denies all the allegations in this case. I intend to prove that the plaintiff is the author of her own misfortune. Thank you, Your Honour. - OR - Good morning, Your Honour. My name is Lou Farnik; that's F-A-R-N-I-K, initial L. I am counsel for the defendant, Mr. Forsake. I intend to show that the plaintiff provoked the fight and is responsible for her own injuries. Thank you, Your Honour.
Good morning, Your Honour. My name is Wayne Bayne; that's B-A-Y-N-E, initial W, the plaintiff. The defendant, Ms. Brown, is here in person. The issue is one of breach of a rental agreement. The defendant was a tenant in the plaintiff's town-house complex. The defendant has agreed to admit the rental agreement into evidence without further proof. The disputes centers around the interpretation of that agreement. Thank you, Your Honour.	Good morning, Your Honour. My name is Pat Brown; that's B-R-O-W-N, initial P, the defendant. My friend has already identified the issue and I am ready to proceed. Thank you, Your Honour.

Techniques for questioning (or examining) witnesses assist the court in hearing testimony that obeys the rules of evidence. Even a self-represented plaintiff and defendant must still work within the rules of evidence (discussed in section 5.2). While you will not be questioning yourself, you will likely be telling your story on the stand. These techniques will help you to act as a good witness as well as help you deal with opposing witnesses. See section 4. for more information on questioning witnesses.

4. Dealing with Witnesses

Use one of the three basic techniques for questioning witnesses:

> Examination-in-chief

> Cross-examination

> Re-examination

In addition, there are special considerations for questioning expert witnesses.

4.1 Examination-in-chief

Examination-in-chief, also known as direct examination, is the process of asking questions of a witness you have called to the stand. These are usually questions that will result in your witness telling the story in his or her own words and in a chronological, complete fashion.

This technique is used to develop the testimony of your witnesses. Likewise, the defendant will use this technique to develop the testimony of the defendant's witnesses. The judge will adopt this technique when he or she must ask the witness a question to clarify the testimony.

Planning your questions in outline form

If you plan a list of questions to ask a witness and rigidly follow them, you may not be able to improvise. Rather, listen carefully to the witness and ask a question that follows through on what he or she is saying.

While a list of questions is a good safeguard for checking to ensure that you have asked all the pertinent questions before the witness leaves the stand, an outline is far more flexible, as it allows you to verify that you have covered all the important issues or question areas before the witness leaves the stand. This, of course, means that you will have to improvise the questions, so if you are not quick on your feet, a list of questions may be a safer approach for you.

Use open-ended questions beginning with "how," "what," "who," "when," "where," "why," and "tell me about." Questions should be brief enough to draw out the story, and the witness should be doing most of the talking.

Do not ask for details about something about which the witness has not yet testified. This is called *leading the witness*, and is not permitted because it is akin to putting words in the witness's mouth. For example, say "Who did you talk to?" not "Did you talk to the man?" if the witness has not yet testified about a man.

Always first ask witnesses a few questions about themselves to assist the court in appreciating who the witnesses are. You may ask questions about the city they live in, their age, occupation, employer's name, length of service, and other details you might like the court to know. Be brief. This is not meant to be a biography of the witness.

Next, deal with the background relationship of the parties (i.e., if the parties knew each other before the event).

Whenever a witness is describing an event, it is best to start with the event itself. Be sure to ask the witness where the event happened, how it happened, who was there when it happened, what happened after the event, and what resulted from the event.

When you have finished questioning a witness, say, "No more questions, Your Honour"; then sit down.

To prepare for an effective examination-in-chief, you should know exactly what the witness has to offer to support your position, and anticipate the story the opposing witnesses may tell. If there is anything that might hurt your case, it is better to bring those facts out from your witness instead of having it come out during the cross-examination or from an opponent's witness.

> When you are asking a witness questions that will not be the source of debate, you may use leading questions. You may lead questions about the witness's name, address, age, occupation, years of service in a particular occupation, and marital status.

🍁 Example

In this example, the plaintiff, Ms. Art, is testifying, while her friend, advocating on her behalf, asks her questions.

Q: Ms. Art, you live in Yellowknife, Northwest Territories, isn't that correct?

A: Yes.

Q: You are the payroll supervisor for Always-Paid Inc., right?

A: Yes.

Q: You've been doing that for five years or so, haven't you?

A: Yes.

Q: Tell me where you were on June 10, 200–.

A: I was at work as usual, just a couple of blocks from where I live. At about 10:00 a.m. I normally take my coffee break, but I was so behind in my work, I worked through it. I happened to look up through the window. Much to my dismay, I saw Ms. Bean taking my bicycle.

Q: Did you know the defendant, Ms. Bean, before that time?

A: Yes, Ms. Bean lives across the street from me.

Q: Why did Ms. Bean take your bicycle?

A: Probably to get some exercise. She would often borrow it for that reason. This time, however, I did not give her permission to borrow it.

Q: What happened next?

A: By the time I got to the window, she had already ridden off. Anyway, quitting time came but I had no bike to ride home from work. I telephoned Ms. Bean to ask her to return my bike. She said she only borrowed it for an hour and returned it to the place where it had been parked outside my workplace window. She said, "Oh, you must have been on lunch when I returned it. You mean, your bicycle wasn't where I left it? Oh no, it must have been stolen."

Q: How did you respond?

A: I was furious. I walked home and went to speak with Ms. Bean.

Q: How did the conversation go, Ms. Art?

A: She became angry with me and said, "How could you accuse me of stealing your bicycle!" I told her that the facts are that my bicycle is missing, she was the last person whom I saw using it, I didn't see her returning it, so I wanted the bicycle back or its value in money. She slammed the door in my face. I left more furious than ever.

and so on . . .

Q. No further questions, Your Honour.

4.2 Cross-examination

Cross-examination is the process of asking questions of a witness whom the opposing party called to the stand. The purpose of cross-examination is to ask questions that will test the truth of the statements the witness made during the examination-in-chief. The plaintiff will cross-examine the defendant's witnesses after they have been examined-in-chief. Likewise, the defendant will use cross-examination to question the plaintiff's witnesses after they have been examined-in-chief.

In a cross-examination, it is best to make short, direct statements or suggestions followed by an ending that invites a "yes" or "no" answer. This is called *leading the witness* because you are the one who is giving the statement and you are trying to get the witness to agree with it.

Sometimes the witness gives more than a "yes" or "no" answer. If that is the case, you probably did not ask a leading question, or you asked a leading question that is complex or consists of more than one question.

Try the following endings: "... isn't that so?", "... isn't that correct?", "... wasn't it?", "... didn't you?", and "... isn't it true?" You, the cross-examiner, should be the person doing most of the talking because the witness's answers will be brief.

Avoid using open-ended questions. They encourage the witness to tell a full story. Use open-ended questions only when you wish to find out a fact that has not come out in the examination-in-chief.

When you have finished questioning a witness, say, "No more questions, Your Honour"; then sit down.

To prepare for an effective cross-examination of a witness, you should know your own witness's story inside out. Anticipate the story the opposing witnesses may tell, and listen ever so carefully to the examination-in-chief for the following:

> Inconsistencies during the examination-in-chief

> Ulterior motives the witness may have for testifying in a certain way

> Statements that may weaken the opposing witness's testimony

> Statements that strengthen your side of the story

🍁 Example

You are the defendant cross-examining the plaintiff's witness, Ms. Art, who has just been examined-in-chief.

Q: Ms. Bean has borrowed your bicycle many times, correct?

A: Yes.

Q: Ms. Bean returned your bicycle every time she borrowed it, didn't she?

A: Yes — except for the last time

Q: You have a very busy job, don't you, Ms. Bean?

A: Yes.

Q: You worked through your coffee breaks that day, isn't that correct?

A: Yes.

Q: You also worked through your lunch break, didn't you?

A: Yes.

Q: Your desk faces away from the window, correct?

A: Yes.

Q: You were tired that day, weren't you? A: A little bit.

Q: It was very foggy that day, wasn't it? A: Yes, it was.

Q: It was foggy. You were tired. You couldn't be sure who took the bicycle, could you? A: No.

Q: Those are my questions for this witness, Your Honour.

This example demonstrates that you could tactfully test the witness's ability to see through fog, especially given that she is an overworked, tired witness.

If you do not wish to cross-examine a particular witness, don't. Simply stand up and say, "No questions for this witness, Your Honour"; then sit down. Use the *Should you cross-examine?* chart to help you decide whether or not to cross-examine a particular witness.

ASK YOURSELF	IF YOU ANSWER	THEN
1. Has the witness damaged your argument?	No	do not cross-examine
2. Is the witness important or significant?	No	do not cross-examine
3. Is the witness credible?	No	do not cross-examine
4. Would the witness be difficult to control?	Yes	do not cross-examine
5. Did the witness withhold information?	Yes	potential for damage — cross-examine
6. Will you be able to weaken credibility?	Yes	cross-examine
7. Is your case weak?	Yes	take a risk — cross-examine

Note: You must consider all the decisions before making a decision not to cross examine.

4.3 Re-examination

Re-examination is the process of asking questions of a witness whom you have called to the stand after the opposing side has cross-examined that witness.

The purpose of a re-examination is to ask questions that will rehabilitate the witness or clarify or develop facts raised during the cross-examination.

A witness is not automatically re-examined, and the judge may not allow re-examination if it is not warranted. The plaintiff and defendant may use re-examination to rehabilitate the witness if his or her credibility has been shattered or the witness's story has been distorted during cross-examination. Re-examination is also warranted when facts are brought out during cross-examination that were not brought out earlier and need to be clarified during re-examination.

As with examination-in-chief, it is best to ask open-ended questions during a re-examination. Stick to the new facts brought out only in the cross-examination. If the cross-examination has weakened your case, you should question your witness with the goal of strengthening it. If cross-examination made facts more confusing or distorted, you should question your witness to clarify the facts.

To prepare for an effective re-examination, listen carefully during the cross-examination for facts or events that the judge has not yet heard from this witness. Make brief notes of facts on which you will need to re-examine.

 Example

During cross-examination, the defendant's counsel made it look like Ms. Art had a habit of harassing Ms. Bean — not a favourable impression to leave with the court. Her representative will now attempt to enlighten the judge during re-examination:

Q: Ms. Art, were you harassing Ms. Bean at any time?

A: No.

Q: Did you place any telephone calls to her other than the day the bike was not returned?

A: No.

Q: Did you visit Ms. Bean?

A: Only to ask for the bicycle back. She told me she had bought it but my sticker from the Finger Lakes was still on the frame.

Q: Did you say anything to Ms. Bean in public?

A: Yes, when I saw her at the grocery store, I approached her and she started to yell at me. The manager asked us both to leave and we did. She refused to speak to me outside. I walked home upset.

Get it down on paper

Good note-taking skills are important to keep track of evidence and the testimony of all witnesses. Do not attempt to write down every word. Write things down if they surprise you, if they are admissions critical for your closing arguments, and if you wish to cross-examine witnesses about them. Some suggested ways of keeping notes during trial include the following:

➤ Use one page per witness.

➤ Write the witness's name at the top of the page.

➤ Draw a line down the centre of the page.

➤ On the left side of the page, write down the gist of what the witness said.

➤ On the right side of the page, write down the gist of what you want to do with this evidence, if anything. You can use a letter X to represent *cross-examine*, and a letter A or another symbol for *closing argument*, if that is when you wish to address the matter.

4.4 Examining expert witnesses

You may need to call an expert witness to provide testimony that requires the knowledge of a person who has knowledge in a particular field. For example, in a personal injury action, the plaintiff may need to call a doctor or specialist to testify about the extent and possible causes of the plaintiff's injuries. In an action over shoddy mechanical work on a vehicle, the plaintiff may hire an expert — a mechanic other than the one who did the shoddy work — to examine the vehicle and testify about the work that appeared to have been done, how the work was defective, and the damage done to the vehicle. A defendant may need to retain (hire) an accident reconstruction expert to show other possible causes of an accident. Other examples of expert witnesses are numerous.

When selecting a witness, you should write to that witness briefly, ask him or her if he or she is interested in providing you with an expert report and possibly testifying at trial. Most expert witnesses will require a substantial fee. These expert fees may or may not be recovered after the trial because the judge may not see fit to reimburse the party for having the report prepared or having the expert testify. This will happen most often when the party could have proved his or her case without calling the witness.

Technically, you need only summons the expert witness. However, you may still have to pay, in advance, a considerable price for your expert witness's written report. The price could range from as low as $50 to higher than $500, depending on the nature of the report and the work required by the expert preparing it.

Special requirements apply when questioning witnesses who are brought in to provide an expert opinion.

Expert reports

▶ British Columbia, New Brunswick, and Prince Edward Island rules permit the judge to order any expert report or to order any expert witness to testify.

▶ In most cases, expert reports must be served on all parties at least 14 days before trial. Estimates about the value of property or repairs are excluded from this rule.

▶ A party served with an expert report may enter evidence in reply, cross-examine the expert witness, or do both. You may need to summons a witness to testify.

4.4.1 When you call the expert

If you are calling an expert witness, you will be conducting an examination-in-chief of that witness. The techniques are the same as for examination-in-chief of other witnesses. However, instead of asking the witness for personal information at the start of the examination-in-chief, you will need to *qualify the witness*. That is, you will need to develop the expert's qualifications, education, training, experience, and fields of specialization. These questions are asked to establish in the judge's mind how qualified your expert witness is in giving opinions on an issue in the trial.

By planning questions thoughtfully, you will be better equipped to build the testimony of your expert witness in your closing arguments. You should develop a set of questions by looking at the expert's résumé. Consider the following questions as a starting point. You can adapt these questions to most expert witnesses by customizing the wording:

▸ What is your name?

▸ What is your occupation?

▸ Do you have an area of specialty? (Describe your area of specialty.)

▸ Where do you do your work (with a firm, for a company, in a laboratory, at a university, or as a consultant)?

▸ How long have you pursued this occupation?

▸ What kind of education did you receive to get into this area of specialty?

▸ What training courses have you taken?

▸ Did you work under any recognized expert in the field? How long?

▸ Do you require a licence or certification to conduct your work? Are you licensed or certified?

▸ At how many trials have you testified before? For the plaintiff? For the defendant?

▸ What other types of work has your occupation led you into (publishing, lecturing)?

Once you have qualified an expert witness, you conduct the examination-in-chief in the same way as described earlier.

4.4.2 When another party calls the expert

If another party called the expert to testify, you will have to cross-examine that expert.

The best ammunition for cross-examining an opposing expert is an expert witness of your very own. If you cannot call your own expert witness, at least try to consult with one who can point out weaknesses in the opposing expert's report.

If neither is possible, you should try to educate yourself on the issue in question. Start with the Internet; then read library textbooks and articles about the subject. This will help you write a list of questions that will challenge the opposing witness's testimony. The technique of cross-examination is the same as discussed in section **4.2**.

5.   Closing arguments

Closing arguments are made after both parties have presented their cases. Sometimes, closing arguments are referred to as *summation*. The closing argument is the last chance you have to address the court. This is your chance to persuade the judge that he or she should rule in your favour based on the evidence before the court. After all evidence has been introduced, the plaintiff gives his or her closing arguments. Then the defendant presents his or her closing arguments.

You should plan your arguments before trial and improvise as necessary after you have heard the opposing party's story. Do not be prepared to read a speech. This is your opportunity to make eye contact with the judge and to answer any questions the judge may ask during your closing arguments.

You are not giving your opinion in the closing argument. Rather, you are submitting to the judge how he or she should consider the evidence of witnesses.

Take the following steps in the closing argument:

(a)   Summarize the issues.

(b)   For each issue, stress the strength of your evidence.

(c)   If the parties presented conflicting evidence, ask the judge to consider your point of view and give the reasons he or she should do so.

(d)   State your belief.

When you finish, thank the judge and sit down.

Sample 11 shows some examples of closing arguments that a plaintiff and a defendant made. After the judge has made his or her decision, the parties will be able to make submissions as to costs (see section **10**).

SAMPLE 11
CLOSING ARGUMENTS

CLOSING ARGUMENTS OF THE PLAINTIFF	CLOSING ARGUMENTS OF THE DEFENDANT
Your Honour, the issues in this case are twofold. First, was the defendant, Mr. Wheeler, negligent in using his rototiller? Second, was the defendant's negligence responsible for damaging the plaintiff's grass?	Your Honour, my friend has already stated the issues in this case.
On the issue of negligence, Mrs. Wiley testified that on March 25, 200–, Mr. Wheeler was working at 9:00 p.m., well past sunset. His property was not fenced off from the plaintiff's property. She testified that he had no exterior lights on and that she was only able to see him by virtue of a fluorescent stripe on his jacket. The plaintiff, Ms. Woe, awoke the next morning to find a large strip of the grass on the east side of her sidewalk ploughed with irreparable damage to the sod. The parties do not dispute the date of the damage.	Your Honour, the defendant denies any wrongdoing. He maintains that he could see properly, that he used the rototiller on his property only, and that he was shocked when Ms. Woe approached him about her lawn.
The defendant testified that he was not negligent, that he could see adequately in the dark, and that it was grubs that ploughed the plaintiff's grass. In support of his assertion, Dr. Annelida, zoologist, testified that grubs most likely caused the ploughing of the grass in a spring resurfacing ritual.	The experts were in disagreement. Dr. Annelida clearly supports the defendant's contention that grubs dug up the plaintiff's lawn. When the grubs prepare for winter, they enter a digging ritual. Their spring resurfacing cannot damage the grass because it is still dormant at that time. Dr. Annelida has been practising for 10 years, some 15 years less than the plaintiff's expert, Dr. Greenwort.
However, Dr. Greenwort, the plaintiff's expert witness, respectfully disagreed with Dr. Annelida. In her view, grubs could not have caused the damage during a resurfacing ritual after winter hibernation. Dr. Greenwort put forth the explanation that grubs could only burrow in such masses in preparation for winter hibernation.	Who's opinion is more compelling? Dr. Greenwort is a generalist, studying insects, grubs, worms, and other invertebrates. However, Dr. Annelida's entire research career has been focused exclusively on grubs, particularly on the European Chafer, a species found in the area in question. This is precisely why Dr. Annelida's opinion should be outweigh Dr. Greenwort's opinion, Your Honour.
Your Honour, I respectfully submit that Dr. Greenwort's evidence should be given greater weight than that of Dr. Annelida. Dr. Greenwort has been a practising zoologist for more than 25 years compared to the 10 years her client has been working in this field.	Dr. Annelida further suggested that a rototiller would produce even rows. The photographs presented by the plaintiffs clearly show no row pattern, further supporting the grub defence proposed by the defendant.
In my respectful submission, the evidence is clear: Mr. Wheeler drove his rototiller over the plaintiff's lawn, clearly damaging the large strip of grass.	I respectfully submit that the plaintiff has not proven on the balance of probabilities that Mr. Wheeler rototilled her lawn. In fact, there is compelling expert testimony that grubs ruined the sod.
Ms. Woe presented two repair estimates, Your Honour, showing that the lowest cost of replacing the sod is $1 345 for the sod itself plus $800 for labour. Before that, the plaintiff must apply a grub-killing chemical at a cost of $37. Therefore, the plaintiff respectfully requests $2 282 as damages.	With respect to damages, the defendant does not dispute the repair estimates.
Thank you, Your Honour.	In conclusion, I respectfully submit that this action be dismissed as against the defendant.
	Thank you, Your Honour.

6. Motions and applications during trial

A motion (or application) is a request that the judge make an order of some kind. Either party may bring a motion during the trial. Motions may generally be brought before the plaintiff presents his or her case, after the plaintiff's case is presented, and after the defendant's case is presented.

Some motions may be brought at trial without prior notice to the court or the other parties. Others must be brought in writing and the parties must be served with notice. Wherever possible, let the opposing party know in advance of the trial that you intend to bring a motion. Table 14 summarizes some of the motions that can be brought, when they can be brought, and whether notice is required.

TABLE 14
BRINGING MOTIONS DURING TRIAL

MOTION TO	BROUGHT BY	NOTICE REQUIRED	BEFORE PLAINTIFF'S CASE	AFTER PLAINTIFF'S CASE	AFTER DEFENDANT'S CASE
Adjourn the Trial	Plaintiff or Defendant	Yes	Most Often	Rarely	Rarely
Amend the Pleadings	Plaintiff or Defendant	Yes	Most Often	Less Often	Less Often
Exclude Witnesses	Plaintiff or Defendant	No	Always	No	No
Exclude Evidence	Plaintiff or Defendant	No	Yes	Yes	No
Dismiss Claim Brought Outside the Limitation Period	Defendant	No	Yes	No	No

If you are requesting an adjournment on the day of trial, try getting the consent of all parties first. If you cannot get the other parties' consent, request one, but be aware of cost consequences.

The court will usually postpone (adjourn) the trial on such terms as are just. However, the judge may order that the party requesting the adjournment pay the other party costs for expenses and inconvenience the adjournment caused. The judge may also order that a party who opposed a request for an adjournment pay costs if reasons given to the party for requesting the adjournment were reasonable.

Chapter 11 provides more information on motions and applications.

7. Evidence

You can produce three types of evidence:

> *Testimonial evidence* is witness testimony.

> *Real evidence* is generally evidence that you can touch or handle. Real evidence is entered as exhibits in the manner demonstrated in section **7.1**. Examples include objects, photographs, audiotapes, videotapes, weapons, and clothing.

> *Documentary evidence* is generally written or typed evidence. Documentary evidence is entered as exhibits in the manner demonstrated in section **7.1**. Examples include documents such as birth certificates, citizenship cards, membership cards, contracts, leases, employment records, hospital records, medical reports, income tax records, bank records, receipts, invoices, cancelled cheques, money orders, and repair estimates.

In Yukon, British Columbia, and Ontario, a document or written statement must be served on all parties at least 14 days before trial. If you have not done this, the judge will decide whether or not the document may be used at trial. Not allowing time for the other parties' review is risky, so pay attention to the 14-day rule.

When serving other parties with documentary evidence, be sure to provide for every document the name, telephone number, and address for service of the witness who made the statement or the person who prepared the document.

If you have had such a document served on you, and you wish to have an opportunity to cross-examine the author or witness, you can either get confirmation from the opposing party that the expert will attend the trial or you can summon the witness to attend trial. Summonsing witnesses is explained in chapter 8.

7.1 Entering exhibits

Real and documentary evidence may be used as exhibits at trial. Certain steps are taken when introducing such evidence through witnesses. The only exception is if the parties give their consent to admit certain documents such as a contract or lease, without taking these steps. In that case the party entering the evidence should inform the judge that, on consent of the parties, the document will be admitted without further proof.

When planning for your trial, you should enter evidence through a witness with the most first-hand knowledge about an object or document.

Be sure to have enough copies of documentary evidence with you: one for the judge, one for each party, and one for you.

7.1.1 Entering real evidence

To enter real evidence as an exhibit, do the following:

(a) Show the photograph (or other real evidence) briefly to the opposing party.

(b) Hold the photograph up briefly to show the judge.

(c) Approach the witness stand.

(d) Show the photograph to the witness by placing it in front of the witness or handing it to the witness. Say, "I am showing you what appears to be a photograph."

(e) Ask the witness, "Do you recognize this photograph?"

(f) Have the witness describe the contents of the photograph by asking, "What is this photograph about?"

(g) Ask the witness additional questions about the photograph, if necessary.

(h) Enter the photograph as an exhibit. Say, "Your Honour, may I have this photograph marked as an exhibit?" The judge will ask the opposing party if there is any objection. If not, the judge will say, "Exhibit 1" (or whatever exhibit number is assigned).

If you have a series of photographs that simply show different views of the same thing, show them to the witness at the same time. Then, when the witness has testified about those photographs, ask the judge to enter them as exhibits 1A, 1B, 1C, and so on.

7.1.2 Entering documentary evidence

To enter documentary evidence as an exhibit, do the following:

(a) Give a photocopy of the letter (or other documentary evidence) to the opposing party.

(b) Pass a copy of the letter to the clerk (or reporter, if no court clerk is present). The court clerk will give it to the judge.

(c) Approach the witness stand.

(d) Show the letter to the witness by placing it in front of the witness or handing it to the witness. Say, "I am showing you what appears to be a letter."

(e) Ask the witness, "Do you recognize it?" Ask them to identify the writer and recipient as well as who signed the letter.

(f) Refer the witness to important passages in the letter and have him or her read them.

(g) Enter the photograph as an exhibit. Say, "Your Honour, may I have this letter marked as an exhibit?" The judge will ask the opposing party if there is any objection. If not, the judge will say, "Exhibit 2" or whatever exhibit number is assigned.

7.1.3 Referring to exhibits

Once an object or document has been marked as an exhibit, it may be referred to as "Exhibit 1," "Exhibit 2A," or whatever exhibit number is assigned. This is the case regardless of which witness is speaking about it and regardless of whether the exhibit is being referred to during examination-in-chief, cross-examination, or re-examination.

7.1.4 Inspection of exhibits

In Ontario, the trial judge may inspect in the presence of the parties any real or personal property during the trial. Although this rarely happens, it basically involves the judge stepping off the bench, walking over to the evidence, and having a look at it.

7.2 Rules of evidence

Rules of evidence exist to ensure that the facts are put before the court in a way that will result in a just verdict. The rules of evidence are not as strict in small claims court as they are in the higher courts. However, you must follow the rules that are listed here.

If the opposing side attempts or has broken a rule of evidence, you should object in the manner outlined for each rule later in this chapter. Sometimes the judge may even point out that certain evidence should not be admitted. This prevents the evidence from prejudicing a self-represented party.

> **The rules of evidence**
>
> ▶ British Columbia and Nova Scotia small claims court rules state that the formal rules of evidence do not apply.
>
> ▶ Saskatchewan rules expressly forbid a judge to accept hearsay evidence.
>
> ▶ Yukon rules state that evidence may be admitted whether or not given under oath or affirmation.
>
> Unless otherwise stated, the rules of evidence are relaxed in small claims court. This does not mean that you can ignore them, but it does mean that if a party errs in introducing certain types of evidence that would otherwise not be admissible if the rules were strictly obeyed, the judge may accept the evidence unless he or she feels it would be improper to do so.

If you intentionally break the rules of evidence and this becomes obvious to the judge, you will lose credibility and that may hamper your chances for a successful trial.

7.2.1 Relevancy rule

All evidence is admissible (i.e., may be used in court) if it is relevant. Evidence is relevant if it matters to the issue for which it is brought forth.

For example, if the issue is whether a former tenant owes rental arrears, then evidence would be as follows:

▶ *Relevant evidence* would include a lease, cheques, money drafts, receipts, bankbook, or cheque book.

▶ *Irrelevant evidence* would include photographs of the rental unit or the fact that the tenant's cheques to people other than the landlord also bounce regularly.

If you hear a witness giving irrelevant evidence, stand up and say, "Your Honour, this is irrelevant"; then sit down. The judge will either agree or disagree with your objection. If the judge agrees with the objection, he or she will not take that evidence into account in the decision-making process.

If someone objects to your witness giving irrelevant evidence and you believe that it is relevant, stand up, say so, and give your reason to the judge. For example, you can say, "Your Honour, the statement is relevant. It goes to the issue of whether or not Ms. Witness was able to see the accident happen."

7.2.2 Privilege rule

You may not wish to produce certain documents as evidence in court. You can avoid using relevant evidence if it is privileged. Privilege may be claimed in these situations:

(a) *Solicitor and client privilege.* If you are represented by a lawyer or law student, you may claim privilege over any correspondence or conversations between you and your lawyer. You may waive the privilege if you wish, but only do so on the advice of counsel.

(b) *Litigation privilege.* Documents prepared for the purpose of this action alone are privileged. Any expert reports or medical reports may be excluded from use at trial on the basis of litigation privilege. You would hold back such evidence if it is not supportive of your claim.

For instance, a medical report that does not support your claim for injuries does not have to be introduced into evidence. You would then seek a second opinion since a claim for personal injuries must be backed up by medical opinion that these injuries were caused as alleged and resulted in pain and suffering as alleged. Likewise, an engineer's report that a pot left on the stove caused a kitchen fire is not favourable if you are a defendant in an action for damages resulting from the fire to the rental unit.

(c) *Settlement attempts.* Settlement discussions and correspondence are privileged. The whole purpose behind settlement negotiations is to encourage full and open discussion between the parties. Sometimes, admissions are made by parties during settlement discussions. At other times, letters of offer to settle contain clauses in which liability is admitted or may be implied. You should not try admitting such discussions and letters into evidence.

(d) *Letters marked "without prejudice."* Any correspondence to which you wish to attach a privilege should be marked "without prejudice." Any letter containing this notation will not be admissible into evidence, so this is a good way of protecting your interests.

If the opposing party attempts to introduce evidence that is of a privileged nature, stand up and object by saying, for example, "Your Honour, this letter is marked 'without prejudice'" or, "Your Honour, I object. This witness is testifying about settlement discussions that are clearly privileged"; then sit down.

7.2.3 *Hearsay rule*

When a witness repeats a statement someone else made out of court, that statement cannot be admitted into evidence if the statement —

(a)   was made outside of court,

(b)   was made by someone who is not a witness in this trial, and

(c)   is now being repeated to prove that the statement is true.

This rule applies to statements both written in expert reports and spoken in conversations.

Hearsay evidence is not admissible into evidence because the person who made the statement is not there to give it nor to refute that how it was repeated by the witness is correct. Furthermore, the person who made the statements cannot be cross-examined.

You can get around the hearsay rule in various ways. The opposing parties may consent to having the hearsay evidence admitted. As well, the small claims court rules do relax the hearsay rule, so written statements may be admitted into court unless a judge orders otherwise. Written statements may be medical reports, expert reports, hospital records, employment records, bank and other financial records, invoices, or repair estimates.

There are also some exceptions to the hearsay rule. Some documentary evidence may be entered as hearsay evidence under certain circumstances. They include the following:

(a)   *Business records*. Evidence legislation allows business records (e.g., bank statements, hospital records, and doctor's notes and records) to be accepted as trial evidence if the following is true:

(i)   They are made in the usual and ordinary course of business.

(ii)   It was in the usual and ordinary course of business to have the records made.

(iii)   The records were made at or around the same time as the event.

If you intend to introduce business records, give the other party at least 14 days' notice before the trial. You may give notice by letter to the other side, advising them that you intend to introduce the attached documents at trial as business records.

(b)   *Medical reports*. Evidence legislation allows notes and records made by medical doctors and health professionals to be entered as evidence with proper notice and without calling these "expert witnesses" to the stand.

(c) *Public documents.* Birth certificates, citizenship cards, and baptismal certificates may be submitted as evidence in small claims court. No notice is required other than disclosure within 14 days of trial.

7.2.4 Opinion rule

All evidence entered through a witness must be known first-hand. That is, the person who is claiming to know something must indeed know it. There is no room for speculation or opinion.

Ordinary people may give an opinion in court if it is about something with which they have repeatedly had experience. For example, most ordinary people would be able to give an opinion about the following:

▶ How fast a car was travelling

▶ Whether someone was drunk

▶ The age of a particular person

▶ Whether certain handwriting is that of a particular person

The only exception to the opinion rule is that experts properly qualified may give an opinion within their expertise. For example, a doctor may give a medical opinion, a fire fighter may give an opinion about the cause of a fire, a mechanic may give an opinion about why an automobile engine malfunctioned, an accident reconstruction specialist may give an opinion about how an accident occurred, and so on. Experts assist the court in understanding complicated details.

Experts must be qualified. In other words, you must convince the court that your expert witness has the appropriate education, certification, and experience to provide an opinion of such a nature.

7.2.5 Character rule

A witness may not testify about the defendant's good or bad character unless it is relevant to an issue. Beyond that, the law of character evidence is complicated and such testimony is best avoided without the advice of a lawyer. Testifying that the defendant is a known spouse abuser is hardly relevant to whether he properly repaired a car. Judges are astute observers and will usually be able to assess a witness's or party's credibility from his or her testimonies.

8. Dealing with Surprises

Even though you may now feel comfortable with trial procedure, evidence, and advocacy skills, you will need to know how to respond to the surprises that occur at the trial.

8.1 Where's my witness?

One of the most unpleasant surprises to deal with is a witness who does not show up or who fails to stay for the balance of the trial. For this reason you should summons witnesses as discussed in chapter 8.

In Ontario, if a witness whose evidence is material to the conduct of an action fails to attend at the trial or to remain in attendance, the trial judge may direct police officers to apprehend the witness and bring that witness promptly before the court. The witness may even be detained in custody until his or her presence is no longer required. The disappearing witness may even be ordered to pay costs.

8.2 Adjournments

Imagine arriving at the courthouse ready to proceed with the trial and being approached by the opposing party to consent to an adjournment. It happens, although not that often. If the person requesting an adjournment has a compelling reason, you may wish to consent to the adjournment. You may also wish to advise that party that you intend to seek costs. The parties will then inform the clerk that an adjournment will be requested.

You may also, even less often, find out right at the beginning of your trial that an adjournment is being requested. Either way, this is an inconvenience and expense for you. You may decide to oppose the adjournment because you are ready to proceed.

A court may order costs for inconvenience and expense as a result of an adjournment. Be sure to seek costs whether you consent to the adjournment or oppose it.

In some circumstances you may not wish to seek costs for compassionate reasons, but stand your ground if you feel the need. If someone is opposing an adjournment because your court interpreter did not show up, you should argue that the interpreter's attendance was arranged, confirmed, and beyond that, not within your control.

Northwest Territories residents, note:
A judge may adjourn a trial to permit further evidence to be gathered and introduced by a party.

9. The Judgment

The judge may decide on the case after he or she has heard all the evidence and closing arguments. In some cases, the judge may *reserve his or her decision*, meaning that the decision will be made at a later date. Some reasons that judges have used to reserve their decisions include the following:

> The judge will need time to consider a novel or evolving point of law.

> The judge has asked one or more of the parties to present him or her with legislation that supports a position advanced at trial, but for which the applicable legislation was not provided.

> The judge is missing a key point of evidence such as a written contract and, therefore, needs more time to reflect on the evidence.

> The judge may wish to review trial transcripts before rendering a decision.

> The judge prefers to provide written reasons because of the complexity of the facts or law governing those facts.

The following are some possible outcomes of the trial:

> You win and are awarded all the relief and costs you requested.

> You win and are awarded some of the relief and costs requested.

> You win and are awarded some or all of the relief you requested but you are not awarded any costs.

> The opposing party wins and is awarded all the relief and costs he or she requested.

> The opposing party wins and is awarded some of the relief and costs he or she requested.

> The opposing party wins and is awarded some or all of the relief he or she requested but no costs are awarded.

10. Speaking to Costs

After the judge has rendered a decision, he or she will usually ask the parties if they wish to speak to costs. Do not speak to costs before the judge asks you to do so. If you win, this is your chance to convince the judge that you should recover all your expenses. If you lose, this is your chance to try to reduce your losses.

A judge may ask the parties to make submissions relating to costs even though the decision has not been made. Sometimes, although rarely, the judge may ask for written submissions relating to costs following the reserved judgment. Even less often is the possibility that the judge will ask the parties themselves to return to court to make cost submissions and, if this happens, it may be something the parties do in the judge's chambers.

When you make a submission relating to costs, simply submit your costs and the applicable small claims court rule that provides the authority for the court to grant it. In some cases, your authority will be based on case law. In other cases, you could argue that costs should be granted in equity (fairness). Be brave. If you do not ask for something, you will not receive it.

 ## Example

[Ontario]

Your Honour, I respectfully submit that the defendant [or plaintiff] ought to pay costs in the amount of $500 [or other amount], which consists of the preparation and filing fee under [Ontario] Rule 19.02, and disbursements in the amount of $75 [or other amount] under [Ontario] Rule 19.01 for which I am now going to pass up receipts. In addition, I have been put to considerable inconvenience and expense and should be compensated for this in the amount of $300 [or other amount].

You should have an idea of the cost you will be seeking before the trial begins. Sample 12 will assist you in collecting your thoughts on costs. While an Ontario spreadsheet is used to shed light on this example, you can prepare much the same list for yourself, taking into consideration the cost rules of your jurisdiction.

The judge may limit an award for costs when it is necessary for the court to rule on a point of law that is novel or unclear at the outset of the trial. Costs may not be awarded if both parties are found equally liable or if both have acted improperly during the course of the proceedings.

11. Immediately after the Trial

Regardless of whether you win or lose the trial, read chapter 10. If you win and are satisfied with the decision, you will need to learn how to collect

SAMPLE 12
DETERMINING COSTS*

COSTS FOR	UNDER RULE	SUBMIT AMOUNT
Preparation and Filing of Pleadings (Plaintiff's Claim, Defence, Defendant's Claim)	19.02	$50 maximum
Disbursements in accordance with the *Administration of Justice Act* (if receipt is presented)		
Photocopying and other administrative fees	19.01(2)	amount on receipt
Service fees for serving court documents	19.01(3)	$20 maximum
Witness summons	19.01(1)	amount on receipt
Counsel Fee		
Lawyer	19.04(a)	$300 maximum
Student-at-Law	19.04(b)	$150 maximum
Compensation for Inconvenience and Expense Available only if the: • successful party is unrepresented; and • amount of the claim is greater than $500; and • court is satisfied that the case has been unduly complicated or prolonged by the unsuccessful party.	19.05	$300 maximum

* This example is for Ontario only. When determining your costs, you should take into consideration the cost rules of your jurisdiction.

your award. If you lose, you will need to know your rights in terms of paying the award to the winning party. You will also learn how to determine whether or not to appeal the decision to the higher court. Sometimes, even a winning party may appeal on a single issue or on the issue of costs.

11.1 Getting your exhibits back

Whether you win or lose, you may wish to have your exhibits returned to you. Write a letter to the court asking for their return. Be sure to tell the clerk whether you are the plaintiff or defendant. If you do so within 45 days, the clerk will likely be able to return the exhibits to you. You will have to pick up real evidence (objects). If you do not claim your exhibits, the court will not be responsible for them for long, so act soon.

11.2 Requesting a new trial

You may bring a motion or application asking the court to grant a new trial. You must do so as soon as possible after the trial. A new trial may be granted in any or all of the following circumstances:

> There was a calculation error in determining damages.

> You were unable to attend the first trial.

> You now have relevant evidence that you could not have reasonably been expected to have at the time of the first trial.

If the judge is not satisfied that your request is supported with good reasons, he or she may dismiss the motion and you will have to live with the judgment of the first trial.

You may also make a motion to the court to set aside or vary a judgment if one was made against you for failing to attend at the trial.

10
After Judgment

This chapter describes proceedings that may arise following judgment.

Judgment may be obtained in the following three ways:

‣ A party wins at trial.

‣ The court clerk signs the default judgment.

‣ The judge grants judgment following a damages assessment hearing.

Types of judgment also differ. For example, a judgment may order any of the following:

‣ A party to complete an action such as —

• performing a service (e.g., repairs),

• returning property owed by another party, or

• delivering goods paid for by another party but not delivered to that party

‣ A party to pay money to another party

‣ That the claim be dismissed without costs to either party, in which case there is no aspect of the judgment to enforce

When judgment is rendered, the party owing the money or obligation becomes the judgment debtor (debtor), and the party entitled to the money or goods becomes the judgment creditor (creditor).

If the judgment is delivered orally, the judge will note the key terms on the endorsement, a sheet that forms part of the official court file.

A judgment should, but does not necessarily, mean that the debtor will comply with its terms. In fact, it is often necessary for the creditor to enforce judgment. This is discussed in the next few sections.

The rules for collections vary greatly among the provinces and territories. While some of the rules outline collection proceedings in great detail, others are silent on these procedures. Various pieces of legislation deal with seizing property and garnishing funds. A complete discussion of the legislation is beyond the scope of this book. Please consult the legislation that applies to your province or territory. You can use the Web sites posted on Self-Counsel Press's Web site at <http://www.self-counsel.com/can-law/smallclaims/resources.html> to find the legislation for your province or territory.

The approaches to collecting money owed to the creditor on a judgment rendered against the debtor follow. These guidelines should provide you with an overview of collection procedures generally available, as well as some collection tips.

1. Enforcing a Judgment Ordering Action

A judgment may order that a party perform a deed such as return goods, re-do work improperly performed under a contract, or perform work not completed in accordance with a contract. If the judgment does not specify a compliance date, you can assume that it is the date of judgment or default judgment. If a judgment orders that personal property be returned or work be performed, it should specify a date by which the action should be completed. If it does not, a reasonable amount of time should be allowed for the work to be completed.

If a debtor does not comply with a judgment ordering the return of personal property (personal belongings, personal items loaned but not returned, items left with a store on consignment, etc.), the creditor may be able to enforce the judgment with a writ of delivery. This is arranged at the court office.

Once issued, the writ of delivery gives the enforcement officer (often referred to as a *bailiff* or *sheriff*) the authority to seize from the debtor the property or goods listed in the judgment. If the goods are seized, they will be returned directly to the creditor.

If an enforcement officer cannot seize the property listed in the writ of delivery, the creditor may bring a motion (or application) to request that other goods or personal property be seized from the debtor. This should be done upon learning that the writ of delivery was unsuccessful.

If the enforcement officer cannot access the premises from which the goods are to be seized, the creditor may bring a motion (or application) requesting an order authorizing the use of force to enter the premises. This is not usually as dramatic as it sounds, for the "force" may simply be authorization to hire a locksmith to remove the lock.

2. Enforcing a Judgment Ordering Payment

If the debtor does not make the payment ordered in the judgment or fails to make payment arrangements, the creditor will have to enforce the judgment.

The creditor should act promptly. It is much harder to enforce a judgment on someone who has spent his or her money, sold his or her house or otherwise changed residences, changed jobs, or filed for bankruptcy. The sooner the creditor acts, the more likely there is to be success in collecting on the judgment.

Usually three enforcement options are available for judgment ordering payment:

(a) Garnishment

(b) Writ of seizure and sale of personal property

(c) Writ of seizure and sale of lands

These options are discussed later in this chapter.

You should review all enforcement options before deciding how to proceed. In fact, unless the creditor believes that the debtor is able to pay the full amount, the creditor might consider agreeing to a schedule of payments. Such a schedule may eventually be ordered by the court in any event, so agreeing on a schedule that is confirmed in writing may save time and money.

If the creditor would rather have the court order the payment schedules, this could be accomplished by requesting a terms of payment hearing. See chapter 11 for more information on terms of payment proceedings.

3. Judgment Debtor Examinations

Before initiating enforcement proceedings, you will need to know something about the debtor's assets (i.e., personal property, real estate, money) and liabilities (i.e., debts, rent payments, mortgage payments, living expenses). Starting with an examination of the debtor is often the best way to proceed, especially if you know little or nothing about the debtor's assets and liabilities.

A judgment debtor examination is a proceeding held before a court official (a judge, deputy judge, or referee) in which the creditor or court official (or both) ask questions of the debtor to allow the creditor to determine the debtor's assets and liabilities. The debtor is obliged to answer these questions under oath.

A creditor may examine the debtor at any time after obtaining judgment if the debtor is not making payments as agreed by the parties or as ordered by the court. If the debtor is a corporation, the creditor may examine an officer or director of that corporation. If the debtor is a partnership, the creditor may examine any of the partners. If the debtor is a sole proprietorship, the creditor may examine the sole proprietor.

3.1 Arranging an examination

To arrange a judgment debtor examination, you must have the court office issue a notice of examination. This will generally involve completing a form, paying a fee to the court office, and then serving the debtor with the notice of examination.

Before you take any enforcement measures, you will have to know how much money you want to recover from the debtor. For the most part, this is easy. You are entitled to the amount the judge ordered or the amount agreed to during settlement. It will also be necessary to calculate how much prejudgment and postjudgment interest you are entitled to claim. Interest rates are either ordered by the judge at the time judgment is given or are available by calling the court office.

3.2 Preparing for the examination

To ensure that the judgment debtor examination unfolds efficiently, the creditor and the debtor should prepare themselves before the court date.

To calculate prejudgment interest:

▶ If you are not sure whether the judge has ordered prejudgment interest, check the endorsement on file with the court, then use this formula:

PJI = A × B × C ÷ D where:

PJI = prejudgment interest

A = principal amount

B = prejudgment interest rate as ordered or in accordance with legislation

C = number of days from the date the claim arose or from the date ordered by the court

D = 365 days (this number is used for all PJI calculations)

To calculate postjudgment interest:

▶ If you are not sure whether the judge has ordered postjudgment interest, check the endorsement on file with the court, then use this formula:

POJ = W × X × Y ÷ D where:

POJ = postjudgment interest

W = principal amount outstanding

X = postjudgment interest rate as ordered or in accordance with legislation

Y = number of days from the date of the judgment

Z = 365 days (this number is used for all POJ calculations)

 Example

Laura obtained judgment in the amount of $500 plus $100 for costs (A = $500 + $100 = $600) and prejudgment interest at the rate of 3.3% (B) since January 2, 1997, and postjudgment interest since the date of judgment, March 10, 1997, at the rate of 5%. She is making interest calculations on June 1, 1997.

PJI = $600 x 0.033 x 66 days ÷ 365 days = $3.58

(Laura has counted 66 days from January 2, 1997, to March 9, 1997.)

POJ = $600 x 0.050 x 83 days ÷ 365 days = $6.82

(Laura has counted 83 days from March 10, 1997, to June 1, 1997.)

3.2.a The creditor

Some officials presiding over the examination prefer to ask the debtor questions rather than having a self-represented creditor run the examination. However, the creditor may not know if this is the case until the examination begins. Therefore, the creditor should prepare as if he or she will be conducting the examination by himself and herself. Both the creditor and the debtor should be aware of the types of questions that are permitted.

You may ask questions pertaining to the following:

- The reason that the debtor has not paid the amount owing
- Whether the debtor intends to obey the order or has any reason for not doing so
- The debtor's income and property
- The debts owed to and by the debtor
- The property the debtor has disposed of before or after any judgment or order
- The debtor's present, past, and future means to satisfy the order
- Debtor's date of birth and driver's licence number
- Any other matter pertinent to the enforcement of the order

In thinking up questions to ask the debtor, the creditor should keep in mind that his or her primary goal is to reveal the assets and liabilities of the debtor while the debtor is under oath. By asking many questions you may potentially increase the number of ways to force the debtor to honour the judgment. For example, by asking both employment and mortgage questions, the creditor is able to gather information that is required for a garnishment and a writ of seizure and sale.

Although there should be a sworn affidavit of service to the examination in the court file, it is a good idea to bring a copy to prove that the debtor was served with notice of the examination.

Sample 13 shows a sample list of questions to be asked at the judgment debtor examination. Keep in mind that you will have to improvise to ensure that you ask the debtor a sufficient number of questions to properly evaluate his or her ability to pay the debt. You may also wish not to ask specific questions if you are certain that they do not apply to the debtor's situation or if you already know the answer.

SAMPLE 13
SAMPLE QUESTIONS FOR A JUDGMENT DEBTOR EXAMINATION

Notes:

- If the debtor does not have the requested documentation or answer on hand, ask for an undertaking that the document or information be produced to you in writing within 10 days of the examination.

- Ask questions relevant to the debtor's situation. You would not, for instance, ask questions about the debtor's employer if he or she already told you that he or she is unemployed or on welfare. Use your common sense to improvise when you get an answer that requires further exploration. Remember, this list is not exhaustive; it is only a start. You may ask the same questions in relation to the debtor's spouse or children.

- You may request that the presiding official make an order as to terms of payment.

- The headings below represent the subjects about which you may ask questions.

A. ANY MATTER PERTINENT TO THE ENFORCEMENT OF THE ORDER

1. What is your full name? Spell it. Are you known by any other name?

2. What is your street address? Do you have different mailing address?

3. What is your date of birth?

4. What is your social insurance number?

5. What is your driver's licence number?

6. Are you single, married, separated, divorced, or otherwise in a cohabitation relationship? If separated, do you have a separation agreement? If so, what are the terms of the agreement? What payments are you obliged to make?

7. Do you have any children? What are their ages? Are any of them living with you? Are you responsible for child support for any of them? If so, how much? Are you paying for their education? If so, how much? Do any of your children have part-time jobs? Do any of your children pay you for room and board?

8. Do you have any dependents such as an elderly or disabled parent or disabled spouse?

B. REASON DEBTOR HAS NOT PAID AMOUNT OWING

1. Why have you not paid the amount owing?

C. WHETHER DEBTOR INTENDS TO OBEY JUDGMENT

1. Do you intend to obey the judgment and pay the money owing?

2. If so, when do you expect to do that?

3. If not, why not?

SAMPLE 13 — Continued

D. DEBTOR'S INCOME AND PROPERTY

1. What is your occupation? Are you employed now? Full-time, part-time, self-employed, or on contract? How long have you worked there? What are your wages and how and when are they paid? Do you receive a cheque or is the amount deposited directly to your bank account? When is your next raise due? Do you receive commissions or bonuses? If so, how much and under what circumstances?

2. Who is your employer? What is your employer's address and telephone number? What is the name of your supervisor?

3. If unemployed, what is your source of income? Are you receiving or expecting to receive money from a previous employer or under a contract or job arrangement?

4. Are you receiving or expecting to receive any social assistance or money from a workers' compensation scheme? Are you receiving money from a family member or friend?

5. Are you entitled to receive money from a judgment, court order, or any other source?

6. Do you have a life insurance policy on anyone? If so, provide details.

7. Do you own any real estate? If so, provide address and detailed description. Is there a loan or mortgage on the property? If so, what amount and when are payments made? Is there a claim or lien on the property?

8. Do you own a car? Provide details for each vehicle (make, model, vehicle identification number, licence plate, amount owing on it, payments being made on it, liens, and so on). What is the car used for (family, work, business, pleasure)?

9. Do you own a recreational vehicle such as a boat, trailer, or camper? Provide details (make, model, vehicle number, licence plate, amount owing on it, payments being made on it, liens, and so on)

10. Do you own any jewelry? If so, provide details and estimate value.

11. Provide a list of all appliances, technical, and computer equipment. Provide a description and serial number for each item.

12. Do you have any valuable artwork (sculptures, paintings, and so on)? If so, describe them and provide the artist's name and estimate the value of the artwork.

13. Do you own any silverware or a coin collection? If so, provide details.

14. Do you own any jewelry or fur coats? If so, provide a detailed description.

E. DEBTS OWED TO AND BY THE DEBTOR

1. Does any person or business owe you money?

2. Do you owe any person or business any money? If so, provide details.

3. Are you expecting to receive an inheritance? If so, from whom? Provide the name and address of the testator.

4. Do you have any loans with a bank or private lending institution? Have you applied for a loan in the past two years? If so, provide a copy of the loan application.

5. Where do you bank? Provide a list of all banks, addresses, and account numbers. Provide a list of any investments (stocks, bonds, gold, and RRSPs).

6. Where do you invest money? Provide details.

7. Did you file an income tax return during the past two years? If so, did you receive a refund? Are you anticipating a refund in the future? Provide details.

8. Do you pay rent or room and board? If so, how much rent do you pay and at what intervals? Provide the name and address of your landlord.

F. PROPERTY DEBTOR HAS DISPOSED OF BEFORE OR AFTER JUDGMENT

1. Did you sell, lend, give away, assign, or transfer any real estate, vehicles, personal property, or other assets before or after judgment? If so, provide details.

G. DEBTOR'S PRESENT, PAST, AND FUTURE MEANS TO SATISFY JUDGMENT

1. What are your plans for earning income in the future? Provide specifics.

2. What is in your budget (vacations, gifts, luxuries, clothes, bills, food, and so on)?

H. QUESTIONS FOR CORPORATE DEBTORS

1. What is your role in this corporation? Director? Officer? Who are the other officers? (If you performed a corporate name search, you would have a list of past directors and officers. If not, ask for that information.)

2. What are the current annual salaries paid to directors and officers?

3. Where does the corporation conduct its business? Provide addresses and specify whether the premises are leased or owned.

4. What were the corporation's revenues for the past two years? Is this typical for every year? If not, please explain.

5. What were the corporation's expenses for the past two years? Is this typical for every year? If not, please explain.

6. What are the corporation's assets (property, office equipment, manufacturing equipment, transportation equipment, investments, bank balances, and so on)?

7. Describe the corporation's shares, their original values, and the number and identity of original and current shareholders.

8. Did the company obtain a bank loan within the past two years? If so, provide particulars.

9. Is the company indebted to any other creditor? If so, provide particulars (including overdrafts and credit line indebtedness).

10. Does the corporation intend to pay this debt? If so, how?

3.2.b *The debtor*

The debtor should bring to the examination proof of his or her assets and liabilities. To prove assets, the debtor should bring any or all of the following documents:

- Bank statements or bank books
- Pay stubs or T4 stubs or letter from the employer confirming salary
- Make, serial number, model of car
- Statements showing value of investments such as guaranteed investment certificates, mutual funds, stocks, registered retirement savings plans, and so on

To prove liabilities, the debtor should bring applicable documents, including any or all of the following documents:

- Bank statements or bank books
- Loan agreements
- Proof of mortgage payments or rental payments
- Proof of car payments
- Credit card statements
- Invoices and receipts
- Judgments or garnishments on which outstanding amounts are owed
- Court orders about child or spousal support payments

3.3 Attendance and co-operation

The debtor must attend the examination, unless it is beyond the debtor's control. The court clerk may deem the debtor to be absent any time after the time scheduled for the examination. Therefore, it is in your best interest to show up on time and, if you are running late (something to be avoided), call the court office ahead of your appointment and let them know that you are on your way.

If the date and time of the examination are inconvenient for the debtor, the debtor should contact the creditor, preferably in writing and as soon as possible after being served, and ask the creditor to consent to an adjournment to a mutually convenient time. If the creditor consents, either the creditor or the debtor must inform the court office, in writing, that the parties have agreed to an adjournment.

Adjournments should be scheduled well in advance. Judgment debtor examinations are held once a week in some jurisdictions, only on evenings in others, and once a month or less often in other areas. Therefore, it is wise to call the court office to find out the next available date.

If the creditor does not consent to an adjournment and the debtor has a very good reason why attendance is impossible, he or she can ask the court directly for an adjournment. Serious illnesses, family funerals, school examinations, and the like should be very good reasons why the court would grant an adjournment even when the creditor does not give his or her consent.

It is in the debtor's best interest to attend and co-operate with the examination. A debtor who willfully does not attend after being served with notice of the examination or who attends and refuses to answer questions may be found in contempt of court.

3.4 Contempt of court

Any person found in contempt of court will receive a notice to attend at a contempt hearing. The court has power to order that the debtor —

> attend an examination,

> make a payment, or

> be jailed for a certain period of time.

The creditor should attend the contempt hearing and make an argument about what he or she deems proper for the court to order. The debtor must attend the contempt hearing to make an argument about why he or she should not be jailed or why he or she should not make payment, or why he or she did not attend at an examination.

If the court finds a debtor in contempt of court and orders the debtor to serve a jail sentence, the court will issue an arrest warrant. This warrant directs and authorizes all police officers in the province or territory to take the debtor to the nearest correctional institution to serve the sentence ordered at the contempt hearing.

The debtor may be taken into custody as soon as the warrant comes to the attention of the police. A debtor may also be arrested when he or she is stopped for a traffic violation, for a routine traffic check, or when the debtor otherwise comes to the attention of the police. The debtor is released when the jail sentence has been served, unless the court orders otherwise.

3.5 Conducting the examination

The judgment debtor examination must take place in the jurisdiction in which the debtor lives or carries on business. Examinations are usually held in private (and in Ontario, they must be in private unless the court orders otherwise). Therefore, examinations are held in the judge's chambers, beyond the limits of the courtroom, and out of hearing range of the people sitting in the courtroom. Sometimes examinations are held inside the courtroom but spectators are not allowed inside while a debtor is being examined.

The creditor and debtor should stay calm and deal with the examination without blame, name calling, or hostility. Both should keep in mind the purpose of the judgment debtor examination and act responsibly. The presiding official tells the debtor that he or she need not answer a question if it is improper.

Once information about the debtor's assets and liabilities has been obtained, you will have a good idea about whether collection efforts will be fruitful. If you decide that the debtor has enough assets or funds to make good on the judgment, you can take measures to seize the funds or assets.

4. Garnishment

You may enforce an order for payment or recovery of money by way of garnishment. Garnishment is a court procedure that allows a creditor to demand money from a business or person whom the creditor expects will either —

> receive money from the debtor (e.g., the debtor's bank, trust company, investment company), or

> pay the debtor (e.g., the debtor's employer, the lottery corporation).

A *garnishee*, the person or business owing the debt to the debtor, for the purpose of this procedure must be in some existing relationship with the debtor at the time the garnishee is served with the notice of garnishment. A creditor cannot, for example, expect co-operation from a future employer or future banker; only the debtor's present employer or present banker is suitable.

Garnishment is the only enforcement option that gives a dollar-for-dollar return. It is the simplest method of collecting on a judgment debt, and is often much faster and often more convenient than seizing personal property or land.

The prevalence of today's automated payroll and pension payment arrangements means that most debtors will receive some proceeds in their bank accounts at some point during the month. The creditor could use the judgment debtor examination as a tool for finding out when and how much the debtor is receiving from various sources.

To initiate garnishment proceedings, the creditor must complete the appropriate forms at the court office and then serve the debtor with notice of the garnishment.

4.1 Limits of garnishment

It is most common for a creditor to garnish wages, bank accounts, and investments. When the debtor owns assets jointly with another individual, only half of the assets jointly owned may be garnished.

The amount of wages that may be garnished is limited. For example, a debtor's wages may already be garnished to recover unpaid family support payments or other garnishments. In those cases, the creditor may wish to look to other sources of garnishment or consider other enforcement options.

No garnishment limit is imposed on bank accounts, regardless of the source of that money. This makes bank accounts attractive garnishment options. The challenge with a bank account is that the debtor must maintain a balance in the account or use the account to cash cheques or receive payments.

Pension laws do not permit the garnishment of pension income. Once a pension cheque is cashed or deposited into an account, however, it loses its pension character and may be garnished.

4.2 The garnishee's role

When the garnishee receives a notice of garnishment, he or she must act on it by redirecting to the creditor the funds that the garnishee owes to the debtor.

The garnishee must forward all garnished funds to the clerk of the court, not directly to the creditor. When the clerk receives payment, the clerk decides the appropriate manner of distributing the garnished funds.

If the garnishee believes that he or she does not owe money as set out in the notice of garnishment, the garnishee may dispute the garnishment by properly notifying the court and the garnishor. For example, a bank acting as a garnishee may dispute a garnishment because the debtor does not have an account with that bank and, therefore, the garnishee does not owe the debtor money.

The garnishee may also dispute the garnishment in a situation in which the entire amount specified in the notice of garnishment cannot be forwarded because the money owed to the debtor is jointly owed to a co-owner (e.g., partnership, joint bank account) or for another reason (e.g., another garnishment is already in place). If the garnishee's statement indicates that there is a co-owner of a debt owed to the debtor, the garnishee must serve the statement on the creditor and debtor.

If a garnishee fails to fulfill garnishment obligations when it was possible to do so, the creditor has the legal right to enforce the judgment on the garnishee. For example, a bank cannot decide to garnish only part of an account in an effort to please its debtor client. Fortunately, banks and other frequent garnishees tend to be aware of their obligations and their rights.

The garnishee can file a garnishee's statement with the court for protection against liability. The statement would indicate why the garnishee is unable to pay the clerk the full amount set out in the notice of garnishment.

4.3 Requesting a garnishment hearing

The creditor, debtor, garnishee, co-owner of a debt, or any other interested person may request a garnishment hearing. A person who has been served with a notice to co-own a debt is not entitled to dispute the enforcement of the creditor's order for the payment or recovery of money or a payment made by the clerk, unless the person requests a garnishment hearing. The court may make a variety of orders relating to the garnishment.

4.4 Claiming funds paid into court

All garnishment payments are payable into court. Once a garnishee has forwarded money to the court clerk in accordance with the notice of garnishment, the debt is considered paid or discharged.

Administering garnishment payments forwarded to the court may take between four and six weeks, depending on the jurisdiction. You may wish to call the garnishee and court office to check on the progress of the garnishment. Bear in mind that you will not receive your money if you have not followed proper court procedure.

When a garnishee owes a debt to the debtor and one or more co-owners, the creditor must take additional steps to claim the funds paid into court, otherwise the money will be returned to the garnishee. Check your local practice with a lawyer or court staff.

If you are unable to garnish funds payable to the debtor by a third party, you may still be able to enforce the judgment with a writ of seizure and sale.

5. Seizure and Sale of Personal Property

Garnishment proceedings are often the simplest and least costly collection procedure to initiate. Unfortunately, the debtor may not have garnishable assets. In that case, a writ of seizure and sale of personal property or of land may be appropriate.

The writ gives the *enforcement officer* (also referred to as a *bailiff* or *sheriff*) the legal right to seize the debtor's personal property. On seizing the items, the enforcement officer then advertises the items and sells them. The proceeds of the sale are first allotted to the enforcement office to cover for expenses incurred as a result of the seizure, storage, and sale of the debtor's items. The remaining money is then paid to the creditor up to the amount to which the creditor is entitled at the time the money is distributed. If any money is left over, it is returned to the debtor.

5.1 How easy is it to seize and sell property?

In many cases, enforcing a judgment with a writ of seizure and sale of personal property is not straightforward:

(a) *You must be able to specifically identify items to be seized.* For example, you will need to name the item and describe it. If an item is identified by a serial number (car, electronic item, appliance, etc.), you will need to know the make, model, and serial number of that item. The best way to obtain this information is by conducting a judgment debtor examination which, as described earlier, has its own fee.

(b) *If you intend to try to seize the debtor's car, you will have to pay a fee to conduct a search with your provincial or territorial ministry*

If you are a judgment creditor, make sure you keep track of any additional court fees required to collect on the judgment debt. You are entitled to recover these costs from the debtor.

governing consumer relations. This search should show if the vehicle is free of liens, debts, or other claims.

(c) *In addition to paying the filing fee, you may also incur a fee for the services of the enforcement office or sheriff's office.* This fee usually covers the cost incurred to seize, advertise, store, and sell the goods.

(d) *If the enforcement officer is unable to enter the debtor's premises peacefully to seize the goods, you may bring a motion (or application) for an order allowing the enforcement officer to use force to enter the debtor's premises.* The enforcement officer would then likely hire a locksmith for assistance in gaining access to the debtor's residence or place of business. A fee is charged to bring a motion or application.

(e) *A writ is valid for a limited period, after which time it must be renewed.* As a general rule, the writ must be renewed at the end of every six-month interval. The writ can be renewed before it expires as long as the judgment is not older than 20 years. If the writ expires, the seizure will be carried out only when the creditor is successful in extending the time for renewal by bringing a motion (or application).

(f) *The debtor may assert to the enforcement officer that the goods identified for seizure are owned not by the debtor but by a co-resident, partner, or family member.* The enforcement officer may take the debtor's word for it and refuse to seize the goods.

(g) *The debtor is allowed to keep certain necessities of life and livelihood.* For example, items such as clothing, household furnishings, and utensils, up to various monetary values, are not subject to seizure. In addition, the debtor can also assume that tools or equipment necessary for his or her livelihood will be safe from seizure. However, tools or equipment used only for the purpose of maintaining a hobby may be seized.

(h) *Executing the writ takes time.* You may not see any money for several months.

(i) *Even if the seizure is successful, there is a chance that you may receive less than you expected or even nothing.* There is no dollar-for-dollar return on a writ of seizure and sale. Obviously, used goods do not sell at the same price as new goods. The creditor will receive the amount that the enforcement officer earned from selling the goods, less the enforcement office's expenses not previously paid.

5.2 Initiating seizure and sale of personal property

To have a writ of seizure and sale of personal property issued, fill out the appropriate form at the court office. You will then need to take the form to the enforcement office. Ask court staff for the original writ if you need to file it in the enforcement office within another jurisdiction.

The writ must be executed to be valid. To have the issued writ executed do the following:

(a) File the issued writ with the enforcement office in the jurisdiction in which the debtor owns the personal property to be seized.

(b) Provide the enforcement office with the list of items to be seized and be sure to identify each item as completely as possible. Provide the make, model, and serial number of any technical equipment, computers, or vehicles.

(c) Pay the security deposit, if required.

The enforcement office now has the authority to attempt to seize and sell the goods. The office must mail to the debtor and the creditor notice about the time and place of the sale of the seized goods. This notice must be provided before the sale and will be advertised in a manner that is likely to bring it to the attention of the public.

The debtor may request that the enforcement officer deliver, within a reasonable time after the request is made, an inventory of personal property seized under the writ.

To renew a writ of seizure and sale of personal property do the following:

(a) Before the writ expires, attend at the court office where the writ was issued. If the writ has expired, you may wish to bring a motion (or application) for the extension of time.

(b) Request that the court clerk renew the writ.

(c) File the renewed writ with the enforcement office where the debtor owns property.

(d) Report promptly to the enforcement office any payments the debtor made in satisfaction of the judgment debt.

If the debtor has paid the debt in full since the writ was issued and filed, write a letter advising the enforcement office that the writ is being withdrawn. Immediately send it to the enforcement office, with a copy to the court office.

6. Seizure and Sale of Lands

If the debtor owns land, vacant or otherwise, the creditor may obtain a writ of seizure and sale of lands. The court will issue this writ as long as any part of the debt remains unpaid. Seizure and sale of lands is the preferred method for collection when it is not possible to garnish funds or seize personal property owned by the debtor.

The debtor will not be able to sell the land until the debt and accumulated enforcement costs are paid in full.

Note: While this approach is simple, inexpensive, and may eventually lead to collection, it may not bring results quickly.

The procedure for seizure and sale of lands varies greatly across Canada. Consult with your local small claims court if you wish to take this approach.

If the debtor has paid the debt making the execution of the writ unnecessary, the enforcement office must be notified immediately. You must then withdraw the writ in writing and forward that letter to the enforcement office, with a copy to the court office.

If the debtor has paid the debt in full since the writ was issued and filed with the enforcement office, write a letter advising the enforcement office that the writ is being withdrawn. Immediately send it to the enforcement office, with a copy to the court office.

7. Enforcing an Order of a Board, Tribunal, Agency, or Other Court

Small claims court may be used to enforce an order made by a board, tribunal, agencies, or other courts. For example, if you obtain an order of a tribunal or another court and the money the debtor owed is within the monetary jurisdiction of the small claims court, you may use that court to enforce that order.

To enforce an order made in a venue other than small claims court, the creditor must do the following:

(a) Obtain from the registrar, court office, tribunal office, board office, or agency office (whichever applies) a certified copy of the order that the creditor wishes to enforce.

(b) Take the certified copy of the order, along with the fee, to the small claims court office in which the debtor lives or carries on business.

(c) Begin enforcement proceedings as described in section **8**.

For example, if you wanted to enforce a restitution order granted under the Young Offenders Act or the Criminal Code, you would file a certified copy of the restitution order with the appropriate civil court, depending on the monetary jurisdiction, and proceed with the available collection measures as if it were a judgment of that court.

8. Tips for Creditors

In many cases, collecting money is a challenge. Nevertheless, judgments must be enforced in accordance with the rules of the court and relevant legislation. Even though collection proceedings may frustrate you, never harass the debtor.

If your claim is related to a motor vehicle accident, contact your provincial or territorial Ministry of Transportation and request that the debtor's driver's licence be suspended until the judgment debt is satisfied. You will need proof of judgment for the ministry to honour your request.

Often the biggest challenge is locating the debtor. Therefore, it is crucial to begin enforcement proceedings as soon as possible. The Internet is an inexpensive first step to try to locate the debtor. Refer to the list of people and business search files posted on Self-Counsel Press's Web site at <http://www.self-counsel.com/canlaw/smallclaims/resources.html>. If you are unsuccessful and your judgment is worth spending additional money on enforcement, you may wish to hire a private investigator. A private investigator may be able to locate the debtor so that you could serve the debtor with court papers such as a notice of examination or notice of contempt hearing.

If you are served with a notice to attend a consolidation hearing, read section **9** to find out more about consolidation orders. Creditors are allowed to make submissions about issues pertaining to the granting of a consolidation order. Make a point of attending the hearing of the motion (or application).

Before attending a consolidation hearing, it may be a good idea to investigate the debtor's ability to pay by, for example, conducting a judgment debtor examination. Knowing that information will assist you in making submissions to the court to support the argument that a consolidation order is not proper in a situation where the debtor is able but unwilling to pay. Read chapter 11 to learn what you will need to do to properly respond to this type of motion (or application).

9. Tips for Debtors

If judgment has been granted against you and you do not plan to appeal the judgment, you should comply with that judgment immediately. Ignoring the judgment is no solution since a creditor may attempt to enforce judgment for 20 years from the date of judgment. If the creditor is forced to take such steps, you will be ultimately responsible for expenses the creditor incurred. If you lost at trial, swallow your pride and pay up.

Do not try to dispose of your assets (sell, lend, give away, transfer, or assign) so as to hide them from the creditor and the court. Such efforts are illegal and will not be lost on the court, which may make an order for the seizure of those assets. You may run into other problems if you disobey court orders or fail to attend a judgment debtor examination. You may even be ordered to serve a jail sentence after which you will still owe the debt.

If default judgment was signed against you, you may be able to get that default judgment struck in certain legitimate circumstances. To do so, bring a motion (or application) immediately. See chapter 11 if this situation applies to you.

9.1 If you are unable to pay

If you have legitimate reasons why you are unable to comply with the judgment, you should bring them to the attention of the creditor and the court. If, for example, you attend at a judgment debtor examination, you should make the presiding official aware of any financial difficulties you have, and try to work out a payment plan before the official makes an order he or she deems appropriate. Asking for a terms of payment hearing will allow you to have some control over your finances.

If you agree to a schedule of payments, be sure to pay according to schedule. Failure to comply with a court order could mean that you will be found in contempt of court and, possibly, spend time in jail.

Pay if you have the capability. If you are unable to pay, approach the court for a consolidation order or a terms of payment hearing, if either is appropriate in your circumstances.

9.2 Consolidation orders

If you are a judgment debtor who owes money on more than one judgment of the small claims court, consider requesting a consolidation order. A consolidation order allows all judgment debts to be combined and distributed equally among judgment creditors according to a schedule.

A consolidation order may set out the following:

▸ A list of unsatisfied orders for the payment of money against the debtor, indicating in each case the date, court, amount, and amount unpaid

▸ The amounts to be paid into court by the debtor under the order

▸ The times of the payments (the schedule)

Once a consolidation order is in effect, the court clerk will distribute the money paid into the consolidation account at least once every six months. The only recourse a creditor has for enforcing a judgment debt while a consolidation order is in effect is to file a writ of seizure and sale of lands with the enforcement office.

Failure to abide by the terms of the consolidation order terminates the order. The court clerk would then notify the creditors by mail. No further consolidation order would be made for at least one year after termination.

You must request a consolidation order by bringing a motion (or application). You will then file an affidavit setting out specific details and serve a notice of motion or notice of application on all creditors within seven days of the hearing date set by the court. The creditor may make submissions at the hearing of this motion (or application) about the amount and times of payments. Attempts to deceive the court about your capability to pay will likely be pointed out by a creditor who has surely investigated your finances.

10. Appealing a Judgment

An appeal is a request made to the higher court to review the decision made by the judge of a lower court. The names of appeal courts differ among provinces and territories. Table 15 outlines the courts where small claims appeals are heard, but it is best to ask small claims court staff about the court in which you should bring the appeal.

In Ontario, you may only appeal a judgment if the amount of the plaintiff's or defendant's claim resulting in that judgment sought to recover is at least $500.

10.1 Grounds for appeal

If you disagree with a judgment of the small claims court, you may appeal the decision provided you have grounds (a legal reason) to appeal the decision. If you feel that the judge has made an error of fact or an error of law, you may have grounds for an appeal. You must also be able to convince the court that the judge was incorrect in reaching that conclusion of fact or in applying the law to the particular set of facts.

10.1.a *Error of fact*

An error of fact occurs when a judge finds, based on evidence and oral testimony, that a certain event occurred or that a certain statement is true. For instance, a witness may have testified that her bicycle was stolen and demolished in the process. If the judge notes in the decision that he or she believes that statement to be true, the judge has made a finding of fact. If you could prove that the judge was incorrect in reaching that conclusion, you may wish to appeal the decision.

However, if the judge makes a decision based on the credibility of a witness, you cannot appeal the decision. Appellate courts base their review on the contents of the trial transcripts and appeal arguments of the parties. Witnesses do not testify at appeal hearings. Therefore, the appellate court cannot assess the credibility of witnesses and will not overturn a finding of credibility.

10.1.b *Error of law*

An error of law may be grounds for appeal if you believe there was an improper application of the common law, questionable interpretation of a statute, or improper consideration of evidence.

Note: You need not disagree with everything that the judge found nor with every treatment of the law or rules of evidence. An appeal may be brought relating to one or more issues. For instance, appeals are sometimes brought on the issue of costs, rather than on the merits (factual and legal aspects) of the case.

10.2 Commencing an appeal

When a case moves out of the jurisdiction of the small claims court, procedures become more complicated. Agents are not permitted to represent parties at the hearing of an appeal. As a result, many people hire a lawyer to handle their appeals.

TABLE 15
WHERE TO APPEAL SMALL CLAIMS JUDGMENTS

PROVINCE	SMALL CLAIMS COURT TRIALS ARE HELD IN:	SMALL CLAIMS APPEALS ARE HEARD IN:
NWT	Territorial	Court
YK	Supreme Court, Small Claims Court	Supreme Court
BC	Provincial Court	Supreme Court
AB	Provincial Court, Civil Division	Court of Queen's Bench
SK	Court of Queen's Bench, Small Claims Court	Court of Queen's Bench
MB	Court of Queen's Bench, Small Claims	Court of Queen's Bench
ON	Superior Court of Justice, Small Claims Court	Superior Court of Justice
NB	Court of Queen's Bench, Small Claims Court	Court of Queen's Bench, Appeal Division
NS	Supreme Court, Small Claims Court	Supreme Court
PEI	Supreme Court, Small Claims Court	Supreme Court, Appeal Division
NFLD	Provincial Court	Supreme Court

Your appeal will operate under the rules of the higher court, not the rules of the small claims court. If you are serious about appealing your case without a lawyer's assistance, obtain a copy of the rules of civil procedure and familiarize yourself with the relevant rules concerning appeals. Self-represented parties are expected to comply with the rules of the court, regardless of their experience or knowledge of the law.

If you plan to conduct your own appeal, be sure to observe deadlines. An appeal must be brought within a short amount of time, usually 30 days of the date of the decision, unless a statute or court rules state a different deadline.

If an appeal is based on an issue related to the Canadian Constitution and, particularly, the Canadian Charter of Rights and Freedoms, then the Attorney General for Canada may make submissions. Even if the Attorney General was not a party at trial, he or she is entitled to be heard at the appeal.

Likewise, if an appeal is based on a statute that gives an official the right to be heard during an appeal of that statute, that official may make submissions.

If the constitutionality of a provincial or territorial statute is an issue in the appeal, both the Attorney General for your province or territory and the Attorney General for Canada should be served with notice of the appeal.

Once an appeal has been commenced, all court orders for payment of money are automatically *stayed*. This means that the judgment is put on hold until the appellate court has reviewed it and made a ruling. In the meantime, if the trial judge has ordered a party to pay money into court or to pay someone else, the party need not comply if an appeal has been commenced.

If the appellate court upholds the judgment, the losing party must comply with the judgment.

11
Other Appearances

1. Motions and Applications

Some words you should know

In this book, the term *motion* is used interchangeably with the word *application*. They serve the same purpose and entail similar procedures when small claims are concerned.

The party bringing the motion is called the *moving party*. A party bringing an application is an *applicant*.

The party responding to the motion is called the *responding party*. A party responding to the application is the *respondent*.

Motions are requests to the court for an order to be made in accordance with the rules of the court, other legislation, or the common law.

Any party who has filed a claim or defence must be notified of the motion before the hearing date unless the court orders otherwise. In urgent circumstances, motions may be brought *ex parte* (without notice) or on short notice. Motions are most often brought in writing. Most jurisdictions have court forms that act as notices of motion and that must be filed with the court and served on all parties.

Motions are dealt with by way of a hearing held in the courtroom, unless a judge chooses to hear the motion in chambers.

British Columbia residents, note:

The registrar may make an order in response to an application if all the parties consent to the order requested in the application. This is called an *over-the-counter application* since the registrar makes the order based on the form submitted without the parties having to appear at a hearing. This is only possible if the particulars about the order requested are sufficient and if it pertains to one of the following orders:

- ▶ An order renewing a claim or third party notice
- ▶ An order changing the date of a settlement conference
- ▶ An order extending the time for certificate of readiness
- ▶ An order permitting the hearing to be conducted by telephone
- ▶ An order permitting service of the claim outside British Columbia
- ▶ An order permitting another method of service
- ▶ An order exempting someone from paying fees
- ▶ Any other order that the registrar is authorized to make without notice to another party

If the registrar is satisfied that the request is urgent, the application may be granted without notice of it being provided to all other parties.

The registrar may refer the application to a judge who may order that the applicant appear before a judge to explain why the order should be made.

A motion should be brought and held in the jurisdiction in which the claim was brought. The exceptions include cases in which all parties consent to another location, in which the court approves of another location, or in which the motion is of an urgent nature.

Motions should not be brought frivolously nor should they be opposed without good reason. If the judge hearing the motion is of the view that the motion should not have been brought, should not have been opposed, or was only necessary as a result of a party's default, the judge may order one or more parties to pay costs of the motion.

A motion is not a trial and, therefore, witnesses play no role at the hearing. Although rare, witnesses may be called on to submit sworn affidavits as part of a party's motion materials. In fact, the parties themselves may introduce evidence by affidavit. Good advocacy skills are nevertheless important and will help you deliver a more persuasive argument. These skills are vital to delivering a solid argument within the brief span of time to which motions are generally restricted. Read the advocacy section of chapter 9 well before you attend the hearing.

You should prepare for the motion properly so as to increase your chance for success. The next few sections outline these preparation techniques as well as how a motion should be arranged, adjourned, and argued. Comments on specific motions are also offered in this chapter.

1.1 Bringing a motion

Before arranging a motion, call the court office to check for local practice. Most courts hear motions on a specific day of the week. Some hear them only once a month or even less often. It is best to call ahead to get an idea of available dates. In some jurisdictions, you must book a motion date by telephone and then file all your motion materials and affidavits of service with the court a certain number of days before the hearing date. If you do not comply with the proper procedures, your motion will be taken off the motions list.

Before bringing a motion, you should, if possible, advise the other parties that you intend to bring a particular motion and agree to three or four dates on which all parties are available to attend. Such contact serves three purposes:

(a) You may be able to resolve the issues in the motion with the other parties and thereby prevent the motion from being brought in the first place.

If you do agree on an issue, confirm it by writing a letter to that party. Later, if the party reneges on your verbal agreement and you are required to bring the motion anyway, you can include the letter as an exhibit to your affidavit to provide evidence that the party earlier agreed on terms that you now have to seek by way of a motion. This is also useful in revealing to the court any intentional delay that the party caused.

(b) You may be able to consent to a motion date and avoid having to consider an adjournment later.

If you schedule a motion and the responding party cannot attend, he or she may seek an adjournment on the day of the motion or, perhaps, earlier. An adjournment ought to be granted for good reason and when it will not prejudice a party's case.

(c) You can ask the court clerk for a date that is mutually convenient and then choose your preferred date from a list of dates.

Before you bring a motion, you must be sure to have grounds (a legal reason) for requesting the order. Some grounds for specific motions are dealt with throughout this chapter.

To bring a motion, take the following steps:

(a) Obtain from the court office the proper form, if required.

(b) Prepare your motion materials, including a notice of motion and the affidavit on which you will be relying at the hearing of the motion. Include both grounds for the request and the facts that support your request. If the space on the form is insufficient, state, "I have set out the facts in support of this motion in my supplementary affidavit, as attached"; then prepare and swear a supplementary affidavit and attach it to the affidavit. Chapter 12 provides guidance on drafting affidavits.

Be sure to attach copies of any exhibits (documents) mentioned in the affidavit. Refer to them as "Exhibit A" (B, C, and so on).

Note: It is a criminal offence to knowingly swear a false affidavit.

Make enough photocopies of the sworn affidavit and any exhibits for each party in the lawsuit, the court, and one for your records.

(c) Take the motion materials, their photocopies, and the fee to the court office where the claim was issued.

(d) The court staff will review the motion materials, write a hearing date on the notice, and then file a copy in the court file.

(e) Serve each party with the motion materials.

Note: In some cases you are required to serve other parties with a notice of motion. For example, in the case of a personal injury lawsuit, if you are asking for an order for a doctor to produce medical records, then you will have to serve the doctor as well as the parties to the lawsuit.

(f) Provide proper proof of service (affidavit or certificate of service).

You may wish to confirm your hearing date by calling the court office before the motion and confirming that your motion is listed for the day specified in the notice of motion.

1.2 Responding to a motion

To respond to a motion, take the following steps:

(a) Obtain from the court office the proper form and supporting affidavit, if required.

(b) Prepare the form and prepare and swear the affidavit containing all the facts in support of your arguments in the motion. If you do not do this, you may be asked to state your version of the facts under oath, which will leave you with much less structure and more unpredictability.

Photocopy the sworn affidavit, making one copy for each party, one for the court, and one for your records.

(c) Serve the form and affidavit on every party served with the notice of motion.

(d) Prepare and swear an affidavit of service for each party you served.

Photocopy the sworn affidavit for your records.

(e) Before the motion hearing date, file the original affidavit and affidavit of service with the court office in which the motion was brought.

You should prepare for the motion before arranging or responding to it, if possible. This will ensure that you have thought about your request thoroughly and have included all evidence in support of your motion.

1.3 Preparing for a motion

To properly prepare to argue a motion you should read the notice of motion and affidavit well before the motion date. Make brief notes on your arguments using the following categories:

(a) *Introduction.* Identify the parties present, state the order being sought, and state that the parties are ready to proceed (or that a party is requesting an adjournment).

(b) *Arguments*. Present the facts, supporting court rule, and any case law of which you are aware. Provide a copy of case law and legislation excerpts to each party, as well as to the judge hearing the motion.

(c) *Costs*. Make an argument for costs of the motion as permitted by the rules.

Be sure to bring the motion materials, your arguments, the pleadings, and correspondence to court. The judge may ask the parties questions that will require you to find these in your file. Chapter 8 suggests a list of items to take to court during trial. The list is useful for any court appearance.

The law does not permit you to argue your own affidavit. Therefore, if a party is knowledgeable about the facts, perhaps that person could swear the affidavit if you wish to argue the motion. In the alternative, if you are the only person with knowledge about the facts set out in the affidavit, someone else should argue the motion for you. The courts have bypassed this difficulty in the past by allowing the moving party to testify rather than submit affidavit evidence. If you are in the predicament of being both the only person who knows the facts set out in the notice of motion and the only person who can argue your motion, inquire with the court office about whether you can testify at the hearing of the motion.

1.4 Arguing a motion

When the case is called, any requests for an adjournment are heard first. Then, if the motion proceeds, the moving party makes his or her arguments. The responding party then has an opportunity to make arguments. Following that, the moving party may ask the judge for permission to respond. The responding party may also request permission to respond.

After the arguments have been made, the judge may do any of the following:

➤ Grant the motion by making the order requested

➤ Grant the motion in part by making an order

➤ Dismiss the motion

➤ Reserve his or her decision for a later date so as to consider the law on the issue or consider other evidence that the parties have undertaken to produce to the court

The judge has discretion to order costs of bringing the motion. The judge may ask one or more of the parties to make submissions relating to costs. If the judge does not ask for cost submissions and the ruling is in your favour, ask for an opportunity to do so. While there is no guarantee that you will be awarded costs, you should argue that costs are payable, if that is appropriate in your circumstances. Be sure to ask for costs to be payable immediately. A party may also request that costs be made payable when the action is finally disposed of by settlement or at trial.

Chapter 9 offers guidance on making cost submissions.

1.5 Dealing with the results of a motion

If you do not understand an order, ask the judge for clarification at the time the order is granted. This will ensure that you are able to abide by the terms of the order.

Following the hearing of the motion, the court clerk sends the typed order to the parties. However, the parties should not wait for that typed order to start abiding by it. The order is effective from the time it is granted unless the judge specifies otherwise. If you refuse to comply with an order, your case may be dismissed, possibly without notice to you and with costs payable by you.

If an order stipulates that you must pay costs to one of the parties, pay them as ordered unless you plan to have the order set aside by way of another motion.

1.6 Withdrawing a motion

Sometimes a motion becomes unnecessary because the party subject to the motion has complied with the request or the parties have settled the motion. In that case, the moving party should write a letter to the other parties withdrawing the motion. A copy should be sent to the court.

2. Dealing with Specific Motions

The success of each motion depends in part on the facts in support of the request. Each case is different, so each motion will depend on a slightly different set of facts. Therefore, you must read the comments on each type of motion as a starting point and improvise as required for your particular set of circumstances.

You will need to show that you have grounds (a legal reason) for requesting the order. Some general arguments that you may wish to apply to your particular set of facts include the following:

> Fairness (equity)

> Prejudice to your case

> Court rules specific to your request

> Rules granting the court general discretion to make or deny an order (as outlined in chapter 5)

The next several pages provide comments on numerous motions but the list is not exhaustive. The facts of your particular case as well as the court rules, rules of equity, and the common law will determine whether or not you are entitled to the order sought in the notice of motion.

2.1 Motions relating to pleadings

2.1.a Actions to be tried together

If you are aware of two actions involving the same set of circumstances, you could bring a motion requesting an order to have the trials held together. One ground for such a motion could be judicial economy (preserving valuable court resources). You may also argue that two related trials would likely inconvenience the witnesses who would be required to testify at both trials. You should attempt to convince the court that the claims are based on the same set of circumstances or that enough common witnesses warrant a common trial. You may have other grounds particular to your set of facts.

Your affidavit should set out the claim number, date of issuance, and parties for each action as well as the grounds and any other relevant facts.

If you are responding to such a motion, be prepared to argue why the trials should not be held together.

❦ Example

The defendant was sued by two different plaintiffs in two separate claims over personal injuries he allegedly caused to each of them. The defendant brings a motion to have the actions tried together given that the identical witnesses would be called if the actions were to be tried separately.

✤ Example

The defendant in Action A is sued for breach of contract. The defendant in Action A then sued another defendant in Action B alleging that his or her actions caused him to breach the contract in Action A. The defendant should have filed this as a defendant's claim but, nonetheless, brings a motion to have the actions tried together.

2.1.b Amendment of pleadings

Chapter 5 outlines the proper method of amending documents. A motion to amend pleadings (plaintiff's claim, defence, or defendant's claim) is only necessary when it is done after the time allowed for amendment. You would be seeking an order permitting the amendment on short notice. Attach a copy of the amended pleading to your affidavit. Your affidavit should outline the changes made and the reason for making them so close to trial. Apply the rules granting the court general discretion to make or deny an order (listed in chapter 5) to strengthen your arguments.

2.1.c Dismissal — Missed limitation period

A defendant could bring a motion seeking an order that the claim be dismissed on the grounds that the limitation period has expired. The defendant should set out in the affidavit the date the claim was issued, whether and when a defence was filed, the limitation period for that particular cause of action, and any other relevant facts. The defendant should present at the hearing a copy of the section of the provincial or territorial Limitations Act or other legislation for each party and for the judge to provide the authority for the assertion that the limitation period was missed.

Courts tend to adhere strictly to limitation periods. They may permit late issuance if there would be a great miscarriage of justice to dismiss a claim outright. Therefore, that argument would be necessary for the plaintiff to succeed. Another argument, although more difficult to accept, is that the plaintiff was unable to bring the claim due to special, extenuating circumstances. The plaintiff must convince the court that the limitation period should be extended, which tends to be a very difficult task.

2.1.d Dismissal — Missed notice period

A defendant could bring a motion seeking an order that the claim be dismissed on the grounds that the notice was improperly given or not given in accordance with relevant legislation. The defendant would set out in the affidavit the date of the cause of action, the date notice was served if it was served, the date the claim was issued, whether and when a defence was filed, and other relevant facts. The defendant should present at the hearing a copy of the section of the provincial or territorial Limitations Act or other legislation for each party and for the judge. The defendant should attach as an exhibit to the affidavit a copy of the notice, if possible.

A plaintiff could seek an extension for filing a notice although, as with requests to extend limitation periods, this is another request that courts are reluctant to grant.

2.1.e Dismissal — Delay

Either party, but more typically the defendant, may bring a motion requesting an order that the claim be dismissed for delay. Grounds for such a motion are that the plaintiff (or other party) has failed to move the action along by failing to comply with a judge's order, failing to provide copies of expert reports or other evidence, or by otherwise causing a delay. The grounds will be specific to your particular set of facts.

You should try to convince the court that the delay will prejudice your right to a fair trial. Your affidavit should set out the events that show the delay as well as any attempts on your part to move the action along. These could be letters to the parties or other attempts. Such attempts on your part help to fortify the argument that an order of this nature is suitable. Short delays of three months are not strong foundations for motions of this nature. However, if several months have passed since the pre-trial conference and the plaintiff has still not set the action down for trial, there would be a stronger case for dismissing the case for delay.

If you are the responding party, you should argue that the delay is not inordinate and would not prejudice the defendant's case. You should also convince the court that the reason for the inactivity was beyond your control (if that indeed was the case).

2.1.f Dismissal — Action improperly brought

Sometimes a claim is inappropriately brought in the small claims court, and this error goes unnoticed by court staff. In that case, you can bring a motion to dismiss the claim for being brought in the wrong forum. For example, suppose the matter should have been resolved at a tribunal. The grounds for such a motion are that the legislation provides that relief sought in the claim must be brought by application to the tribunal. You should set out the facts surrounding this situation and support it during the hearing with sections of the relevant legislation.

If you are the responding party, and the motion for dismissal has not yet been brought but the defendant has brought the error to your attention, verify that the moving party is making a valid request. If so, you should withdraw the action on a "without prejudice" basis. You can do this by writing a letter to the court with a copy to the defendant. You should probably first discuss this with the defendant to ensure that the defendant will not be seeking costs. If the motion has already been brought, advise the defendant by letter that you are willing to consent to the motion if the claim is dismissed on a "without prejudice basis, without costs".

2.1.g Dismissal — No cause of action

Some claims do not reveal a reasonable cause of action. A typical example is a claim in which the plaintiff is suing because the defendant allegedly behaved in a way that embarrassed the plaintiff. The tort of embarrassment is unknown in Canada, so one could argue that the claim does not disclose a reasonable cause of action. On the other hand, if other, legitimate issues are claimed, then the defendant could instead bring a motion to strike only the portion of the claim that does not disclose a reasonable cause of action or leave that matter for determination at a settlement conference or at trial.

If you are the responding party, and the motion has not yet been brought but the defendant has brought it to your attention, verify that the moving party is making a valid request. If so, you should withdraw the action on a "without prejudice" basis. You can do so by writing a letter to the court with a copy to the defendant. You should probably discuss this approach with the defendant first to ensure that the defendant will not be seeking costs. If the motion has already been brought, advise the defendant by letter that you are willing to consent to the motion if the claim is dismissed on a "without prejudice" basis.

2.1.h Dismissal — Defendant improperly named

Claims in which the defendant is improperly named may be dismissed. Grounds for such a motion are that the defendant named is not the person served. For example, corporations are typically misnamed when corporate searches are not conducted before issuing a claim.

The responding party could ask the court to permit an amendment of pleadings instead of a dismissal of the claim outright. However, he or she will have to provide evidence that the defendant's name will be properly shown on the amended claim. The responding party should also try to convince the court that there would be injustice in dismissing the claim.

See chapter 5 for the proper amendment procedure that may be possible without bringing a motion.

2.1.i Extension of time for issuing or filing

If you have missed the deadline for issuing a claim or filing a defence, you may bring a motion to the court for an extension of time. It is best if this motion is brought before the time for issuance or filing expires but, often, the deadline is skipped and the motion is brought afterward. You should support your request with a good reason why the deadline was missed and what measures, if any, you have taken to expedite this task. You should also seek a new deadline for issuance or filing that is reasonable, something in the order of seven to 10 days.

Note: The defendant may file a defence without motion up until the plaintiff notes the defendant in default.

If you are opposed to this type of motion, you will be expected to convince the court that an extension of time is not appropriate and be able to support it with reasons. If you have none, you may wish to consider consenting to a brief extension of 10 days so as to avoid attending at the motion and paying costs yourself.

2.1.j Separate trials

In actions involving a plaintiff's claim and defendant's claim, any of the parties may bring a motion requesting an order for separate trials of the two claims. This may be desirable if the parties in one claim are ready for trial and would be prejudiced by a delay in awaiting the parties in the other claim to be ready for trial. It may also be desired when the issues in one claim are more complicated and lengthy and would unnecessarily prolong or complicate the trial of the issues in the other claim. The success of the motion will also depend on your ability to demonstrate the practicality of holding separate trials. Both sides should make arguments to that effect. Note that when the events in the plaintiff's claim and defendant's claim are intertwined, the judge may order that the claims be tried together.

2.1.k Striking a pleading or part of a pleading

Either party may bring a motion to strike a pleading or any part of the pleading by reason that it was improperly served or fails to comply with one or more court rules. You should rely on specific rules breached as well as the general rules of discretion to make your argument.

If you are a responding party, you could argue that striking an entire pleading would be a drastic order and that an amendment to the pleading would be a just and proper alternative to the order sought.

2.2 Motions relating to default proceedings

2.2.a Seeking default judgment

If a defendant to a defendant's claim has been noted in default, judgment may only be granted at the trial of the action pertaining to the plaintiff's claim or on motion to the court. A motion would be most appropriate when the plaintiff's claim settles and a trial is not needed. In setting out the facts in the affidavit, be sure to include the fact that the defendant was properly served (if that is true). The court will not grant judgment if service was improper or cannot be proven.

2.2.b Extension of time for filing a defence

If you missed the time limit for filing a defence, you may bring a motion for an order granting an extension of time to file the defence. If your failure to file a defence is the result of sheer inadvertence (negligence) on your part, argue that one of the rules of general discretion listed in chapter 5 applies.

If you are opposing a motion for extension, you will need to convince the court that the defendant had ample time to file a defence and that the defendant was served properly and within the prescribed time frame. Your affidavit should include a copy of the affidavit of service (or certificate of service).

2.2.c Setting aside consequences of default

If you have been noted in default or if judgment has been granted against you, bring a motion requesting that the noting in default or default judgment (or both, whichever applies to your case) be set aside and that a reasonable time extension for filing a defence be ordered. You will need grounds for this request, although mere inadvertence (negligence) is known to be an effective factual basis for having the order granted. You should try to show that the defence you wish to put forth in response to the claim has merit. It is very helpful to argue the rules of general discretion set out in chapter 5.

If you wish to oppose such a motion, include a copy of the affidavit of service in your motion materials, proving that service was effected properly. Otherwise, the court may be inclined to set aside the noting of default or the default judgment.

2.3 Motions relating to forum or jurisdiction

Court staff usually know if a claim is being commenced in the proper jurisdiction. Nevertheless, some claims are occasionally brought in the improper jurisdiction. Other claims are brought in the proper jurisdiction but the defendant has since moved or relocated his or her business to another jurisdiction. In still other claims, the jurisdiction is correct but is an inconvenient location in which to hold a trial of the action. For example, a court location may not provide proper access for people with disabilities.

2.3.a Transfer to another jurisdiction

If one or more of the parties wish to have the trial held in a particular location, perhaps different from that specified in the notice of trial, the parties need simply indicate, in a letter to the court, that they consent to a change. However, if the parties disagree about where to hold the trial, a judge can make a ruling on that issue in a jurisdictional hearing.

A *jurisdictional hearing* is a motion to the court requesting an order that the trial be held in a specific location. The moving party must arrange a hearing date and motion materials as described in section **1**.

Both parties should be prepared to argue why the balance of convenience substantially favours holding the trial in a particular location.

In determining the balance of convenience, the judge will evaluate a number of factors:

> The locale where most of the witnesses live

> The area in which the plaintiff and defendant live

> Whether evidence or witnesses can be relocated with relative ease, especially if there are access issues for witnesses or a disabled party

> Other factors brought to the attention of the judge

Arguments for both sides must be persuasive, requiring a review of the law in this area. Often, common sense prevails. If your side of the argument is based on a common sense evaluation of these factors, you have a good chance of being successful in persuading or dissuading the judge to change the forum.

As with any motion or hearing, costs may be awarded against the unsuccessful party. Be sure that you want to risk requesting a hearing or opposing it.

Note: The issue of jurisdiction could also be resolved at trial on motion or at the judge's request.

2.3.b Transfer to the higher court

If you wish to increase the monetary value of your claim to an amount greater than that permitted by the small claims court rules, you may bring a motion to the small claims court to transfer your file to the higher court. Be prepared to show why the amount of your claim is increasing. You may wish to argue that a denial of your request would bring injustice to your case.

If you are opposing a motion to transfer to a higher court, look carefully at the moving party's affidavit to identify arguments to counter the transfer. The court will likely grant such a request unless no grounds support it. You may, therefore, wish to consider consenting to the motion.

Another reason for bringing a motion is if the subject matter is outside the jurisdiction of the small claims court, but this goes unnoticed by court staff at the time the claim is issued. See chapter 2 for examples of the types of claims that may be heard in small claims court.

2.4 Motions relating to service

A number of motions could be brought relating to service. Refer to chapter 13 for insights into service issues that might be resolved on motion to the court. Some examples are discussed later.

2.4.a Extension of time for service

You may bring a motion requesting an extension of time for service. One scenario behind such a motion may involve being unable to serve a party for reasons beyond your control. For example, you may not be able to locate the party, or you have been ill or out of the country.

2.4.b Substituted service

A motion for substituted service is an ex parte motion typically brought to deal with a party who is evading service, or when personal service or alternative to personal service has been attempted more than once with unsuccessful results. Your affidavit should specify the date, time, and manner in which service was attempted. You would request an order allowing service in a manner that is likely to come to the attention of the party you were attempting to serve. You would have to specify the manner of service and why it is likely to come to the party's attention.

In most cases, the court order will provide the effective date of the substituted service as well as the details.

Read chapter 13 for more insight into substituted service.

2.5 Motions relating to settlement

You may request that the court approve of a settlement made by a litigation guardian (or next friend) as well as enforce a settlement agreement made but later retracted by one of the parties.

2.5.a *Court approval of settlement of party under disability*

The court must approve of all settlements made on behalf of parties under disability. Either party may make a motion to the court for approval. Your affidavit would have to set out the following:

› A brief statement of the cause of action and the date the events occurred

› When settlement was reached with the litigation guardian

› The minutes of settlement

› Any correspondence relevant to the settlement (except that marked "without prejudice")

› The amount and other terms of settlement

› Some statement of belief that the settlement is in the best interests of the party under disability

2.5.b *Enforcement of settlement*

If you are faced with a situation in which you have settled a matter either verbally or in writing and the other party then reneges on the agreement, you may bring a motion to the court to enforce the settlement. You should be prepared to show the following in your affidavit:

› The facts pertaining to the settlement

› The minutes of settlement

› The names and addresses of any witnesses to the settlement and affidavits from them relaying what they witnessed

› Any correspondence between the parties relating to the settlement (except that marked "without prejudice")

▶ Any other facts that you may find necessary to include

You should use the rules of general discretion set out in chapter 5, as well as the rules of settlement set out in chapters 6 and 7, to fortify your argument.

If you are the party who reneged on the settlement and you are opposing the motion, your job will be to counter the arguments of the moving party. You may not have had, in your opinion, a valid agreement, or you may not have had the authority to make the agreement on behalf of the party. Use the rules of general discretion in your defence. The judge has discretion to make the order, but you must convince the court that the order should not enforce the settlement and provide a solid reason for that assertion.

2.5.b Removal of litigation guardian

You may bring a motion to remove a litigation guardian. You will have to show that you have a valid reason for making that request and, if possible, suggest a replacement litigation guardian or ask the court to appoint one.

This motion is generally not required if a minor has reached the age of majority. When this happens, the minor is then at liberty to continue any action on his or her own behalf without any application. It is a good idea, however, to advise the court in writing that the minor-now-adult is continuing the action without the further assistance of his or her litigation guardian and you should amend the pleadings to reflect that.

2.6 Motions relating to orders or judgments

An order or judgment made by a small claims court judge, court clerk, or registrar may be varied or set aside in certain circumstances.

2.6.a Setting aside a finding of contempt

If you have been found in contempt, you may be able to have that finding set aside if you have a sound reason as to why the finding is invalid. For instance, you may not have received notice of an examination, thereby having a good reason for not having attended. You may also not have received notice of an order made against you for the same reason. You must convince the court that the finding is inappropriate and unjust. If you missed a proceeding, you should indicate a willingness to co-operate by attending another such proceeding.

2.6.b Setting aside or varying a judgment

Judgments will seldom be set aside. However, if evidence previously un-available or unanticipated has come to light, you may have grounds to bring a motion to have the judgment set aside. A judgment is more likely to be varied than it is to be set aside. Therefore, carefully consider what you would like to accomplish by bringing this motion.

Argue the rules of general discretion listed in chapter 5, as well as any other applicable rule that may have been broken or applied incorrectly, so as to yield the order you are trying to vary.

2.6.c Setting aside an order

You must bring a motion if you wish to have an order set aside. Such motions are not taken lightly. You will have to show the court that the order ought not to have been made in the first place or that it is inappropriate in light of new facts that have come to your attention since the order was made. Orders for payment and enforcement orders are examples of orders that might be set aside if the grounds and supporting facts are compelling. Carefully review the rule or rules under which to bring the motion.

2.7 Motions relating to trial

Even though motions are brought during trial, they should still be brought with proper notice to the parties, whenever possible.

2.7.a Adjournment

Adjournments are sought for many reasons and for any number of proceedings. If a party requests an adjournment and it will not prejudice the other side's case, it is proper to consent to the adjournment. However, if a party believes that the adjournment is inappropriate because it appears to be a delay tactic or because it was brought too late in the day, the request will be opposed and the party denied the adjournment will have to bring the request before the court. Motions for adjournment should always be on notice unless time is insufficient.

2.7.b Exclusion of evidence

If a party is attempting to enter documentary evidence that has not been disclosed within the amount of time permitted by the rules, you could move during the trial, before the evidence is tendered, that the evidence should be excluded on the ground that it was not disclosed according to the particular rule.

2.7.c Exclusion of witnesses

Before any evidence is introduced at trial, either party may request an order excluding witnesses. This order is usually granted unless the judge believes the order is unnecessary. When this happens, the presiding judge will order that all witnesses leave the courtroom and wait outside until they are called in to testify. The purpose of requesting such an order is to allow witnesses to attain more credibility, presumably because they will not have heard other witnesses testify and will not have been influenced by earlier testimony. Notice that such a motion will be brought at trial is not necessary, nor need motion materials be prepared.

2.7.d Improper jurisdiction

See section 2.3. You should bring a motion related to improper jurisdiction at the outset of the trial before evidence is heard and on notice to the parties.

2.7.e Limitation period expired

A motion related to an expired limitation period is discussed in section 2.1.c. This motion may be argued at trial but, again, it is best done on notice to the parties. For greater likelihood of success, you should have pleaded in your defence that the action is statute-barred (no longer legally enforceable).

2.7.f New trial or judgment

A new trial may be requested on motion on the grounds that the rules provide. Typically, however, new trials are seldom granted and arise mainly out of appeals. Your affidavit should set out the facts that support both arguments: an order for a new trial or an order for a new judgment.

2.7.g Production of evidence

If a party has failed to produce documents to be introduced at trial, you may bring a motion for an order compelling that party to produce those documents. In some cases, if the party has made an earnest attempt at obtaining the evidence but a person who is not a party is not releasing those documents, try to obtain an order compelling that nonparty to produce documents. You will need to show that the documents are relevant to the pleadings. It is helpful to argue that continuing without such productions would not allow you to properly prove your case or provide a full and fair defence.

❖ Example

Mort was injured in a snowmobile accident. He sued the driver, Bart, for damages caused to his right leg. Mort's medical records are a relevant piece of evidence for damages. Bart contacted Mort to ask for the records since the trial was coming up in the next few weeks. Mort told Bart that he had made earnest attempts to contact his family doctor, once by a letter that was accompanied by an authorization for the release of those records, and once by telephone. Mort was unsuccessful in requesting that the doctor send him a copy of his medical file. Bart decides to serve notice of motion on both the doctor and Mort. Bart is seeking an order compelling the doctor to produce the requested records. Bart includes a copy of the letter and authorization form that Mort kindly sent him. Mort advised Bart that he would not oppose the motion since it was in his best interests to introduce the records at trial.

2.8 Motions relating to enforcement

You may bring a number of motions related to enforcement proceedings. Since enforcement varies vastly across the country, discussion of these motions is beyond the scope of this book. We suggest that you review the legislation on debt collection and enforcement of judgments and review the court rules. If you are still unsure about whether you can bring a motion, ask the court office staff if a motion can assist you with your particular enforcement issue, or get legal advice. Some general ideas for motions follow.

2.8.a Consolidation of judgment debts

When more than one outstanding small claims court judgment is held against the debtor, he or she may make a motion for a consolidation order that will combine the debts and set out a schedule of payments to be distributed equally among creditors.

The debtor's affidavit must set out the following facts:

(a) The names and addresses of the creditors who have obtained an order for the payment of money against the debtor

(b) The amount owed to each creditor

(c) The amount of the debtor's income from all sources, identifying them

(d)   The debtor's current financial obligations and any other relevant facts

2.8.b Extension of time to renew writ

An order for the extension of a writ of seizure and sale of personal property or of lands is rarely granted. However, there may be a compelling reason why the writ could not be renewed before it expired; or perhaps it was not renewed due to sheer inadvertence. If you do not mind risking the cost of the motion, you may try bringing this motion.

2.8.c Interim recovery of personal property

If you would urgently like to recover personal property, bring an ex parte motion for the interim recovery of personal property. Such an order would require a detailed list of belongings that you claim are yours and ought to be recovered from another party. This motion is typically brought by evicted or locked-out tenants whose personal belongings may be on the landlord's premises. Prepare your motion materials, take them to the court office, and tell the staff that it is an urgent matter. A judge may be able to make the order within a short time.

2.8.d Renewal of warrant of committal

If an arrest warrant or warrant of committal was issued and the debtor has not been taken into custody during the year while the warrant is valid, the creditor may bring a motion ordering that the warrant be renewed for another year. The motion must be brought before the warrant expires.

2.8.e Seizure of other goods — Writ of delivery

If an enforcement officer advises that he or she is unable to enforce a writ for seizure and sale of personal property, the creditor may be able to bring a motion authorizing the enforcement officer to seize personal goods other than those specified in the writ.

2.8.f Setting aside enforcement proceedings and orders

You could request that an enforcement proceeding be set aside on a number of grounds. Read chapter 10 for some hints. The motion is typically brought by a party who is entitled to notice of a proceeding but has not been served with such notice. The party may then seek to set aside enforcement proceedings such as writs, garnishments, or orders for payment.

An *ex parte* proceeding is brought and conducted without notice to the other party who, therefore, does not attend the proceeding.

2.8.g Use of force — Writ of seizure and sale

If an enforcement officer notifies you that he or she was unable to seize goods following a writ because he or she could not gain entry into the premises, bring a motion for an order authorizing the enforcement officer to use force to enter the debtor's premises. You should show in the affidavit the letter from the enforcement officer indicating the problem of entry and that the order ought to allow a locksmith to handle the matter. The key to bringing this motion is bringing it quickly, before the debtor absconds with any personal property. You may try bringing an ex parte motion on an urgent basis.

2.8.h Terms of payment

If the presiding official refuses to make an order for terms of payment at the end of a judgment debtor examination, the debtor or creditor may bring a motion asking the court to make such an order. While the court will seldom overrule the decision of one of its officials, it may do so if new information has come to light since the examination. Of course, the court will not have had the benefit of participating in the judgment debtor examination and may order a terms of payment hearing instead. The advantage of bringing the motion, at least in some jurisdictions, is that your motion will likely be heard well before a payment hearing can be scheduled.

2.8.i Satisfaction of undertakings

During the course of a judgment debtor examination, a debtor may have undertaken to produce certain documentation as proof of assets and liabilities. If the debtor fails to do this, the creditor may bring a motion asking for an order compelling the debtor to satisfy those undertakings within a certain number of days or be compelled to re-attend at a judgment debtor examination.

3. Damages Assessment Hearing or Adjudication Hearing

A damages assessment hearing (or adjudication hearing) is a trial in which the plaintiff must prove damages alleged in the claim. Liability need not be proven, just the amount of the claim. If the defendant failed to file a defence within the time permitted and the court noted the defendant in default at the request of the plaintiff, then the plaintiff may be required to prove damages before a judge. This would occur during a damages assessment hearing.

Whether or not an assessment hearing is required depends on whether the action involves liquidated or unliquidated damages. Table 16 explains the difference.

❦ Example

If the plaintiff claimed that his ankle was injured in an assault, the plaintiff would have to prove the ankle injury since an amount cannot be determined by examining the claim itself.

❦ Example

If the plaintiff claimed that she lost money as a result of a breach of contract, the plaintiff would have to prove the loss if the amount cannot be determined by examining the claim itself.

❦ Example

If the plaintiff claimed that property was damaged, the plaintiff would have to prove the monetary value of the damages since this amount cannot be determined by examining the claim itself.

You may have to request a hearing by paying a court fee and advising the court in writing that you wish to have the matter set down for an assessment hearing or adjudication. A sample of such a letter appears in chapter 12. Some jurisdictions require that a court form be used for that request.

The clerk does not notify the defendant of this hearing. Defendants do not participate in these hearings because, by failing to file a defence, they have lost their rights to dispute any part of the claim.

3.1 Preparing for an assessment hearing

To prepare for an assessment hearing, prepare an affidavit setting out the details of your damages. Attach as exhibits all receipts, estimates, and other information relevant to the issue of damages. Be sure to mention in

TABLE 16
LIQUIDATED VERSUS UNLIQUIDATED DAMAGES

Liquidated Damages	Unliquidated Damages
Liquidated damages refer to damages for amounts that are easily determined by the court, thereby allowing the court to grant damages without further proof.	*Unliquidated damages* refer to damages for amounts that are not easily determined by the court, thereby requiring that evidence as to damages be presented to the court before damages can be granted.
Examples include:	Examples include:
▶ damage resulting from a breach of contract when the contract specifies what happens in the event of a breach (e.g., how much money will have to be paid in the event of a breach)	▶ damage resulting from a breach of contract when the contract does not specify what happens in the event of a breach
▶ damages in the form of failing to pay an invoice, if that invoice makes it clear that the person invoiced is responsible for paying the amount requested	▶ damage done by a service person (e.g., back hoe driver, dry cleaner, hairdresser, tradesperson, etc.) — court must be convinced that repairs were reasonable, that repair costs were applied only to remedy the damage done and not to add to the value of the object or property repaired (that repairs were not done to gain economic advantage)
▶ damages in the form of a debt when the debt could be a loan or a credit card balance and when the terms of the agreement are certain	▶ damages for an injury, in a case in which medical proof and proof of medical expenses and loss of income are required
Liquidated Damages ⇨ Default Judgment (Quick Judgment)	Unliquidated Damages ⇨ Damages Assessment ⇨ Judgment

your affidavit that any repairs made did not serve to better what was there before, but simply to restore it to pre-incident condition (if that is true). You should also state that no element of profit motivates your claim for damages (if that is true). Damages will not be awarded if the repair led to betterment (property improvement) or profit.

Your affidavit should also provide proof of loss of income or loss of profit, proof of injury, proof of loss of enjoyment of life, or loss of livelihood (if any of these are part of your claim). In other words, be prepared to support your claim with concrete evidence. Accident reports and photographs of injuries or damaged property are also extremely useful toward proving your case for damages.

Note: The law does not permit you to argue your own affidavit. Therefore, if a party is knowledgeable about the damages and costs, perhaps that person could swear the affidavit so that you could present it to the court as evidence. Alternatively, if you are the only person with knowledge of the damages and costs, you will have to ask a friend, agent, law student, or lawyer to appear at the assessment hearing or, if your jurisdiction permits it, you may be able to give testimony under oath and argue your motion at the same hearing.

3.2 Appearing at an assessment hearing

At the assessment hearing, you will introduce yourself and then pass your affidavit to the judge. The judge will take time to read it. In some courts, you may give the affidavit to the clerk of the court before the court is in session so that the judge will read the affidavit before your appearance. Familiarize yourself with the advocacy techniques described in chapter 9. You will not need to know how to examine witnesses, but the other advocacy techniques will enhance your presentation during the hearing.

4. Judgment Debtor Examination

The judgment debtor examination is discussed fully in chapter 10.

5. Terms of Payment Hearing

The debtor or creditor may request a payment hearing after a defence has been filed with the court. To request a terms of payment hearing, take the following steps:

(a) Obtain from the court office a form, if required.

(b) Prepare the form and provide the reason for requesting certain terms of payment or disputing terms of payment sought by the defendant (e.g., defendant is capable of paying more than proposed in the terms of payment). Photocopy the completed form for your records.

(c)   File the form with the court office.

The court will schedule a hearing and send the parties a notice of the hearing. In some jurisdictions this process may take a few months.

The hearing will proceed similar to a judgment debtor examination except that the presiding official will be in control. The official will try to ascertain how much of the debt the debtor is capable of paying and what payments would be possible for the debtor to make. The creditor and debtor may both make submissions about what would constitute a fair payment schedule. The official will then make an order relating to terms of payment.

The creditor should keep track of amounts of payments received and the dates on which they were received. The debtor must make payments according to the order. If, while the payment schedule is in effect, either party wishes to vary the terms of the order, the party may bring a motion to the court. This would happen if the debtor becomes capable of paying either more or less than that ordered due to a change in the debtor's financial circumstances.

To ensure you are prepared, use Checklist 7.

CHECKLIST 7
CHECKLIST FOR OTHER APPEARANCES

BRINGING A MOTION

❑ Did you read the appropriate sections of chapter 11 to prepare to bring the motion?

❑ Did you check with your local court office about the exact procedure for bringing a motion?

❑ Did you prepare a notice of motion, on a pre-printed form if required?

❑ Did you prepare and swear an affidavit or arrange for oral testimony, where permitted?

❑ Did you serve the notice of motion and affidavit on all parties within the time provided by the rules?

❑ Did you prepare and swear an affidavit of service for each party you served?

❑ Did you file the affidavit of service with the court within the time provided by the rules?

❑ Did you pay the court fee, if required?

RESPONDING TO A MOTION

❑ Did you prepare an affidavit setting out your version of the facts?

❑ Did you swear the affidavit before a commissioner of oaths?

❑ Did you serve your affidavit on all parties served with the notice of motion?

❑ Did you prepare an affidavit of service for each party served with your affidavit?

❑ Did you prepare your arguments?

DAMAGES ASSESSMENT HEARING

❑ Did you set the matter down for trial on the damages (damages assessment hearing) by sending a written request to the court, on a pre-printed form if required?

❑ Did you pay the court fee?

❑ Did you prepare an affidavit setting out the particulars of your damages?

❑ Did you swear the affidavit before a commissioner of oaths?

❑ Did you make a photocopy for your records?

❑ Did you prepare for the damages assessment hearing by reading the appropriate section in chapter 11?

❑ Did you prepare for the damages assessment hearing by reading the advocacy section in chapter 9?

TERMS OF PAYMENT HEARING

❑ Did you request the payment hearing by sending a written request to the court?

❑ Did you prepare for the payment hearing by reading the appropriate section in chapter 11?

12
Preparing Documents

1. Writing Demand Letters

No rule or statute in any of the small claims court rules requires a plaintiff to send a demand letter before commencing a lawsuit. Sometimes, however, a demand letter can be an effective way of resolving the dispute without resorting to legal action.

In the demand letter, the writer demands that payment be made, that personal or business property be returned, or that the recipient do something or stop doing something that forms the basis of a lawsuit.

A demand letter primarily serves to —

‣ bring the demand to the attention of the person who is allegedly doing something the writer does not appreciate;

‣ put the wrongdoer on notice that, if the demand is not met, consequences such as a lawsuit or a penalty of some kind will result; and

‣ allow the wrongdoer to take corrective steps so that court action does not become necessary.

The demand letter should contain the following general elements:

‣ The writer's name, address, telephone number, and fax number, if available, all clearly printed or typed

‣ The recipient's name, address, telephone number, and fax number, if available, all clearly printed or typed

- The date that you sent the letter
- The manner in which the letter will be sent (by regular mail, by fax, by registered mail, by courier, by hand)
- A paragraph that identifies the writer and the recipient
- A paragraph that outlines the problem and includes an invoice number, cheque number, contract number, or identifier for any other document that is at the core of the alleged wrongdoing
- A paragraph that makes the demand
- A paragraph that states the consequences for failing to respond to the demand
- A paragraph that ends the letter in a tone that will encourage the recipient to meet the demand
- A signature

Writing a good demand letter takes practice. If a demand letter comes on too strong, it may discourage the recipient from co-operating and may, indeed, make legal action necessary. You should attempt to achieve a balance between being firm and being reasonable. Have no reservation about asking that your rights be upheld, money paid, or personal property returned, but give the debtor a reasonable time within which to respond to your demand. You should consider all the facts about your situation and those of the debtor in order to determine what is reasonable.

Since a demand letter is not required in the first instance, the number of demand letters you send is also a personal choice. If you think that the first demand letter has not come to the attention of the recipient, you may wish to follow it up with one or more subsequent letters. Although in practice it is rare to send more than one demand letter, it is worthwhile to consider sending at least one.

Review a demand letter before finalizing it. While reviewing it, do the following:

- Check to see if the recipient will understand the circumstances described in the letter.
- If you are writing a demand letter to a particular individual for the first time, try to end on a positive note, if possible. This will encourage a response to or settlement of the matter.
- If you are writing a second or third demand letter, your tone should become more stern each time. If you are writing a final

demand letter, make that clear to the recipient and state a deadline by which you expect a reply before proceeding with a lawsuit.

> If you are writing a second or third demand letter, state in those letters that you have not received a response to your previous letter and indicate the date of that letter.

Sample 14 shows three demand letters written to the same debtor. Although you may only write one demand letter, read through these samples to get an idea about the tones and styles in which demand letters can be written.

2. Writing Complaint Letters

In some situations a complainant wishes to bring a complaint to someone's attention without threatening legal action or even considering it. Legal action may not be possible or desirable in some cases. When relationships should be preserved, when no cause of action exists, or when suing is undesirable, it is best to try to resolve a dispute in an alternative way before resorting to legal action.

The letter of complaint is used to encourage dialogue between the parties and should be worded diplomatically. The letter of complaint is also useful in preserving relationships between family members, friends, business associates, or acquaintances in small towns.

The complaint letter should contain the following general elements:

> The writer's name, address, telephone number, and fax number, if available, all clearly printed or typed

> The recipient's name, address, telephone number, and fax number, if available, all clearly printed or typed

> The date that you sent the letter

> The manner in which the letter will be sent (by regular mail, by fax, by registered mail, by courier, by hand)

> A paragraph that identifies the writer and the recipient

> A paragraph that specifies the complaint

> A paragraph that offers a solution for the recipient's consideration

> A paragraph that ends the letter in a tone that will encourage the recipient to respond favourably or make their own suggestions

> A signature

SAMPLE 14
DEMAND LETTERS

A   Filomena is a hair stylist who worked on a customer's beehive hairdo more than three months ago. Although her customer, Beatress Bliss, produced a cheque that same day, Filomena's bank notified her that the chequing account did not contain sufficient funds to honour the cheque. Not willing to lose a customer, Filomena thought carefully about how to make a demand for payment.

This is Filomena's first demand letter.

Filomena's Fancy Frizzes
Filomena Falimena, Owner/Stylist
200 Solution Street
Regina, SA S4N 2K2
(306) 555-9999

Beatress Bliss
99 Tin Haven
Regina, SA S4P 1V1

June 28, 200–

Re: Cheque No. 13 in the amount of $90, dated June 12, 200–

Dear Ms. Bliss:

When you were in my shop a couple of weeks ago for your usual monthly appointment, you provided a cheque for $90 as payment for your hairdo.

Unfortunately, your bank has returned the cheque saying there are insufficient funds in your chequing account. Perhaps you could contact your bank to straighten out the confusion.

In the meantime, my accountant has requested that you replace the cheque with a money draft within the next 10 days. I am sending a self-addressed, stamped envelope to save you time. If you prefer, you may replace the cheque with cash by bringing it to your next appointment on July 12, 200–.

I look forward to hearing from you and working on your hair next month. Thank you.

Sincerely yours,

Filomena Falimena

Filomena Falimena
Owner/Stylist

SAMPLE 14 — Continued

B   It is July 14, 200–, and Filomena has not seen or heard from Beatress. She requires payment and has carefully drafted a reminder letter so as not to lose Beatress as a customer. The body of her reminder letter reads:

When you were in my shop a couple of weeks ago for your usual monthly appointment, you provided a cheque for $90 as payment for your hairdo. I also sent you a letter informing you that the cheque could not clear your account due to insufficient funds or confusion with your banking arrangements.

In my letter dated June 28, 200–, I asked you to replace the cheque in time for your appointment scheduled for July 12, 200–. I was looking forward to doing your hair on that date but I haven't seen you. I hope you haven't encountered further problems.

If you have accidentally overlooked my request, please forward your payment in the above amount. So as not to complicate my accounting, may I please receive your payment by July 31, 200–.

Thank you.

C   It is August 1, 200-, and Filomena has not seen or heard from Beatress. Her letters have not been returned, so she assumes Beatress has been receiving them. She is not keen on going to court for a $90 debt, so she decides to make another attempt at collecting the money. She must be more stern since two previous letters have not produced the payment.

The body of Filomena's third and final demand letter reads:

This is my third and final request for payment in lieu of the NSF cheque that you provided me with on July 12, 200–. I have waited patiently, but business does not run on patience alone; it requires income.

My letters of June 28, 200–, and July 14, 200–, have not been returned to me, so I assume you have received them. In the event that you have not received them, please consider this your final notice that a payment of $90 in the form of a bank draft, certified cheque, money order, or cash is due by August 15, 200–. If you prefer to pay by cash, please bring it in; do not mail it.

If I do not receive your payment by August 15, 200–, I will have no choice but to start a lawsuit in small claims court. Should this unfortunate step be necessary, I will also be asking the court to compensate me for service fees and administrative expenses incurred in attempting to receive your payment, interest as of July 12, 200–, and any loss of income as a result of my absence from the business on the day of trial. I will also be bringing my assistant, Mina, as a witness and will be demanding reimbursement for my witness fees.

May I please hear from you by August 15, 200–?

Sample 15 shows a sample complaint letter.

3. Writing Letters to the Court

On several occasions you may have to correspond with the court, depending on the length and complexity of your lawsuit. You may write to the court to do any of the following:

- ❯ Request an adjournment
- ❯ Request that a matter be set down for trial
- ❯ Request a pre-trial or settlement conference
- ❯ Request a damages assessment hearing
- ❯ Request a terms of payment hearing
- ❯ Request that the matter be withdrawn
- ❯ Request that the defendant be noted in default
- ❯ Confirm the date of a proceeding
- ❯ Inform the court office or confirm any number of items related to the proceedings

Style of cause

The *style of cause* refers to the title of proceedings or the title of the lawsuit. For example, if the plaintiff's surname is Bozo and the defendant's surname is Soho, then the style of cause is *Bozo v. Soho*. Or, for another example, if multiple plaintiffs or defendants are involved and the plaintiffs' surnames are Charise, Morisse, and Clarise and the defendants' names are Kiehl and Peil, the style of cause is *Charise et al. v. Kiel et al. Et al.* is a short form of the Latin phrase *et alia* which means *and others*. The style of cause is a convenient way of referring to a particular lawsuit without listing all the names of all the parties.

Since small claims actions usually involve one plaintiff and one defendant, the first names may also be used in the style of cause. For example, it would not be unusual to refer to a simple lawsuit as *Pocohontis v. John Smith*.

SAMPLE 15
COMPLAINT LETTER

Lomer is a fruit farmer who lives on a small farm next door to Martha and Peter Moody, a couple with three energetic children. For the past two years, the children have played outside in their backyard. Lomer enjoys their shrills and shrieks. However, almost every weekend in the summer, Lomer finds their kites stuck in his apricot trees, damaging the sensitive fruit. He also finds sticks and stones beneath the trees. Lomer relies on his small orchard to supplement a meager pension income and is no longer able to tolerate this behaviour. Yet he is sensitive to the importance of maintaining good neighbourhood relations.

Here is Lomer's carefully worded complaint letter:

Lomer Homer
Lot 5, Concession 10
Apricotville, NS B4C 0V0
(808) 888-9999

Martha and Peter Moody
Lot 7, Concession 10
Apricotville, NS B4C 0V0

May 10, 200–

Re: My Orchard

Dear Mr. and Mrs. Moody:

Since you have moved next door, your children have brought a refreshing liveliness to the neighbourhood. I enjoy watching them play and am careful not to discourage them.

However, as you know, many kites have been stuck in my apricot trees. I have discarded many bushels of apricots over the years because they have been damaged when the kites are removed or when the children throw sticks and stones to try to dislodge their kites. Since I rely on my orchard for much-needed income, I would appreciate having healthy, salesworthy fruit.

Although the children mean well, they may not understand how sensitive apricots are. Would you explain to the children the difficulties of growing apricots and the hazards that result from their kites, sticks, and stones? Perhaps a solution is to ask the children to play a little farther from the orchard.

Unfortunately, I do not know your telephone number. However, I would be pleased to discuss this some more. Please feel free to call me anytime at 888-9999.

Yours truly,

Lomer Homer
Lomer Homer

Whenever you are writing to the court, you should include the following elements:

- ▶ The writer's name, address, telephone number, and fax number, if available, all clearly printed or typed
- ▶ The court file number
- ▶ The names of the parties, or style of cause (e.g., *Bif v. Mif Enterprises*)
- ▶ The court's address clearly printed or typed
- ▶ The date of writing or typing
- ▶ The manner in which the letter will be sent (by regular mail, by fax, by registered mail, by courier, by hand)
- ▶ A paragraph that identifies the writer as a plaintiff or as a defendant
- ▶ A paragraph that outlines the problem or request
- ▶ A signature

Samples 16 to 22 show examples of various letters to the court.

4. Drafting Authorizations

A signed (or executed) authorization is permission to release confidential information to yourself, the court, or another party in the lawsuit. Authorizations are often necessary to obtain reports, records, or other information from your file. You will most often make this kind of request from institutions such as a corporate employer, government office, financial institution, hospital, medical office, utility office, or social organization. Authorizations are also necessary to respond to a court order to produce certain records, file them with the court, and serve them to other parties.

Before sending an authorization, call the institution to find out if they charge a fee for this service. Often, you will need to provide the fee at the same time as the authorization. Ask the institution what information you should provide in your authorization. Think carefully before providing your social insurance number and other personal information to institutions other than the government. It is not recommended. If nongovernment institutions or organizations ask for your social insurance number, state that you are reluctant to divulge that information and ask if another piece of information would facilitate the institution's search for your file.

Verify with the institution the address and department to which the authorization should be sent. Ask the institution for an estimate about when you might expect to receive the requested disclosure.

SAMPLE 16
LETTER REQUESTING THAT COURT NOTE THE DEFENDANT IN DEFAULT

The plaintiff has called the court office, whose staff advised him that the defendant has failed to file a defence within the allotted time. The plaintiff is now writing to the court to request that the clerk note the defendant in default and sign default judgement.

Ursula Pont
67 Tribl Avenue
Mississauga, ON M7M 3K3
(905) 111-1111

Clerk of the Court
Mississauga Small Claims Court
2301 Haines Road
Mississauga, ON L4Y 1Y5

HAND DELIVERED

February 8, 200–

Re: Pont v. Hunn, Court File No. M555/99

Dear Madam/Sir:

Today I was advised by court office staff that the defendant, A. Hunn, has not filed a defence within the period allowed by the small claims court rules. Kindly note the defendant in default.

This case deals with an NSF cheque. It should not be necessary to proceed to a damages assessment hearing in this case. Would you kindly sign default judgment?

Thank you.

Ursula Pont
Ursula Pont
Plaintiff

SAMPLE 17
LETTER REQUESTING DAMAGES ASSESSMENT HEARING

The court has advised Yuri that the defendant in his case was noted in default as requested, but that default judgment cannot be obtained without a damages assessment. He replies:

Yuri Makinin
203 Pantry Lane
St. Catharines, ON J8J 7H7
(905) 222-2222

Clerk of the Court
St. Catharines Small Claims Court
59 Church, 1st Floor
St. Catharines, ON L2R 7N8

SENT BY REGULAR MAIL

December 20, 200–

Re: Makinin v. Smilee, Court File No. 674/00

Dear Madam/Sir:

Thank you for your letter dated November 30, 200– in which you advised me that the defendant in the above action has been noted in default.

Kindly arrange a damages assessment hearing for March or April 200–. For this I enclose a cheque for $100 in accordance with the small claims court fee schedule.

Thank you.

Yuri Makinin
Yuri Makinin
Plaintiff

SAMPLE 18
LETTER REQUESTING AN ADJOURNMENT

Alexis is the plaintiff in a small claims court action. She has a scheduling conflict and, after consulting with the defendant's agent, Quint, writes to the court to request an adjournment of the pre-trial in the matter since the defendant has given his consent. This example can be applied to adjourn a trial as well, provided the adjournment is on consent. However, note that you should call the court office before arranging mutually convenient dates since the court office may be booking months ahead, depending on the jurisdiction.

Alexis Pleat
202 Court Blvd., Suite 202
Edmonton, AB T4N 1C3
(403) 444-4444

Trial Scheduling Coordinator
Provincial Court of Alberta, Civil Division
Main Floor, Law Courts
1A Sir Winston Churchill Square
97th Street & 102A Avenue
Edmonton, AB T5J 0K2

SENT BY REGULAR MAIL and
BY FAX TO (403) 999-9999

April 10, 200–

Re: Broom v. Boor, Court File No. 777/00

Dear Sir or Madam:

Please be advised that the parties in the above action have consented to adjourn the pre-trial conference scheduled for May 10, 200–. Please adjourn the pre-trial conference to any of the following dates agreed upon by the parties:

July 5, July 12, July 14, July 20, July 25, 200–.

Thank you.

Alexis Pleat

Alexis Pleat

Copy to: Mr. Blair Quint
            Paisley Court Agents

SAMPLE 19
LETTER REQUESTING SCHEDULING OF PRE-TRIAL CONFERENCE

Vincent is the plaintiff in a small claims court action. At a settlement (pre-trial) conference, he was ordered to produce a medical report about his alleged injuries. Vincent is now advising the court that the medical report has been served on all parties and that they are ready to resume that portion of the pre-trial conference that was adjourned to await this report.

Vincent New
202 Podium Place, Suite 4000
Toronto, ON M7M 8M8
(416) 333-3333

Trial Scheduling Coordinator
Whitby Small Claims Court
605 Rossland Street East
Whitby, ON L1N 9G7

SENT BY REGULAR MAIL and
BY FACSIMILE TO (416) 999-9999

August 21, 200–

Re: Wolfe v. Chairs 'n' Tables Inc., Court File No. W111/00

Dear Sir or Madam:

On February 10, 200–, the parties attended a pre-trial conference with Deputy Judge Broist presiding. Deputy Judge Broist ordered that the plaintiff in the above action produce a medical report detailing his injuries.

Please find enclosed a copy of that report, written by Dr. Ankle, for the court file. We have served this report on the defendant pursuant to s.3.5 of the Ontario Evidence Act.

Since we have complied with Deputy Judge Broist's order, kindly schedule the pre-trial conference for any Monday in the months of September, October, or November, as agreed to by the parties.

Thank you.

Vincent New
Vincent New

SAMPLE 20
LETTER REQUESTING AN ACTION BE SET DOWN FOR TRIAL

Anthony is a self-represented plaintiff. He was unable to settle the action at the settlement conference. He writes a letter to the court requesting that the matter be set down for trial.

Anthony Smart
900 Cerebellum Street
Nanaimo, BC   V2M 3X5
(204) 111-1111

Trial Scheduling Coordinator
Provincial Court of British Columbia
Fifth floor, 408 York Avenue
Nanaimo, BC V3C 0P9
(204) 945-3461

SENT BY REGULAR MAIL

July 10, 200—

Re: Smart v. Part, Court File No. H999/00

Dear Sir or Madam:

Please set the above matter down for trial. I enclose a money order as the fee for this service.

Thank you.

Anthony Smart
Anthony Smart
Plaintiff

SAMPLE 21
LETTER WITHDRAWING A CLAIM (Provincial Court)

Ursula Pont
67 Trible Avenue
Bathurst, NB E2A 4W8
(506) 111-1111

BY REGULAR MAIL

Clerk of the Provincial Court
P.O. Box 5001
Bathurst, NB E2A 3Z9
(506) 547-2580

February 8, 200–

Re: *Pont v. Hunn*, Court File No. M555/99

Dear Madam/Sir:

Please be advised that the above matter has settled and the claim is being withdrawn.

Thank you.

Ursula Pont
Ursula Pont
Plaintiff

SAMPLE 22
LETTER WITHDRAWING A CLAIM

Ursula Pont
67 Trible Avenue
Bathurst, NB E2A 4W8
(506) 111-1111

Clerk of the Court
P.O. Box 5001
Bathurst, NB E2A 3Z9
(506) 547-2580

February 8, 200–

Re: Pont v. Hunn, Court File No. M555/99

Dear Madam/Sir:

Please be advised that I have decided to withdraw the above claim. Accordingly, the settlement conference scheduled for April 10, 200- is no longer required.

Thank you.

Ursula Pont
Ursula Pont
Plaintiff

The properly drafted authorization should include the following information:

- ▶ The institution's name and address, all clearly printed or typed
- ▶ Your name
- ▶ Information necessary for the institution to locate your file and understand your request, for example:
  - ▶ A doctor's office will most likely require your date of birth.
  - ▶ A hospital will most likely require your social insurance number.
  - ▶ Canada Customs and Revenue Agency and Human Resources and Development Canada will most likely require your social insurance number.
  - ▶ A bank will most likely require your account number and transit number.
  - ▶ The police will most likely require your date of birth and an accident or occurrence date.
  - ▶ An insurance company will most likely require an accident date or occurrence date and, perhaps, your file number. If you know the adjuster's name, that would be helpful as well.
  - ▶ An employer will most likely require your employee number or date of birth. Other useful information is the period of employment.
- ▶ A paragraph that makes the request for reports, records, or other information in your file, specifying the time period for which you wish to have information
- ▶ The date that the authorization was signed in front of a witness
- ▶ Your signature (this makes it an executed authorization)
- ▶ The signature of a person who witnessed your signature being made

Finally, you should send a cover letter along with the authorization. The cover letter is important as it may become necessary to prove to the court that you have requested records in an attempt to move the lawsuit along, the date you made the request, and to whom the request was made.

A properly drafted cover letter should include the following information:

- ▶ The writer's name, address, telephone number, and fax number, if available, all clearly printed or typed

> The institution's name, address, telephone number, and fax number, if available, all clearly printed or typed

> The date that you sent the letter

> The manner in which the letter will be sent (by regular mail, by fax, by registered mail, by courier, by hand)

> A paragraph that identifies the writer as a party in a lawsuit

> The nature of the lawsuit (personal injury, breach of contract, etc.)

> The date of the cause of action (event out of which the lawsuit arose)

> A paragraph that makes the request for reports, records, or other information in your file, specifying the time period for which you wish to have information

> A paragraph that states that the appropriate fee for this service is enclosed, if a fee is necessary, or a description of some other payment arrangement

> Your signature

Samples 23 to 26 show examples of suitable cover letters and authorizations.

If you have not received information that you requested within four to six weeks, follow up with another letter and a copy of the first letter and authorization. Stress in your follow-up letter that you are involved in litigation and would like a prompt reply. A follow-up telephone call tends to be less effective unless you are contacting someone with whom you are already acquainted.

5. Preparing the Plaintiff's Claim

Many provinces and territories have pre-printed claim forms that you must complete. Ask at your local court office if such a form is necessary and, if so, acquire a copy. In addition to preparing a claim form, you should prepare a "Schedule 'A'" on a separate sheet that you should attach to the form. Include the following information in Schedule 'A':

(a) State the remedy being sought — general, special, punitive damages, prejudgment interest.

(b) Identify the parties.

(c) State the facts in chronological order.

SAMPLE 23
AUTHORIZATION FOR THE RELEASE OF MEDICAL RECORDS FROM A PHYSICIAN

Anthony Smart
900 Cerebellum Street
Winnipeg, MB R2M 3X5
(204) 111-1111

Dr. Quiezze
Winnipeg Heart Clinic
1111 Artery Avenue
Winnipeg, MB R2R 1V3

SENT BY REGULAR MAIL

July 10, 200–

Re: Smart v. Part, Court File No. H999/00

Dear Dr. Quiezze:

I am the plaintiff in a personal injury court action arising out of a slip and fall accident outside the premises of Oliver's Oil Ltd. In order to move this action along, I require copies of parts of my medical file. Accordingly, please find enclosed an authorization for the release of my complete clinical notes and records dated June 1, 200–, to the present.

I enclose a cheque for $25 for photocopying as requested by Ms. Rice of your office.

Thank you.

Anthony Smart
Anthony Smart
Plaintiff

Enclosure

Authorization

TO: Dr. Quiezze
        Winnipeg Heart Clinic
        1111 Artery Avenue
        Winnipeg, MB R2R 1V3

RE: Anthony Smart
        Date of Birth, July 22, 1975

You are hereby directed and authorized to release to me, Anthony Smart, 900 Cerebellum Street, Winnipeg, Manitoba, R2M 3X5, copies of my complete clinical notes and records from June 1, 1993, to the present, and this shall be your good and sufficient authority.

Dated at Winnipeg, this 10th day of July 200–.

I.M. Witness
_____
Witness

Anthony Smart
_____
Anthony Smart

AUTHORIZATION FOR THE RELEASE OF MEDICAL RECORDS FROM A HOSPITAL

Anthony Smart
900 Cerebellum Street
Saskatoon, SK R2M 3X5
(204) 111-1111

Help'em Hospital
911 Ambulance Drive
Saskatoon, SK R1R 0V0

SENT BY REGULAR MAIL

July 10, 200–

Attention: Patient Records Department

Re: Smart v. Part, Court File No. H999/98

I am the plaintiff in a personal injury court action arising out of a slip and fall accident outside the premises of Oliver's Oil Ltd. I attended the emergency ward at your hospital on October 12, 200–. I believe that Dr. Woerble treated me.

I require copies of my complete hospital file. Please find enclosed an authorization for the release of those records.

I enclose a cheque for $15 as the photocopying fee for this service.

Thank you.

Anthony Smart
Anthony Smart
Plaintiff

Enclosure

SAMPLE 24

Authorization

TO: Help'em Hospital
        911 Ambulance Drive
        Saskatoon, SK R1R 0V0

RE: Anthony Smart
        Date of Birth, July 22, 1975
        Health Card No. 38492839482983

You are hereby directed and authorized to release to me, Anthony Smart, 900 Cerebellum Street, Saskatoon, SK R2M 3X5, copies of my complete hospital file, and this shall be your good and sufficient authority.

Dated at Saskatoon, this 10th day of July, 200–.

I.M. Witness
_____
Witness

Anthony Smart
_____
Anthony Smart

SAMPLE 25

AUTHORIZATION FOR THE RELEASE OF RECORDS HELD BY AN INSURANCE COMPANY

Amanda Lamb
900 Fare Court
Brampton, ON M8L 8M8
(905) 450-4545

Street Harm Auto Insurance Company
200 Premium Crescent
Toronto, ON M09 9M9

SENT BY REGULAR MAIL

May 12, 200–

Re: Lamb v. Georgetown Bus Company, Court File No. B777/98

I am the plaintiff in a personal injury court action arising out of an automobile accident on March 21, 200–. I enclose an authorization for the disclosure of my file to the defendant, Georgetown Bus Company.

I require copies of my complete hospital file. Please find enclosed an authorization for the release of those records.

The defendant, Georgetown Bus Company, has agreed to pay fee for this service. Please send your invoice to its attention at:

Georgetown Transportation Company
900 Manifold Boulevard
Brampton, ON M8M 7M7

Thank you.

Amanda Lamb
Amanda Lamb
Plaintiff

Authorization

TO: Street Harm Auto Insurance Company
200 Premium Crescent
Toronto, ON M09 9M9

RE: Amanda Lamb
Motor Vehicle Accident: March 21, 200–
Adjuster: Bob Bobovich

You are hereby directed and authorized to release to the Georgetown Bus Company, 900 Manifold Boulevard, Brampton, Ontario, M8M 7M7, solicitors for the defendant in court action number B777/98, copies of all property damage documentation in your possession, including photographs taken of the vehicles involved in the above motor vehicle accident, and this shall be your good and sufficient authority.

Dated at Brampton, this 12th day of May, 200–.

I.M. Witness	_Amanda Lamb_
Witness	Amanda Lamb

SAMPLE 26
AUTHORIZATION FOR THE RELEASE OF RECORDS
FROM AN EMPLOYER

Amanda Lamb
900 Fare Court
Brampton, ON M8L 8M8
(905) 450-4545

Knitter's Knick-knack Limited
200 Wooly Lane
Aurora, ON M09 9M9

SENT BY REGULAR MAIL

May 12, 200–

Re: *Lamb v. Georgetown Bus Company*, Court File No. B777/98

I am the plaintiff in a personal injury court action arising out of an automobile accident on March 21, 200–. In accordance with a court order, I require proof of loss of income and require that portions of my file be produced for me.

Please find enclosed an authorization for the release of those records.

Thank you.

Amanda Lamb
Amanda Lamb
Plaintiff

Enclosure

Authorization

TO: Knitter's Knick-knack Limited
200 Wooly Lane
Aurora, ON M09 9M9

RE: Amanda Lamb
Date of Birth: November 3, 1975
Employed as of September 1, 200-

You are hereby directed and authorized to release to me copies of my employment file as related to income and benefits only, and this shall be your good and sufficient authority.

Dated at Brampton, this 12th day of May, 200-.

_____
I.M. Witness
Witness

_____
Amanda Lamb
Amanda Lamb

(d) State the allegation that a contract has been breached.

(e) State the allegation that damages result from the breach.

(f) List any legislation on which the plaintiff relies.

(g) Show that —

    (i) the contract was valid,

    (ii) the contract was breached,

    (iii) at least one demand was made to the defendant to honour the contract,

    (iv) damages resulted from the breach (specifically state the reasons punitive damages apply, if alleged), and

    (v) you attempted to mitigate damages (reduction of loss through plaintiff's actions), if you did.

(h) Include as attachments to the claim —

    (i) a photocopy of the contract,

    (ii) a photocopy of any demand letters that were sent, and

    (iii) a photocopy of the sections of legislation on which the plaintiff relies.

Sample 27 shows an example of a plaintiff's claim for breach of contract. You may wish to compare it with Sample 28, which shows a corresponding defence for breach of contract. **Note:** These samples use the Ontario forms. The forms for your province or territory may look slightly different. An additional sample claim is shown in the sample pleadings in Sample 35.

6. Preparing the Defence

Many provinces and territories have pre-printed defence forms that you must complete. Ask at your local court office if such a form is necessary and get a copy. In addition to preparing a defence form, you should prepare the following on a separate sheet and attach it to the form:

(a) Photocopy the plaintiff's claim and work from that copy, leaving the original intact.

(b) Place the letter *A* next to any statement that you wish to admit.

(c) Place the letter *D* next to any statement that you wish to deny.

(d) Place the letter *U* next to any statement about which you know nothing.

PLAINTIFF'S CLAIM FOR BREACH OF CONTRACT

Superior Court of Justice
Cour supérieure de justice

Plaintiff's Claim
Demande du demandeur
Form/*Formule* 7A Ont. Reg. No./*N° du règl. de l'Ont.* : 258/98

Claim no. / *N° de la demande*

Sealed/*Scellé*

Kaladar
Small Claims Court / *Cour des petites créances de*
Highway 7, P.O. Box 88
Address / *Adresse*
Kaladar, Ontario

K0H 1Z0

Plaintiff No. 1 / *Demandeur N° 1*

Full name / *Nom et prénoms*

SAFE-T-STORE INC.

Address for service (street & number, city, postal code)
Domicile élu (numéro et rue, ville, code postal)

19 Mill St.

Hamilton ON L8L 3Y3

Phone no. *Numéro de téléphone*	Fax no. (if any) *Numéro de télécopieur (le cas échéant)*
(905) 555-1212	(905) 545-2121

Plaintiff's Lawyer/Agent (Full name)
Avocat/mandataire du demandeur (nom et prénoms)

Harvey Law

Lawyer/Agent's address for service (street & number, city, postal code)
Domicile élu de l'avocat/du mandataire (numéro et rue, ville, code postal)

200 Main St. W., Suite 1

Hamilton ON L7L 2Z2

Lawyer/Agent's phone no. *Numéro de téléphone de l'avocat/du mandataire*	Lawyer/Agent's fax no. (if any) *Numéro de télécopieur (le cas échéant)*
(905) 444-1212	(905) 555-2121

Plaintiff No. 2 (if applicable) / *Demandeur N° 2 (le cas échéant)*

Full name / *Nom et prénoms*

Address for service (street & number, city, postal code)
Domicile élu (numéro et rue, ville, code postal)

Phone no. *Numéro de téléphone*	Fax no. (if any) *Numéro de télécopieur (le cas échéant)*

Plaintiff's Lawyer/Agent (Full name)
Avocat/mandataire du demandeur (nom et prénoms)

Lawyer/Agent's address for service (street & number, city, postal code)
Domicile élu de l'avocat/du mandataire (numéro et rue, ville, code postal)

Lawyer/Agent's phone no. *Numéro de téléphone de l'avocat/du mandataire*	Lawyer/Agent's fax no. (if any) *Numéro de télécopieur (le cas échéant)*

Defendant No. 1 / *Défendeur N° 1*

Full name / *Nom et prénoms*

Gregory Toke

Address for service (street & number, city, postal code)
Domicile élu (numéro et rue, ville, code postal)

1000 Mill Way

Mill Haven ON M3M 2L2

Phone no./ *Numéro de téléphone*	Fax no. (if any) *Numéro de télécopieur (le cas échéant)*
(905) 333-3333	

Defendant's Lawyer/Agent (Full name)
Avocat/mandataire du défendeur (nom et prénoms)

Lawyer/Agent's address for service (street & number, city, postal code)
Domicile élu de l'avocat/du mandataire (numéro et rue, ville, code postal)

Lawyer/Agent's phone no. *Numéro de téléphone de l'avocat/du mandataire*	Lawyer/Agent's fax no. (if any) *Numéro de télécopieur (le cas échéant)*

Defendant No. 2 (if applicable)/ *Défendeur N° 2 (le cas échéant)*

Full name / *Nom et prénoms*

Address for service (street & number, city, postal code)
Domicile élu (numéro et rue, ville, code postal)

Phone no./ *Numéro de téléphone*	Fax no. (if any) *Numéro de télécopieur (le cas échéant)*

Defendant's Lawyer/Agent (Full name)
Avocat/mandataire du défendeur (nom et prénoms)

Lawyer/Agent's address for service (street & number, city, postal code)
Domicile élu de l'avocat/du mandataire (numéro et rue, ville, code postal)

Lawyer/Agent's phone no. *Numéro de téléphone de l'avocat/du mandataire*	Lawyer/Agent's fax no. (if any) *Numéro de télécopieur (le cas échéant)*

Note: For additional defendants, please list on attached sheet with all the necessary information as requested above.
Rem. : *S'il y a d'autres défendeurs, veuillez indiquer leurs noms et tous les renseignements demandés ci-dessus sur une feuille séparée.*

SCR 7.01-7A (REV. 99/10) *(formerly/anciennement SCC 0061)*

SAMPLE 27 — Continued

TO THE DEFENDANT(S) / AU(X) DÉFENDEUR(S) :

The plaintiff claims from you $ __900.00__ plus $ _____
Le demandeur vous demande ___(amount of claim)___ $ plus ___(interest claimed to date (if any))___ $
___(montant de la demande)___ ___(intérêts réclamés à ce jour (le cas échéant))___

and costs for the reason(s) set out below.
ainsi que des dépens, pour le/les motif(s) énoncé(s) ci-dessous.

The plaintiff further claims from you pre-judgment interest and post-judgment interest in accordance with the *Courts of Justice Act*.
Le demandeur vous demande également des intérêts antérieurs et postérieurs au jugement conformément à la Loi sur les tribunaux judiciaires.

You may attend at the nearest Small Claims Court to obtain the "How to Make Small Claims Court Work for You" booklet as well as "Your Guide to Making a Defence."
Vous pouvez obtenir la brochure Comment profiter pleinement de la Cour des petites créances de même que le Guide sur la défense auprès de la Cour des petites créances la plus proche.

IF YOU DO NOT FILE A DEFENCE WITH THE COURT WITHIN TWENTY (20) CALENDAR DAYS AFTER YOU RECEIVED THIS CLAIM, JUDGMENT MAY BE ENTERED AGAINST YOU.
JUDGMENT MAY BE ENTERED WITHOUT FURTHER NOTICE TO YOU.
SI VOUS NE DÉPOSEZ PAS DE DÉFENSE AUPRÈS DU TRIBUNAL AU PLUS TARD VINGT (20) JOURS CIVILS APRÈS AVOIR REÇU LA PRÉSENTE DEMANDE, UN JUGEMENT PEUT ÊTRE INSCRIT CONTRE VOUS SANS AUTRE AVIS.

TYPE OF CLAIM / NATURE DE LA DEMANDE

☐ Unpaid Account / *Compte impayé*	☐ Promissory Note / *Billet*	☐ Damage to Property / *Dommages causés à des biens*
☒ Contract / *Contrat*	☐ Services Rendered / *Services rendus*	☐ Lease / *Contrat de location*
☐ Motor Vehicle Accident / *Accident de véhicule automobile*	☐ N.S.F. Cheque / *Chèque sans provision*	☐ Other _____ / *Autre*

REASONS FOR CLAIM AND DETAILS / MOTIFS DE LA DEMANDE ET PRÉCISIONS
Explain what happened, where and when **and** the amounts of money involved.
*Expliquer ce qui est arrivé, indiquer le lieu et le moment de l'incident **et** préciser les sommes d'argent en cause.*

SEE ATTACHED SCHEDULE 'A'

_____

If more space is required, attach separate sheet(s)./*Si vous avez besoin de plus d'espace, annexez une feuille supplémentaire.*

If the claim is based in whole or in part on a document(s), **you must attach** a copy of the document(s) to the claim, or if the document(s) is lost or unavailable, **you must explain** why it is not attached in the space provided below.
Si la demande est fondée en tout ou en partie sur un document, vous devez annexer une copie de celui-ci à la demande. Si le document est perdu ou n'est pas disponible, vous devez expliquer ci-dessous pourquoi il n'est pas annexé.

_____

_____   _____
(Date)   (Signature of clerk/*Signature du greffier*)

SCR 7.01-7A (REV. 99/10) *(formerly/anciennement SCC 0061)*

SAMPLE CLAIM	EXPLANATIONS

## Schedule 'A' 	
### Plaintiff's Claim 	
 	
1. The plaintiff claims:
  a) General damages in the amount of $200;
  b) Special damages in the amount of $200;
  c) Punitive damages in the amount of $500;
  d) Prejudgment interest at the rate of 24% in accordance with the agreement between the parties; and
  e) Postjudgment interest pursuant to the Courts of Justice Act.
 	
2. The plaintiff, Safe-T-Store, is a corporation incorporated under the Corporations Act of Ontario. At all material times, the plaintiff was operating a storage depot located at 19 Mill Street, Hamilton.
 	
3. The defendant, Gregory Toke, is a resident of Millhaven, Ontario.
 	
4. On June 1, 200–, the defendant formed a contract with the plaintiff. The contract was for the rental of a storage garage in the plaintiff's depot for the period of June 1, 200–, to August 1, 200–. The contract entitled the defendant unlimited access to his storage garage by way of a combination locking system known only to the plaintiff and the defendant. The contract is attached to this claim as Schedule 'B'.
 	
5. The defendant paid to the plaintiff a deposit of $200 in accordance with clause 10 of the contract. According to clause 12 of the contract, the defendant was to pay the plaintiff $200 on July 1, 200–, and $200 on August 1, 200–.
 	
6. The contract stipulated that the rental agreement was for a three-month period, ending on August 31, 200–, with an option to renew the contract for a further deposit of $200, to be provided one day prior to the expiration of the contract. Under the contract, the defendant was responsible for removing his belongings from the plaintiff's depot by 6:00 p.m. on August 31, 200–, unless he paid the additional $200 by that date.
 	
7. The defendant did pay the plaintiff $200 on July 1, 200–, and August 1, 200–, in accordance with the contract.
 	
8. On August 21, 200–, the plaintiff attempted to contact the defendant to remind him that the contract was nearing an end and that a further $200 deposit could extend the contract by 90 days. A message to that effect was left on the defendant's answering machine.
 	
9. On August 31, 200–, the contract expired. The defendant failed to provide an additional deposit in accordance to the contract. The defendant also failed to remove the belongings stored in the plaintiff's depot.
	► State the remedy being sought — general, special, punitive damages, or prejudgment interest. If an interest rate is stipulated in the contract between the parties, then you should demand this interest rate instead.
	
	► Identify the parties.
	
	► State the facts in chronological order.

10. The plaintiff attempted to call the defendant on August 31, 200–, leaving a detailed message on the defendant's answering machine.

11. On September 1, 200–, the plaintiff sent a demand letter to the defendant asking that he pay the additional deposit and rental charges and remove his belongings immediately. The letter is attached to this claim as Schedule 'C'.

12. To the knowledge of the plaintiff, no response was received to either the letter or the telephone messages sent to the defendant.

13. On September 1, 200–, the plaintiff changed the combination on the locking system to the location rented by the plaintiff, in accordance with the contract.

14. On September 21, 200–, the defendant arrived at the office of the plaintiff, demanding that his goods be released to him. The plaintiff refused to do so unless a further $200 was paid by the defendant.

15. The defendant refused to pay any additional monies and left.

16. The plaintiff's staff sent a further demand letter for payment, threatening that the plaintiff's goods would be removed and auctioned off in accordance with the contract.

17. To the knowledge of the plaintiff, no response to the additional demand letter was received from the defendant.

18. The defendant was clearly in breach of the contract formed with the plaintiff.
   ▶ State the allegation that a contract was breached.

19. The plaintiff had no recourse but to remove his belongings and put them up for auction. However, the defendant was not storing items that could be auctioned; the defendant was storing dried marijuana. On October 10, 200–, the plaintiff notified the police who, on the same day, removed 100 boxes of the substance from the storage garage rented by the defendant.

20. The defendant again breached clause 17, stating that illegal goods were not allowed to be stored in the plaintiff's depot.

21. The plaintiff states that the defendant owes the plaintiff $200 for the additional rent for the month of September 200–.
   ▶ State the allegation that damages resulted from the breach.

22. The plaintiff states that the defendant owes the plaintiff $200 for the loss of business income in the amount of $200 for the month of October.

23. The plaintiff pleads that this is a proper case for the defendant to pay punitive damages in the amount of $500, considering the administrative expense to which the plaintiff was put to enforce the contract and that illegal goods were stored in the plaintiff's depot.
   ▶ Specifically state the reason you believe punitive damages should apply (of alleged).

   ▶ List any legislation the plaintiff relies on (not applicable here).

(e)   On a separate sheet, state that the defendant admits the allegations contained in paragraphs with the letter *A* next to them.

(f)   State that the defendant denies the allegations contained in paragraphs with the letter *D* next to them.

(g)   State that the defendant has no knowledge of the allegations contained in paragraphs with the letter *U* next to them.

(h)   Plead that the claim is statute-barred (no longer legally enforceable by reason of the lapse of time), if applicable to your case.

(i)   State the defendant's version of events for each allegation that the defendant denies.

(j)   Provide a defence for each allegation about liability that the defendant denies.

(k)   State that the defendant denies or knows nothing about the damages the plaintiff claims.

(l)   State that the plaintiff failed to mitigate (minimize) damages, if this is applicable to your case.

(m)   Plead any legislation that the defendant is relying on.

(n)   Plead any costs that the defendant wishes to recover.

(o)   Include as attachments to the defence —

    (i)   a photocopy of the contract (if written and if the plaintiff has not attached it to the claim),

    (ii)   a photocopy of any letters sent to the defendant about this action (if the plaintiff has not attached them to the claim), and

    (iii)   a photocopy of the sections of legislation on which the defendant relies.

Sample 28 shows an example of a defence for breach of contract. It corresponds to the claim for breach of contract in Sample 27. An additional sample defence is shown in the sample pleadings in Sample 35.

7. Preparing Defence-Related Claims

Although many of the same principles involved in preparing the plaintiff's claim may be applied to preparing a defence-related claim, the elements vary slightly.

SAMPLE 28
DEFENCE FOR BREACH OF CONTRACT

Superior Court of Justice
Cour supérieure de justice

Defence / *Défense*

Form/*Formule* **9A** Ont. Reg. No./*N° du règl. de l'Ont.* : 258/98

Claim no. / *N° de la demande*

H 3255/93

Sealed/Scellé

Kaladar
Small Claims Court / *Cour des petites créances de*
Highway 7, P.O. Box 88
Address / *Adresse*
Kaladar, Ontario

K0H 1Z0

Plaintiff No. 1 / *Demandeur N° 1*

Full name / *Nom et prénoms*

SAFE-T-STORE INC.

Address for service (street & number, city, postal code)
Domicile élu (numéro et rue, ville, code postal)

19 Mill St., Hamilton ON L8L 3Y3

(905) 555-1212   (905) 545-2121

Phone no. *Numéro de téléphone*	Fax no. (if any) *Numéro de télécopieur (le cas échéant)*

Harvey Law

Plaintiff's Lawyer/Agent (Full name)
Avocat/mandataire du demandeur (nom et prénoms)

200 Main St.W., Suite 1

Lawyer/Agent's address for service (street & number, city, postal code)
Domicile élu de l'avocat/du mandataire (numéro et rue, ville, code postal)

(905) 444-1212   (905) 555-2121

Lawyer/Agent's phone no. *Numéro de téléphone de l'avocat/du mandataire*	Lawyer/Agent's fax no. (if any) *Numéro de télécopieur (le cas échéant)*

Plaintiff No. 2 (if applicable) / *Demandeur N° 2 (le cas échéant)*

Full name / *Nom et prénoms*

Address for service (street & number, city, postal code)
Domicile élu (numéro et rue, ville, code postal)

Phone no. *Numéro de téléphone*	Fax no. (if any) *Numéro de télécopieur (le cas échéant)*

Plaintiff's Lawyer/Agent (Full name)
Avocat/mandataire du demandeur (nom et prénoms)

Lawyer/Agent's address for service (street & number, city, postal code)
Domicile élu de l'avocat/du mandataire (numéro et rue, ville, code postal)

Lawyer/Agent's phone no. *Numéro de téléphone de l'avocat/du mandataire*	Lawyer/Agent's fax no. (if any) *Numéro de télécopieur (le cas échéant)*

Defendant No. 1 / *Défendeur N° 1*

Full name / *Nom et prénoms*

GREGORY TOKE

Address for service (street & number, city, postal code)
Domicile élu (numéro et rue, ville, code postal)

1000 Mill Way, Millhaven ON M3M 2L2

Phone no./ *Numéro de téléphone*	Fax no. (if any) *Numéro de télécopieur (le cas échéant)*

(905) 333-3333

Defendant's Lawyer/Agent (Full name)
Avocat/mandataire du défendeur (nom et prénoms)

Lawyer/Agent's address for service (street & number, city, postal code)
Domicile élu de l'avocat/du mandataire (numéro et rue, ville, code postal)

Lawyer/Agent's phone no. *Numéro de téléphone de l'avocat/du mandataire*	Lawyer/Agent's fax no. (if any) *Numéro de télécopieur (le cas échéant)*

Defendant No. 2 (if applicable)/ *Défendeur N° 2 (le cas échéant)*

Full name / *Nom et prénoms*

Address for service (street & number, city, postal code)
Domicile élu (numéro et rue, ville, code postal)

Phone no./ *Numéro de téléphone*	Fax no. (if any) *Numéro de télécopieur (le cas échéant)*

Defendant's Lawyer/Agent (Full name)
Avocat/mandataire du défendeur (nom et prénoms)

Lawyer/Agent's address for service (street & number, city, postal code)
Domicile élu de l'avocat/du mandataire (numéro et rue, ville, code postal)

Lawyer/Agent's phone no. *Numéro de téléphone de l'avocat/du mandataire*	Lawyer/Agent's fax no. (if any) *Numéro de télécopieur (le cas échéant)*

Note: For additional defendants, please list on attached sheet with all the necessary information as requested above.
Rem. : *S'il y a d'autres défendeurs, veuillez indiquer leurs noms et tous les renseignements demandés ci-dessus sur une feuille séparée.*

This Defence is being filed on behalf of: _____
Cette défense est déposée au nom de :

[X] I/We dispute the full claim made by the plaintiff.
Je conteste/Nous contestons la totalité de la demande présentée par le demandeur.

[ ] I/We admit the plaintiff's full claim and propose the following terms of payment:
Je reconnais/Nous reconnaissons être redevable(s) de la totalité de la demande du demandeur et propose /proposons les modalités de paiement suivantes :

$ _____ per _____ commencing _____
$ *par* *à compter du*

[ ] I/We admit part of the plaintiff's claim amounting to $ _____
Je reconnais/Nous reconnaissons être redevable(s) d'une partie de la demande du demandeur, soit

and propose the following terms of payment:
et propose/proposons les modalités de paiement suivantes :

$ _____ per _____ commencing _____
$ *par* *à compter du*

I/We dispute the balance of the claim.
Je conteste/Nous contestons le reliquat de la demande.

NOTE: Payments to be made directly to Plaintiff or the Plaintiffs Lawyer/Agent.
REMARQUE : *Les paiements doivent être versés directement au demandeur ou à l'avocat/mandataire du demandeur.*

REASONS FOR DISPUTING THE CLAIM AND DETAILS / *MOTIFS DE CONTESTATION DE LA DEMANDE ET PRÉCISIONS*

_____
SEE ATTACHED SCHEDULE 'A'
_____
_____
_____
_____
_____
_____
_____
_____

If the defence is based in whole or in part on a document(s), **you must attach** a copy of the document to the defence, or if the document(s) is lost or unavailable, **you must explain** why it is not attached in the space provided below.
*Si la défense est fondée en tout ou en partie sur un document, **vous devez annexer** une copie de celui-ci à la défense. Si le document est perdu ou n'est pas disponible, **vous devez expliquer** ci-dessous pourquoi il n'est pas annexé.*

_____
_____
_____

NOTE: If the defence contains a proposal for terms of payment, the plaintiff is deemed to have accepted the terms unless the plaintiff, in writing to the clerk, disputes the proposal and requests a hearing within 20 calendar days of service of a copy of the DEFENCE.

The notice of hearing will be served (delivered) on the parties.

REMARQUE : *Si la défense comprend une proposition à l'égard des modalités de paiement, le demandeur est réputé les avoir acceptées, sauf s'il conteste, par écrit auprès du greffier, la proposition en demandant la tenue d'une audience dans les 20 jours civils de la signification d'une copie de la DÉFENSE.*

L'avis d'audience sera signifié (remis) aux parties.

- IF THE DEFENDANT FAILS TO ATTEND AT THE HEARING, THE CLERK MAY SIGN JUDGMENT FOR THE UNPAID BALANCE ADMITTED; **OR**
- IF THE DEFENDANT FAILS TO MAKE PAYMENT IN ACCORDANCE WITH THE TERMS OF PAYMENT PROPOSED, THE CLERK UPON RECEIPT OF THE PLAINTIFF'S AFFIDAVIT MAY SIGN JUDGMENT FOR THE UNPAID BALANCE.

- *SI LE DÉFENDEUR N'ASSISTE PAS À L'AUDIENCE, LE GREFFIER PEUT INSCRIRE UN JUGEMENT POUR LE SOLDE RECONNU;* **OU**
- *SI LE DÉFENDEUR N'EFFECTUE PAS LES PAIEMENTS CONFORMÉMENT AUX MODALITÉS PROPOSÉES, LE GREFFIER PEUT, SUR RÉCEPTION DE L'AFFIDAVIT DU DEMANDEUR, CONSIGNER UN JUGEMENT POUR LE SOLDE IMPAYÉ.*

NOTE: If the address set out in the claim is incorrect, you must notify both the plaintiff(s) and the court (in writing) of your correct address.
REMARQUE : Si l'adresse indiquée dans la demande est inexacte, vous devez informer le(s) demandeur(s) et le tribunal, par écrit, de votre adresse exacte.

January 30, 1999
_____
(Date)   (Defendant's signature or Solicitor/Agent's name
                           Signature du défendeur ou de son procureur/mandataire)

SCR 9.01-9A (REV. 99/10) *(formerly/anciennement SCC 0071)*

© Queen's Printer for Ontario, 2000. This is an unofficial version of Government of Ontario legal materials.

SAMPLE DEFENCE	EXPLANATIONS
Schedule 'A' **Defence** 1. The defendant admits the allegations contained in paragraphs 2, 3, 4, 5, 7, 14, and 15 of the plaintiff's claim. 2. The defendant denies the allegations contained in paragraphs 6, 8, 9, 17, 18, 20, 21 and 22 of the plaintiff's claim. 3. The defendant has no knowledge of the allegations contained in paragraphs 1, 10, 11, 12, 13, 16, and 19 of the plaintiff's claim. 4. The defendant pleads that the plaintiff's claim is barred for being served on the plaintiff more than six months after being issued. The defendant seeks that this action be dismissed for being in breach of Rule 8.01(2) of the Small Claims Court Rules. 5. The defendant states that he acted in accordance with the contract until he was denied access to the storage garage he rented. On August 31, 200-, the defendant attempted to remove his belongings at approximately 5:45 p.m. but the combination lock was changed without notice to the plaintiff and the plaintiff's office was closed for the day. 6. The defendant specifically denies that a contract was breached. 7. The defendant denies storing any illegal goods and puts the plaintiff to the strict proof of that allegation. 8. The defendant denies that the plaintiff suffered damages as alleged and puts the plaintiff to strict proof of those damages. 9. The defendant states that if the plaintiff did suffer damages, which the defendant specifically denies, the amount claimed is excessive. 10. The defendant states that if the plaintiff did suffer damages, which the defendant specifically denies, the plaintiff failed to mitigate his damages. 11. The defendant pleads and relies on the Repair and Storage Liens Act, R.S.O. 1990, c. R.25. 12. The defendant pleads that the action be dismissed as against the defendant with costs.	▶ State those allegations to which the defendant admits. ▶ State those allegations that the defendant denies. ▶ State those allegations about which the defendant knows nothing. ▶ Plead that the claim is statute-barred (no longer legally enforceable by reason of the lapse of time), if applicable to your case. ▶ State the defendant's version of events for each allegation that the defendant denies. ▶ Provide a defence for each allegation of liability that the defendant denies. ▶ State that the defendant denies or knows nothing about the damages claimed. ▶ State that the plaintiff failed to mitigate damages. ▶ Plead any legislation on which the defendant is relying. ▶ Plead any costs that the defendant wishes to recover.

Some provinces and territories require you to complete a pre-printed form, which you can obtain from the court registry. In addition to preparing the form, you should attach to the form a separate sheet listing the following information:

(a) State the remedy being sought (e.g., general, special, punitive damages, prejudgment interest).

(b) Identify the parties and explain that the claimant is a defendant in a particular plaintiff's claim.

(c) State the facts in chronological order.

(d) State the allegations that are the source of this claim.

(e) State the allegation that there were resulting damages.

(f) List any legislation on which you rely.

(g) Include as attachments to the claim —

(i) a photocopy of the contract,

(ii) a photocopy of any demand letters that were sent, and

(iii) a photocopy of the sections of legislation on which the plaintiff relies.

8. Preparing an Affidavit

An affidavit is written evidence appearing as a series of statements that tells the story of the deponent (the person making it) and is sworn before a commissioner of oaths. The most frequent use of original affidavits rather than ones created using pre-printed forms is an affidavit sworn in support of a notice of motion or notice of application.

The *deponent* is the person who tells the story in his or her own words. However, sometimes the agent representing the deponent prepares the affidavit. Nonetheless, the deponent must swear under oath that the facts set out in the affidavit are true. Therefore, it is critical that the deponent read the affidavit carefully before swearing to it. The deponent should check that all facts are true. If the deponent does not understand a portion of the affidavit, he or she should insist that the writer explain and rewrite that portion so that its meaning is clear.

A commissioner of oaths may be a lawyer or another person designated as a commissioner of oaths. You may try to get your affidavit sworn at the court office, if a commissioner of oaths is present at the time you attend.

Some indictable offences

Section 131 of the Criminal Code of Canada provides that one who knowingly swears a false affidavit is committing perjury. Section 132 makes perjury an indictable offence, thereby making imprisonment on conviction a possibility.

Section 138 also makes it an indictable offence to act as a commissioner of oaths without being so appointed. A commissioner of oaths is a person appointed under provincial authority who may witness the swearing of an affidavit.

8.1 Purpose of an affidavit

The affidavit is a story. It presents a statement of the deponent's facts. Since it is a sworn document, it is used in place of oral testimony in motions, damages assessment hearings, and jurisdictional hearings.

An opposing party may cross-examine the deponent about the statements he or she made in the affidavit. Therefore, the affidavit is best presented in the story-teller's vocabulary and style and with sufficient detail to make the story clear. The more clearly an affidavit is written, the more likely it will not be called into question and, therefore, the more likely the opposing party will not cross-examine the deponent.

8.2 Structure of an affidavit

Some types of affidavits are available as forms that a deponent can fill out. A set of forms can be obtained from the small claims court office, or you may find the relevant legislation for your province or territory on one of the Web sites listed on the Self-Counsel Press's Web site at <http://www.self-counsel.com/canlaw/smallclaims/resources.html>. These specific forms provide the appropriate structure. The deponent need only provide the necessary information for each particular style of "story." When a form is provided by the court, simply complete the form and have it sworn before a lawyer or commissioner of oaths.

If you require a very detailed or lengthy affidavit, create an original one from scratch. The following sections provide some pointers on creating an original affidavit.

8.3 Creating an original affidavit

In some instances you may choose to prepare an original affidavit from scratch as opposed to using a pre-printed form. For example, you may not have the appropriate form on hand, or the form may not lend itself to the task at hand (it may not have enough space for all the details of damages required to be proven by affidavit evidence at a damages assessment hearing). You may also wish to describe difficulties in serving a party.

An affidavit must contain the following contents in the order specified:

(a) *General heading.* The general heading should contain the court file number (claim number), name of the court, identification of the parties (i.e., Between Plaintiff or Plaintiffs and Defendant or Defendants)

(b) *Title.* The title should read *Affidavit*

(c) *Statement of oath* or affirmation

(d) *Statement of who you are* and why you have knowledge of the contents of the affidavit

(e) *The story* told in the following manner:

    (i) Use your own words.

    (ii) Just like any other story, begin at the beginning, give the facts in the order they occurred, and end at the end.

    (iii) Use one thought per paragraph.

    (iv) Number all of the paragraphs.

(f) *Your reason for preparing the affidavit* using the following standard line or a variation: "I make this affidavit in support of the relief sought and for no other or improper purpose."

(g) *Jurat.* The jurat is a statement that the affidavit was made under oath in the presence of a commissioner of oaths and consists of the signature of the deponent and the signature of the commissioner of oaths or a lawyer.

Samples 29 and 30 show two sample affidavits.

9. Preparing an Affidavit of Service

If a pre-printed form is not available from your local court office, you may draft an original affidavit of service. The same principles apply as when drafting any other affidavit. However, certain contents must be included in addition to the general contents.

AFFIDAVIT FOR A DAMAGES ASSESSMENT HEARING

Mr. Georgey Porgy, the defendant, failed to file a defence. Mr. Porgy was noted in default. The action proceeded to a trial for damages assessment since the damages were not easily ascertainable. In such a trial, evidence is usually entered by affidavit.

Affidavit evidence is crucial. The judge cannot assess the credibility of the deponent nor ask further questions about the story told in the affidavit if the deponent is not present. Therefore, the affidavit must be complete, easy to understand, and persuasive.

In this scenario, the plaintiff has prepared an affidavit to persuade the court that the damages are as alleged in the plaintiff's claim. The defendant, on being notified of the damages assessment, decided to create an affidavit in reply to provide his or her own version of the story about the alleged damages.

The plaintiff obtaining default judgment presents his or her affidavit evidence to the judge. In some jurisdictions, the plaintiff can pass it to the court clerk, who will pass it to the judge to read before the hearing. The judge would read it before making a ruling. The judge may have questions for the plaintiff; then the successful party would be asked to speak to costs of the action.

SUPPLEMENTARY AFFIDAVIT	EXPLANATIONS
File No. N99999-98 SUPERIOR COURT OF JUSTICE NEWMARKET SMALL CLAIMS COURT BETWEEN: WIDGETS INC. Plaintiff - and - GEORGEY PORGY and 1111111 Ontario Ltd., c.o.b. as Georgey's Gorgeous Lawns Defendant **A F F I D A V I T** I, Anna Banana, of the City of Barrie, in the County of Simcoe, MAKE OATH AND SAY:	• court file number assigned by the court office when they issue the Statement of Claim • general heading — identifies appropriate court and parties in the action • title of the document • statement of oath made by deponent

SAMPLE 29 — Continued

1. At all material times, I was Manager of the Accounting Department of Widgets Inc. and as such have knowledge of the facts in this affidavit.

   - states who the deponent is
   - "at all material times" is important because it shows how the deponent knows the information

2. On August 14, 200-, the defendant, Georgey Porgy, an independent contractor and sole owner of 1111111 Ontario Ltd., carrying on business as Georgey's Gorgeous Lawns, was cutting grass on our business premises, at 121 Pretty Street, Newmarket, using a lawn tractor.

   - beginning of story

3. On that day, Mr. Porgy, while operating the tractor, knocked down a flowering cherry tree on the back east end of the business property.

4. I am informed by Rodney Stewart, Property Manager of Widgets Inc., and do verily believe that he approached Mr. Porgy and asked him to replace the damaged tree. Mr. Stewart advises, and I do verily believe, that Mr. Porgy said that he would consider it and get back to him.

   - when the deponent has gained knowledge through a third party, this knowledge is qualified by using "I do verily believe" — without that phrase, the statement is hearsay

5. Mr. Stewart advises, and I do verily believe, that he has personally made three telephone calls to Mr. Porgy about the damaged tree. Mr. Stewart further advises, and I do verily believe, that Mr. Porgy has not returned any of his calls.

6. As of today's date, I am informed by Mr. Stewart, and do verily believe, that Mr. Porgy has never, in any way, contacted Mr. Stewart or any other employee of Widgets Inc. about the damaged tree.

7. I do verily believe that Mr. Porgy does not intend to replace the tree.

   - end of the story

8. I do verily believe that this is a just and proper case to order Mr. Porgy to pay for the cost of the new tree.

   - "just and proper" — argumentative but often included to make the affidavit more persuasive

9. I make this affidavit in support of the relief sought and for no other or improper purpose.

   - reason for preparing the affidavit

   - left-hand column: jurat — provides the date and place of oath and person who commissioned it

   - right-hand column: signature of deponent

SWORN BEFORE ME AT The City of Barrie, County of Simcoe, this 24th day of September, 200–

I.M. Commissioner
_____
Commissioner of Oaths

Anna Banana
_____
ANNA BANANA

NOTE: The deponent's signature is mandatory and must be made in the presence of a Lawyer or Commissioner of Oaths

SAMPLE 30

AFFIDAVIT IN SUPPORT OF A MOTION TO DISMISS AN ACTION FOR DELAY

Ms. Kalivani Goor, the plaintiff, failed to take steps to move along her lawsuit. Six months have passed since the pre-trial was held and the defendant, Ms. Lucy Dale, feels prejudiced by the delay. She brings a motion to dismiss the plaintiff's claim for delay. In support of her motion she prepares the affidavit shown on the next page. It will serve as evidence during the hearing of the motion.

SUPPLEMENTARY AFFIDAVIT	EXPLANATIONS
File No. H77-97	► court file number assigned by the court office when they issue the Statement of Claim
SUPERIOR COURT OF JUSTICE HAMILTON SMALL CLAIMS COURT BETWEEN: KALIVANI GOOR Plaintiff - and - LUCY DALE Defendant	► general heading — identifies appropriate court and parties in the action
A F F I D A V I T	► title of the document
I, Lucy Dale, of the City of Hamilton, in the Regional Municipality of Hamilton-Wentworth, MAKE OATH AND SAY:	► statement of oath made by deponent
1. I am the defendant in this action for trespass.	► states who the deponent is
2. The plaintiff's claim was issued on February 12, 200–, and I received the claim by mail on June 25, 200–.	► beginning of story
3. The parties attended at a pre-trial conference on October 30, 200–, before The Honourable Judge Lee.	
4. At the end of the pre-trial conference, Judge Lee made two orders. Judge Lee first ordered that the plaintiff, Ms. Lucy Dale, produce to the court and the defendant copies of the security surveillance videotape that she claimed showed the alleged trespass taking place on her property. This was to be done within 45 days of the pre-trial conference. The Judge also ordered that the plaintiff set the action down for trial within 60 days. Attached as Exhibit 'A' to this affidavit is a copy of Judge Lee's orders, dated October 30, 200–.	► when the deponent has gained knowledge through a third party, this knowledge is qualified by using "I do verily believe" — without that phrase, the statement is hearsay

5. Six months have passed since the pre-trial conference was held. On September 5, 200–, I attended at the court office. My review of the court file in this matter indicates, and I do verily believe, that the plaintiff, Ms. Lucy Dale, has failed to set this matter down for trial and has not produced a copy of the videotape to the court as Judge Lee ordered.

6. I, too, have not been served with a copy of the videotape as Judge Lee ordered.

7. My only witness for trial, Ms. Celia Barnam, was an elderly neighbour whose residence was situated between the houses of the plaintiff and defendant. Unfortunately, Ms. Barnam died on September 2, 200–. Attached as Exhibit 'A' to this affidavit is a copy of Ms. Barnam's death certificate.

   ▶ end of the story

8. I do verily believe that the plaintiff is responsible for the delay that has seriously prejudiced my ability to defend myself in a trial of this matter. In addition, the plaintiff has failed to comply with Judge Lee's order dated October 30, 200–. Therefore, I do verily believe that this is a just and proper case to dismiss the plaintiff's claim with costs.

   ▶ "just and proper" — argumentative but often included to make the affidavit more persuasive

9. I make this affidavit in support of the relief sought in the Notice of Motion and for no other or improper purpose.

   ▶ reason for preparing the affidavit

SWORN BEFORE ME AT The City of Hamilton, Regional Municipality of Hamilton-Wentworth, this 12th day of July 200–

I.M. Commissioner
—————————————————
Commissioner of Oaths

Lucy Dale
—————————————————
LUCY DALE

An affidavit of service must contain the following contents in the order specified:

(a) General Heading

   (i)   Court File No. (claim number)

   (ii) Name of Court

   (iii) Between Plaintiff or Plaintiffs and Defendant or Defendants — identify the parties

(b) Title — "Affidavit of Service"

(c) Statement of oath or affirmation

(d) State who you are — "I am the plaintiff, friend, process server, etcetera."

(e) State the facts relating to service, as follows:

   (i)   State how the document was served.

   (ii) State when the document was served.

   (iii) State upon whom the document was served.

   (iv) If served by mail, specify that the mail has not been returned to the sender.

(f) Jurat — The jurat states that the affidavit was made under oath in the presence of a commissioner of oaths and consists of the following:

   (i)   Signature of deponent

   (ii) Signature of commissioner of oaths or a lawyer

Sample 31 shows some examples of phrases to use in an affidavit of service.

You are not required to write a letter to accompany a court document that you intend to serve on a party in the lawsuit. However, such letters are often written by lawyers and agents to accompany documents served by mail.

You may wish to use the following phrases if you choose to write an accompanying letter:

➤ "Please find enclosed the plaintiff's claim, served on you under the small claims court rules."

➤ "Please find enclosed the notice of examination, which we serve on you in accordance with the small claims court rules."

WORDING FOR AFFIDAVIT OF SERVICE

Affidavit of Service by Mail (use standard headings)

I, Humphrey Logan, the plaintiff in this action, have served the Plaintiff's Claim upon the defendant, Mequilia Bona, on December 10, 200-, by sending the claim by regular mail to the defendant's last known address, 999 Awol Avenue, Nanaimo, British Columbia. Twenty days have since passed and the letter was not returned to me.

Affidavit of Service By Personal Delivery (use standard headings)

I, June April, am a process server with At Your Service Unlimited. On August 1, 200-, I served personally the Plaintiff's Claim upon the defendant, Mequilia Bona, by leaving a copy with an adult at 100 Walnut Street, Charlottetown, Prince Edward Island, who identified herself as being the defendant.

Affidavit of Service by Fax (use standard headings)

I, Humphrey Logan, the plaintiff in this action, served the Amended Plaintiff's Claim upon the defendant, Mequilia Bona, on January 2, 200-, by sending a copy by telephone transmission to the fax number (807) 999-9999 for the defendant's solicitor located in Yellowknife, Northwest Territories. The proof of the completed transaction is attached to this affidavit and is labelled Exhibit 'A'.

10. Preparing a Supplementary Affidavit

A supplementary affidavit is used to correct or add to information provided in an affidavit previously sworn by the same deponent.

The basics of preparing affidavits outlined earlier apply to supplementary affidavits with a few differences:

(a) You need not and should not repeat all the paragraphs of your original affidavit to which you are adding or correcting, but mention that the affidavit is supplementary.

(b) If you are correcting the original affidavit, state —

  (i) the paragraph that contains the error,

  (ii) the reason you made the error,

(iii) the correct version of the facts, and

(iv) that all other paragraphs of the original affidavit are correct as sworn.

(c) If you are adding to the original affidavit, state —

(i) the facts that have come to your attention since the original affidavit was sworn, and

(ii) the date or approximate date that you discovered the additional facts.

Sample 32 shows a supplementary affidavit.

11. Preparing an Affidavit in Reply

An affidavit in reply is prepared in response to an affidavit that an opposing party made. Sample 33 shows an example of an affidavit in reply.

12. Drafting a Notice Letter

Notice may be required before you commence a claim. Chapter 2 provides an explanation of notice and notice periods. Notice may be in the form of a letter with the following characteristics:

(a) Clearly show your name, address, telephone number, and fax number.

(b) Clearly show the name, address, telephone number, and fax number of the person or entity you are suing. If you are suing a municipality, address the letter to the clerk of the town or city against which you intend to make a claim. If you are suing the provincial or territorial government, address the letter to the Attorney General for your province or territory.

(c) Set out what happened, when it happened, where it happened, and how it happened.

(d) State that you intend to take legal action.

(e) Date the letter.

(f) Sign the letter, and photocopy it for your records.

(g) Send the letter via registered mail within seven days of the event.

Sample 34 shows a notice letter.

Sample 35 shows a complete set of sample pleadings. Use these and Checklist 8 to prepare your own pleadings.

SAMPLE 32
SUPPLEMENTARY AFFIDAVIT

SAMPLE SUPPLEMENTARY AFFIDAVIT	EXPLANATIONS
File No. N99999-98	▶ court file number assigned by the court office when they issue the Statement of Claim
ONTARIO COURT (GENERAL DIVISION) NEWMARKET SMALL CLAIMS COURT BETWEEN: ANNA BANANA Plaintiff - and - GEORGEY PORGY Defendant	▶ general heading — identifies appropriate court and parties in the action
A F F I D A V I T	▶ title of the document
I, Anna Banana, of the City of Barrie, in the County of Simcoe, MAKE OATH AND SAY:	▶ statement of oath made by deponent
1. At all material times, I was Manager of the Accounting Department of Widgets Inc. and as such have knowledge of the facts in this affidavit.	▶ mention that this affidavit is a supplement
2. I prepared this affidavit as a supplement to my affidavit sworn on September 24, 200–.	▶ new facts
3. On June 10, 200–, Mr. Stewart purchased a similar flowering cherry tree of approximately the same age to replace the damaged tree. The cost of the new tree was $378.45. Attached to this affidavit and marked as Exhibit 'A' is a copy of the receipt for the replacement tree.	▶ mention that this is a supplement so that the reader knows to read the original affidavit first
4. I do verily believe that this is a just and proper case to order Mr. Porgy to pay for the cost of the new tree.	▶ "just and proper" — argumentative but often included to make the affidavit more persuasive
5. I make this affidavit in support of the relief sought and for no other or improper purpose.	▶ reason for preparing the affidavit
SWORN BEFORE ME AT The City of Barrie, County of Simcoe, this 24th day of September, 200– *I.M. Commissioner* ——————————— Commissioner of Oaths *Anna Banana* ——————————— ANNA BANANA	▶ left-hand column: jurat — provides the date and place of oath and person who commissioned it ▶ right-hand column: signature of deponent NOTE: Jurat and deponent's signature are mandatory and must be made in the presence of a lawyer or Commissioner of Oaths

SAMPLE 33
AFFIDAVIT IN REPLY

SAMPLE AFFIDAVIT IN REPLY	EXPLANATIONS
File No. N99999-98	▶ court file number assigned by the court office when they issue the Statement of Claim
ONTARIO COURT (GENERAL DIVISION) NEWMARKET SMALL CLAIMS COURT BETWEEN: Anna Banana Plaintiff - and - Georgey Porgy Defendant	▶ general heading — identifies appropriate court and parties in the action
A F F I D A V I T I N R E P L Y I, Georgey Porgy, of the City of Hamilton, in the Regional Municipality of Hamilton-Wentworth, AFFIRM:	▶ title of the document ▶ affirmation made by deponent ▶ states who the deponent is ▶ beginning of story
1. I am an Independent Contractor working in the landscaping business.	
2. During the summer of 200–, I cut grass for Widgets Inc. at their 121 Pretty Street location.	
3. On August 14, 200–, I knocked down a flowering cherry tree on the back east end of that property during the course of my work.	
4. I informed Rodney Stewart, Property Manager of Widgets Inc., that I knocked down the cherry tree. He replied that I should pay for it. I told him that it was diseased and would have fallen soon anyway.	
5. I felt badly because the area looked awful without a tree. I informed Mr. Stewart that I would see if I could find a similar tree for him through my landscaping business. However, I could not find one as they were worth a lot more than the diseased tree that I knocked down.	
6. Mr. Stewart left me three phone messages about replacing the tree. I was in the old country when he called each time. When I returned, I heard the messages but ignored them because I believed his request was unreasonable.	

7. The tree that I knocked down was worth nothing.

8. The tree that Widgets Inc. replaced it with was a better quality flowering cherry tree than the original tree.

9. I do verily believe that I should not have to pay for their landscaping improvements.

10. I make this affidavit in response to the affidavit by Ms. Anna Banana and for no other or improper purpose.

SWORN BEFORE ME AT The City
Hamilton, Regional Municipality
of Hamilton-Wentworth, this 27th
day of September, 200–

_____
I.M. Commissioner
Commissioner of Oaths

_____
Georgey Porgy
GEORGEY PORGY

► end of the story

► reason for preparing the affidavit

► left-hand column: jurat — provides the date and place of oath and person who commissioned it

► right-hand column: signature of deponent

NOTE: The jurat and deponent's signature, which must be made in the presence of a lawyer or Commissioner of Oaths, must be included on all affidavits

SAMPLE 34
NOTICE LETTER

Martino slipped on a sidewalk and broke his index finger. He now wishes to sue the municipal office, City of Slippery Slopes, which is responsible for keeping the sidewalk in good repair. Martino checks the Municipal Act and discovers, much to his amazement, that he must provide formal, written notice within seven days of the accident. The Act requires that Martino deliver this notice to the City Clerk by registered mail, postmarked no later than seven days after the fall. Martino, a two-finger typist, rolls up his sleeves and uses his healthy index finger to type the notice.

Martino Bocca 123 Banana Lane Oopsville, PE C0B 1K0 Telephone: (902) 999-9999	▶ your name and address
<div align="right">January 3, 200–</div> <div align="center">WITHOUT PREJUDICE</div>	▶ date of letter ▶ to ensure that this letter is not used against you at a later date
City of Slippery Slopes P.O. Box 8888 Oopsville, PE C0B 1K0	▶ address of potential defendant
Re: Slip and Fall on Municipal Property, January 2, 200–	
To the Clerk of the City of Slippery Slopes:	▶ letter must be addressed to the City Clerk
Please consider this good and proper notice that on the 2nd day of January, 200-, I was walking down the east sidewalk of Main Street when I caught my foot in a deep crack in the sidewalk. Had this sidewalk been properly maintained and repaired, I would not have fallen and broken my index finger.	▶ contents must include: – what happened – when it happened – where it happened – how it happened, to the best of your recollection
I intend to sue the City of Slippery Slopes for damages arising out of this incident.	▶ state intention to sue
Yours truly, *Martino Bocca* Martino Bocca	▶ sign the letter

SAMPLE 35
PLEADINGS

Monty called his neighbour Ilya, a carpenter, to assist him in repairing the roof of his summerhouse at Waterton Lakes. Ilya brought over a ladder to do the job. Monty began climbing the ladder but fell off the ladder and down the 60-metre slope of a forested ravine and sustained injuries. Monty filed a plaintiff's claim against Ilya because he thinks that Ilya is responsible, either because he did not properly inform Monty on the use of a ladder or because he deliberately jostled the ladder to scare Monty as a sick joke.

Superior Court of Justice
Cour supérieure de justice

Plaintiff's Claim
Demande du demandeur

Form/*Formule* 7A Ont. Reg. No./*N° du règl. de l'Ont.* : 258/98

Claim no. / *N° de la demande*

Sealed/*Scellé*

Toronto
Small Claims Court / *Cour des petites créances de*
444 Yonge Street, 2nd Floor
Address / *Adresse*
Toronto, ON M5B 2H4

Plaintiff No. 1 / *Demandeur N° 1*

Full name / *Nom et prénoms*

Monty Fall

Address for service (street & number, city, postal code)
Domicile élu (numéro et rue, ville, code postal)

200 Pellitier Street

Windsor, ON N9A 7A5

Phone no./ *Numéro de téléphone*   Fax no. (if any) *Numéro de télécopieur (le cas échéant)*

(519) 555-1212

Plaintiff's Lawyer/Agent (Full name)
Avocat/mandataire du demandeur (nom et prénoms)

Lawyer/Agent's address for service (street & number, city, postal code)
Domicile élu de l'avocat/du mandataire (numéro et rue, ville, code postal)

Lawyer/Agent's phone no. *Numéro de téléphone de l'avocat/du mandataire*   Lawyer/Agent's fax no. (if any) *Numéro de télécopieur (le cas échéant)*

Plaintiff No. 2 (If applicable) / *Demandeur N° 2 (le cas échéant)*

Full name / *Nom et prénoms*

Address for service (street & number, city, postal code)
Domicile élu (numéro et rue, ville, code postal)

Phone no. *Numéro de téléphone*   Fax no. (if any) *Numéro de télécopieur (le cas échéant)*

Plaintiff's Lawyer/Agent (Full name)
Avocat/mandataire du demandeur (nom et prénoms)

Lawyer/Agent's address for service (street & number, city, postal code)
Domicile élu de l'avocat/du mandataire (numéro et rue, ville, code postal)

Lawyer/Agent's phone no. *Numéro de téléphone de l'avocat/du mandataire*   Lawyer/Agent's fax no. (if any) *Numéro de télécopieur (le cas échéant)*

Defendant No. 1 / *Défendeur N° 1*

Full name / *Nom et prénoms*

Ilya Pushdim

Address for service (street & number, city, postal code)
Domicile élu (numéro et rue, ville, code postal)

500 County Way

Essex, ON N8A 3Y7

Phone no./ *Numéro de téléphone*   Fax no. (if any) *Numéro de télécopieur (le cas échéant)*

(519) 444-2121

Defendant's Lawyer/Agent (Full name)
Avocat/mandataire du défendeur (nom et prénoms)

Lawyer/Agent's address for service (street & number, city, postal code)
Domicile élu de l'avocat/du mandataire (numéro et rue, ville, code postal)

Lawyer/Agent's phone no. *Numéro de téléphone de l'avocat/du mandataire*   Lawyer/Agent's fax no. (if any) *Numéro de télécopieur (le cas échéant)*

Defendant No. 2 (If applicable)/*Défendeur N° 2 (le cas échéant)*

Full name / *Nom et prénoms*

Address for service (street & number, city, postal code)
Domicile élu (numéro et rue, ville, code postal)

Phone no./ *Numéro de téléphone*   Fax no. (if any) *Numéro de télécopieur (le cas échéant)*

Defendant's Lawyer/Agent (Full name)
Avocat/mandataire du défendeur (nom et prénoms)

Lawyer/Agent's address for service (street & number, city, postal code)
Domicile élu de l'avocat/du mandataire (numéro et rue, ville, code postal)

Lawyer/Agent's phone no. *Numéro de téléphone de l'avocat/du mandataire*   Lawyer/Agent's fax no. (if any) *Numéro de télécopieur (le cas échéant)*

Note: For additional defendants, please list on attached sheet with all the necessary information as requested above.
Rem. : *S'il y a d'autres défendeurs, veuillez indiquer leurs noms et tous les renseignements demandés ci-dessus sur une feuille séparée.*

SCR 7.01-7A (REV. 99/10) *(formerly/anciennement SCC 0061)*

TO THE DEFENDANT(S) / *AU(X) DÉFENDEUR(S) :*

The plaintiff claims from you $ __1,450.00__ plus $ _____
Le demandeur vous demande   (amount of claim) $ plus   (interest claimed to date (if any)) $ _____
                              (montant de la demande)   *(intérêts réclamés à ce jour (le cas échéant))*
and costs for the reason(s) set out below.
ainsi que des dépens, pour le/les motif(s) énoncé(s) ci-dessous.

The plaintiff further claims from you pre-judgment interest and post-judgment interest in accordance with the
Courts of Justice Act.
Le demandeur vous demande également des intérêts antérieurs et postérieurs au jugement conformément à la
Loi sur les tribunaux judiciaires.

You may attend at the nearest Small Claims Court to obtain the "How to Make Small Claims Court Work for You" booklet as
well as "Your Guide to Making a Defence."
Vous pouvez obtenir la brochure Comment profiter pleinement de la Cour des petites créances *de même que le* Guide sur
la défense *auprès de la Cour des petites créances la plus proche.*

> **IF YOU DO NOT FILE A DEFENCE WITH THE COURT WITHIN TWENTY (20) CALENDAR DAYS AFTER
> YOU RECEIVED THIS CLAIM, JUDGMENT MAY BE ENTERED AGAINST YOU.**
> **JUDGMENT MAY BE ENTERED WITHOUT FURTHER NOTICE TO YOU.**
> *SI VOUS NE DÉPOSEZ PAS DE DÉFENSE AUPRÈS DU TRIBUNAL AU PLUS TARD VINGT (20) JOURS
> CIVILS APRÈS AVOIR REÇU LA PRÉSENTE DEMANDE, UN JUGEMENT PEUT ÊTRE INSCRIT CONTRE
> VOUS SANS AUTRE AVIS.*

TYPE OF CLAIM / *NATURE DE LA DEMANDE*

☐ Unpaid Account *Compte impayé*	☐ Promissory Note *Billet*	☐ Damage to Property *Dommages causés à des biens*
☐ Contract *Contrat*	☐ Services Rendered *Services rendus*	☐ Lease *Contrat de location*
☐ Motor Vehicle Accident *Accident de véhicule automobile*	☐ N.S.F. Cheque *Chèque sans provision*	☒ Other Personal Injury *Autre*

REASONS FOR CLAIM AND DETAILS / *MOTIFS DE LA DEMANDE ET PRÉCISIONS*

Explain what happened, where and when **and** the amounts of money involved.
Expliquer ce qui est arrivé, indiquer le lieu et le moment de l'incident **et** *préciser les sommes d'argent en cause.*

SEE ATTACHED SCHEDULE 'A'

_____

If more space is required, attach separate sheet(s)./*Si vous avez besoin de plus d'espace, annexez une feuille supplémentaire.*

If the claim is based in whole or in part on a document(s), **you must attach** a copy of the document(s) to the claim, or if
the document(s) is lost or unavailable, **you must explain** why it is not attached in the space provided below.
Si la demande est fondée en tout ou en partie sur un document, **vous devez annexer** *une copie de celui-ci à la demande.*
Si le document est perdu ou n'est pas disponible, **vous devez expliquer** *ci-dessous pourquoi il n'est pas annexé.*

_____   _____
(Date)   (Signature of clerk/*Signature du greffier*)

SCR 7.01-7A (REV. 99/10) *(formerly/anciennement SCC 0061)*

Plaintiff's Claim for Commission of a Tort

SAMPLE CLAIM	EXPLANATIONS

## Schedule 'A' 	
### Plaintiff's Claim 	
 	
The Relief Sought: *(Headings are optional)*
 	
1. The plaintiff seeks the following relief:
 	
   a) General damages in the amount of $450;
 	
   b) Special damages in the amount of $500;
 	
   c) Punitive damages in the amount of $500;
 	
   d) Prejudgment interest under the Courts of Justice Act;
 	
   e) Postjudgment interest under the Courts of Justice Act; and
 	
   f) Its costs of this action.
	▶ State the remedy being sought — general, special, punitive damages, pre-judgment interest. Postjudgment interest is usually pleaded even though it is awarded upon judgment pursuant to the Courts of Justice Act.

The Parties 2. The plaintiff, Monty Fall, is a resident of Windsor, Ontario. 3. The defendant, Ilya Pushdim, is a resident of Essex, Ontario.	▶ Identify the parties.
Liability 4. On May 30, 200-, the defendant, a carpenter by trade and the next door neighbour of the plaintiff at the material times, attended at the plaintiff's residence on 928 Renovation Drive in Windsor, Ontario, to assist the plaintiff with roof work needed on his summer house. 5. The defendant arrived at the plaintiff's residence carrying a 10-metre aluminum ladder. 6. The defendant propped the ladder against the summer house and indicated that it was safe to climb. The plaintiff joked that the plaintiff should climb on the roof first to test the ladder. 7. The plaintiff began to climb the ladder when, suddenly and without warning, the ladder gave way, causing the plaintiff to fall from the ladder and down the 60-metre slope of a forested ravine. 8. On his descent, the plaintiff heard sounds of laughter emanating from the defendant's direction. 9. After his fall, the plaintiff tried to climb up the side of the ravine but was seriously injured and unable to do so unassisted. Firefighters hoisted the plaintiff to safety and an ambulance transported the plaintiff to the emergency ward of a local hospital.	▶ State the facts relating to liability in chronological order.

10. The plaintiff states that the fall and resulting injuries were solely the result of the negligence as follows:
 	
(a) he owed a duty to the plaintiff to educate him about the safety issues surrounding ladder usage;
 	
(b) he failed to take the reasonable care of an experienced carpenter because he failed to:
 	
   (i) ensure that the ladder was properly secured;
 	
   (ii) ensure that the rungs of the ladder were free of debris and moisture;
 	
   (iii) inform the plaintiff that the circumstances warranted the use of a safety harness; and
 	
   (iv) inform the plaintiff that the circumstances warranted the use of a safety helmet.
	► State the allegations of negligence.

11. In the alternative, the plaintiff pleads that the defendant deliberately moved the ladder in a darkly comic effort to frighten and embarrass the plaintiff, an action the plaintiff pleads constitutes battery and caused him to fall.	► State any alternative allegations such as intentional torts.
General Damages	
12. The plaintiff sustained numerous serious injuries including, but not limited to, a sprain to his cervical muscles and ligaments, a broken ankle, numerous cuts, scratches, bruises, numerous headaches, and pain and suffering. He also suffered an aggravation of his ulcer. His enjoyment of life has been impaired as a result of continuing headaches and his new fear of climbing ladders.	► State the general damages.
Special Damages	
13. As a result of the injuries sustained, the plaintiff was unable to perform the duties of his normal occupation as a grave digger and lost one month's worth of wages.	► State the special damages.
14. The plaintiff has been put to medical and other out-of-pocket expenses.	
Punitive Damages	
15. The plaintiff pleads that, if the court finds this to be a case of the intentional tort of battery, this is a proper case for the defendant to pay punitive damages in the amount of $500, considering the severe consequences suffered at the defendant's hand.	► State the punitive damages.
Legislation	
16. The plaintiff pleads and relies upon the relevant provisions of the Negligence Act, R.S.O. 1990, c. N.1.	► List any legislation on which the plaintiff relies.

SAMPLE 35 — Continued

Superior Court of Justice
Cour supérieure de justice

Defence / *Défense*

Form/*Formule* 9A Ont. Reg. No./*N° du règl. de l'Ont.* : 258/98

Claim no. / *N° de la demande*
T1111/91

Sealed/Scellé

Toronto
Small Claims Court / *Cour des petites créances de*
444 Yonge Street, 2nd Floor
Address / *Adresse*
Toronto, ON M5B 2H4

Plaintiff No. 1 / *Demandeur N° 1*

Full name / *Nom et prénoms*
Monty Fall

Address for service (street & number, city, postal code)
Domicile élu (numéro et rue, ville, code postal)
200 Pellitier Street

Windsor ON N9A 7A5

Phone no.
Numéro de téléphone
(519) 555-1212

Fax no. (if any)
Numéro de télécopieur (le cas échéant)

Plaintiff's Lawyer/Agent (Full name)
Avocat/mandataire du demandeur (nom et prénoms)

Lawyer/Agent's address for service (street & number, city, postal code)
Domicile élu de l'avocat/du mandataire (numéro et rue, ville, code postal)

Lawyer/Agent's phone no.
Numéro de téléphone de l'avocat/du mandataire

Lawyer/Agent's fax no. (if any)
Numéro de télécopieur (le cas échéant)

Plaintiff No. 2 (if applicable) / *Demandeur N° 2 (le cas échéant)*

Full name / *Nom et prénoms*

Address for service (street & number, city, postal code)
Domicile élu (numéro et rue, ville, code postal)

Phone no.
Numéro de téléphone

Fax no. (if any)
Numéro de télécopieur (le cas échéant)

Plaintiff's Lawyer/Agent (Full name)
Avocat/mandataire du demandeur (nom et prénoms)

Lawyer/Agent's address for service (street & number, city, postal code)
Domicile élu de l'avocat/du mandataire (numéro et rue, ville, code postal)

Lawyer/Agent's phone no.
Numéro de téléphone de l'avocat/du mandataire

Lawyer/Agent's fax no. (if any)
Numéro de télécopieur (le cas échéant)

Defendant No. 1 / *Défendeur N° 1*

Full name / *Nom et prénoms*
Ilya Pushdim

Address for service (street & number, city, postal code)
Domicile élu (numéro et rue, ville, code postal)
500 County Way

Essex, ON N8A 3Y7

Phone no./ *Numéro de téléphone*
(519) 444-2121

Fax no. (if any)
Numéro de télécopieur (le cas échéant)

Defendant's Lawyer/Agent (Full name)
Avocat/mandataire du défendeur (nom et prénoms)

Lawyer/Agent's address for service (street & number, city, postal code)
Domicile élu de l'avocat/du mandataire (numéro et rue, ville, code postal)

Lawyer/Agent's phone no.
Numéro de téléphone de l'avocat/du mandataire

Lawyer/Agent's fax no. (if any)
Numéro de télécopieur (le cas échéant)

Defendant No. 2 (if applicable)/ *Défendeur N° 2 (le cas échéant)*

Full name / *Nom et prénoms*

Address for service (street & number, city, postal code)
Domicile élu (numéro et rue, ville, code postal)

Phone no./ *Numéro de téléphone*

Fax no. (if any)
Numéro de télécopieur (le cas échéant)

Defendant's Lawyer/Agent (Full name)
Avocat/mandataire du défendeur (nom et prénoms)

Lawyer/Agent's address for service (street & number, city, postal code)
Domicile élu de l'avocat/du mandataire (numéro et rue, ville, code postal)

Lawyer/Agent's phone no.
Numéro de téléphone de l'avocat/du mandataire

Lawyer/Agent's fax no. (if any)
Numéro de télécopieur (le cas échéant)

Note: For additional defendants, please list on attached sheet with all the necessary information as requested above.
Rem. : S'il y a d'autres défendeurs, veuillez indiquer leurs noms et tous les renseignements demandés ci-dessus sur une feuille séparée.

SCR 9.01-9A (REV. 99/10) *(formerly/anciennement SCC 0071)*

SAMPLE 35 — Continued

This Defence is being filed on behalf of: _____
Cette défense est déposée au nom de :

[X] I/We dispute the full claim made by the plaintiff.
Je conteste/Nous contestons la totalité de la demande présentée par le demandeur.

[ ] I/We admit the plaintiff's full claim and propose the following terms of payment:
Je reconnais/Nous reconnaissons être redevable(s) de la totalité de la demande du demandeur et propose
/proposons les modalités de paiement suivantes :

$ _____ per _____ commencing _____
$ par   *à compter du*

[ ] I/We admit part of the plaintiff's claim amounting to $ _____
Je reconnais/Nous reconnaissons être redevable(s) d'une partie de la demande du demandeur, soit

and propose the following terms of payment:
et propose/proposons les modalités de paiement suivantes :

$ _____ per _____ commencing _____
$ par   *à compter du*

I/We dispute the balance of the claim.
Je conteste/Nous contestons le reliquat de la demande.

NOTE: Payments to be made directly to Plaintiff or the Plaintiffs Lawyer/Agent.
REMARQUE : *Les paiements doivent être versés directement au demandeur ou à l'avocat/mandataire du demandeur.*

REASONS FOR DISPUTING THE CLAIM AND DETAILS / *MOTIFS DE CONTESTATION DE LA DEMANDE ET PRÉCISIONS*

_____

SEE ATTACHED SCHEDULE 'A'

_____
_____
_____
_____
_____
_____
_____
_____

If the defence is based in whole or in part on a document(s), **you must attach** a copy of the document to the defence, or if the document(s) is lost or unavailable, **you must explain** why it is not attached in the space provided below.
*Si la défense est fondée en tout ou en partie sur un document, **vous devez annexer** une copie de celui-ci à la défense.*
*Si le document est perdu ou n'est pas disponible, **vous devez expliquer** ci-dessous pourquoi il n'est pas annexé.*

_____
_____
_____

NOTE: If the defence contains a proposal for terms of payment, the plaintiff is deemed to have accepted the terms unless the plaintiff, in writing to the clerk, disputes the proposal and requests a hearing within 20 calendar days of service of a copy of the DEFENCE.

The notice of hearing will be served (delivered) on the parties.

REMARQUE : *Si la défense comprend une proposition à l'égard des modalités de paiement, le demandeur est réputé les avoir acceptées, sauf s'il conteste, par écrit auprès du greffier, la proposition en demandant la tenue d'une audience dans les 20 jours civils de la signification d'une copie de la DÉFENSE.*

L'avis d'audience sera signifié (remis) aux parties.

- IF THE DEFENDANT FAILS TO ATTEND AT THE HEARING, THE CLERK MAY SIGN JUDGMENT FOR THE UNPAID BALANCE ADMITTED; **OR**
- IF THE DEFENDANT FAILS TO MAKE PAYMENT IN ACCORDANCE WITH THE TERMS OF PAYMENT PROPOSED, THE CLERK UPON RECEIPT OF THE PLAINTIFF'S AFFIDAVIT MAY SIGN JUDGMENT FOR THE UNPAID BALANCE.
- *SI LE DÉFENDEUR N'ASSISTE PAS À L'AUDIENCE, LE GREFFIER PEUT INSCRIRE UN JUGEMENT POUR LE SOLDE RECONNU; **OU***
- *SI LE DÉFENDEUR N'EFFECTUE PAS LES PAIEMENTS CONFORMÉMENT AUX MODALITÉS PROPOSÉES, LE GREFFIER PEUT, SUR RÉCEPTION DE L'AFFIDAVIT DU DEMANDEUR, CONSIGNER UN JUGEMENT POUR LE SOLDE IMPAYÉ.*

NOTE: If the address set out in the claim is incorrect, you must notify both the plaintiff(s) and the court (in writing) of your correct address.
REMARQUE : *Si l'adresse indiquée dans la demande est inexacte, vous devez informer le(s) demandeur(s) et le tribunal, par écrit, de votre adresse exacte.*

January 31, 2000
_____   _____
(Date)   (Defendant's signature or Solicitor/Agent's name
             Signature du défendeur ou de son procureur/mandataire)
SCR 9.01-9A (REV. 99/10) (formerly/anciennement SCC 0071)

© Queen's Printer for Ontario, 2000. This is an unofficial version of Government of Ontario legal materials.

SAMPLE 35 — Continued

Defence for Commission of a Tort

SAMPLE DEFENCE	EXPLANATIONS

Schedule 'A'
Defence
 	
1. The defendant admits the allegations contained in paragraphs 2, 3, 4, and 5 of the Plaintiff's Claim.
 	
2. The defendant denies the allegations contained in paragraphs 6 through 15, inclusive, of the Plaintiff's Claim.
 	
3. The defendant has no knowledge of the allegations contained in paragraphs 1 and 16 of the Plaintiff's Claim.
 	
4. The defendant pleads that the plaintiff's claim is scandalous, frivolous, vexatious, and an abuse of the court's process. The defendant seeks that this action be dismissed for being in breach of Rule 12.02(1) of the Small Claims Court Rules.
 	
5. The defendant states that this incident was a mere accident, beyond the control of the defendant.
 	
6. In the alternative, if this honourable court does not agree that this incident was a mere accident, the defendant states that the plaintiff was the author of his own misfortune as follows:
 	
    (a) he failed to observe common sense rules of using a ladder such as wearing proper footwear instead of clogs;
 	
    (b) he ought not to have attempted climbing the ladder if he lacked reasonable skill and self-command to do so;
 	
    (c) he was climbing the ladder while his ability to do so was impaired by alcohol, drugs, stress, illness, or fatigue; and
 	
    (d) he failed to wear corrective lenses when he knew or ought to have known that he required them in order to climb the ladder safely.
 	
7. The defendant further states that he owed no duty of care to the plaintiff above and beyond that of a reasonable neighbour.
 	
8. The defendant specifically denies that he had a duty to educate the plaintiff on ladder safety.
	➤ State those allegations to which the defendant admits.
	
	➤ State those allegations that the defendant denies.
	
	➤ State those allegations about which the defendant knows nothing.
	
	➤ Plead that the claim is statute-barred (no longer legally enforceable by reason of the lapse of time) or should be dismissed on other grounds.
	
	➤ State the defendant's version of events for each allegation that the defendant denies.
	
	➤ Provide a defence for each allegation of liability that the defendant denies.

9. The defendant specifically denies that he deliberately acted in a way that caused the plaintiff to fall. The defendant also denies laughing at the plaintiff's fall.

10. The defendant denies that the plaintiff suffered damages as alleged and puts the plaintiff to strict proof of both general and special damages.

► State that the defendant denies or knows nothing about the damages claimed.

11. The defendant states that if the plaintiff did suffer damages, which the defendant specifically denies, the amount claimed is excessive and remote.

12. The defendant states that if the plaintiff did suffer damages, which the defendant specifically denies, the plaintiff failed to mitigate his damages by attempting to climb up the ravine when emergency crews warned him not to do so.

► State that the plaintiff failed to mitigate damages.

13. The defendant specifically denies that the plaintiff suffered a loss of income as he was compensated for his time off work by virtue of a sick benefits plan offered by his employer.

14. The defendant specifically denies that the plaintiff incurred medical and out-of-pocket expenses since his employer's health benefit plan would have paid such expenses.

15. The defendant specifically denies that this is a case of intentional battery and puts the plaintiff to strict proof thereof.

• Plead any legislation on which the defendant is relying. (none in this case)

16. The defendant pleads that the action be dismissed as against the defendant with costs.

• Plead any costs that the defendant wishes to recover.

SAMPLE 35 — Continued

<table>
<tr>
<td colspan="2">
Superior Court of Justice
Cour supérieure de justice
</td>
<td colspan="2" align="right">
Defendant's Claim
Demande du défendeur
</td>
</tr>
</table>

Form/*Formule* 10A   Ont. Reg. No./*N° du règl. de l'Ont.* : 258/98

Claim no. / *N° de la demande*

T1111/91

Sealed / *Scellé*

Toronto
Small Claims Court / *Cour des petites créances de*
444 Yonge Street, 2nd Floor
Address / *Adresse*
Toronto, ON   M5B 2H4

Plaintiff No. 1 / *Demandeur N° 1*

Full name / *Nom et prénoms*

Ilya Pushdim

Address for service (street & number, city, postal code)
Domicile élu (numéro et rue, ville, code postal)

500 County Way

Essex, ON   N8A 3Y7

Phone no. / *Numéro de téléphone*   Fax no. (if any) / *Numéro de télécopieur (le cas échéant)*

(519) 444-2121

Plaintiff's Lawyer/Agent (Full name)
Avocat/mandataire du demandeur (nom et prénoms)

Lawyer/Agent's address for service (street & number, city, postal code)
Domicile élu de l'avocat/du mandataire (numéro et rue, ville, code postal)

Lawyer/Agent's phone no. / *Numéro de téléphone de l'avocat/du mandataire*   Lawyer/Agent's fax no. (if any) / *Numéro de télécopieur (le cas échéant)*

Plaintiff No. 2 (if applicable) / *Demandeur N° 2 (le cas échéant)*

Full name / *Nom et prénoms*

Address for service (street & number, city, postal code)
Domicile élu (numéro et rue, ville, code postal)

Phone no. / *Numéro de téléphone*   Fax no. (if any) / *Numéro de télécopieur (le cas échéant)*

Plaintiff's Lawyer/Agent (Full name)
Avocat/mandataire du demandeur (nom et prénoms)

Lawyer/Agent's address for service (street & number, city, postal code)
Domicile élu de l'avocat/du mandataire (numéro et rue, ville, code postal)

Lawyer/Agent's phone no. / *Numéro de téléphone de l'avocat/du mandataire*   Lawyer/Agent's fax no. (if any) / *Numéro de télécopieur (le cas échéant)*

Defendant No. 1 / *Défendeur N° 1*

Full name / *Nom et prénoms*

Aladdin Ladder Inc.

Address for service (street & number, city, postal code)
Domicile élu (numéro et rue, ville, code postal)

100 Rung Road

Hamilton, ON   N7A 7B7

Phone no./ *Numéro de téléphone*   Fax no. (if any) / *Numéro de télécopieur (le cas échéant)*

Defendant's Lawyer/Agent (Full name)
Avocat/mandataire du défendeur (nom et prénoms)

Lawyer/Agent's address for service (street & number, city, postal code)
Domicile élu de l'avocat/du mandataire (numéro et rue, ville, code postal)

Lawyer/Agent's phone no. / *Numéro de téléphone de l'avocat/du mandataire*   Lawyer/Agent's fax no. (if any) / *Numéro de télécopieur (le cas échéant)*

Defendant No. 2 (if applicable)/ *Défendeur N° 2 (le cas échéant)*

Full name / *Nom et prénoms*

Address for service (street & number, city, postal code)
Domicile élu (numéro et rue, ville, code postal)

Phone no./ *Numéro de téléphone*   Fax no. (if any) / *Numéro de télécopieur (le cas échéant)*

Defendant's Lawyer/Agent (Full name)
Avocat/mandataire du défendeur (nom et prénoms)

Lawyer/Agent's address for service (street & number, city, postal code)
Domicile élu de l'avocat/du mandataire (numéro et rue, ville, code postal)

Lawyer/Agent's phone no. / *Numéro de téléphone de l'avocat/du mandataire*   Lawyer/Agent's fax no. (if any) / *Numéro de télécopieur (le cas échéant)*

Note: For additional defendants, please list on attached sheet with all the necessary information as requested above.
Rem. : *S'il y a d'autres défendeurs, veuillez indiquer leurs noms et tous les renseignements demandés ci-dessus sur une feuille séparée.*

SCR 10.01-10A (REV. 99/10) *(formerly/anciennement SCC 0076)*

TO THE DEFENDANT(S) IN THE DEFENDANT'S CLAIM:
AU(X) DÉFENDEUR(S) DANS LA DEMANDE DU DÉFENDEUR :

The plaintiff in the Defendant's Claim in this action claims from you
Le demandeur dans la demande du défendeur présentée dans le cadre de l'action vous demande paiement de,

$ __1,450.00__ ___ plus $ _____ , and costs for the reason(s) set out below.
  (amount of claim)   (interest claimed to date (if any))
  (montant de la demande)   **$ plus** *(intérêts réclamés à ce jour (le cas* $, *ainsi que des dépens, pour le/les motif(s) énoncé(s) ci-dessous.*
                             échéant))

The plaintiff further claims from you pre-judgment interest and post-judgment interest in accordance to the
Courts of Justice Act.
Le demandeur vous demande également des intérêts antérieurs et postérieurs au jugement conformément à la
Loi sur les tribunaux judiciaires.

> **IF YOU DO NOT FILE A DEFENCE WITH THE COURT WITHIN TWENTY (20) CALENDAR DAYS AFTER YOU HAVE RECEIVED THIS DEFENDANT'S CLAIM, JUDGMENT MAY BE ENTERED AGAINST YOU. JUDGMENT MAY BE ENTERED WITHOUT FURTHER NOTICE TO YOU.**
> *SI VOUS NE DÉPOSEZ PAS DE DÉFENSE AUPRÈS DU TRIBUNAL AU PLUS TARD VINGT (20) JOURS CIVILS APRÈS AVOIR REÇU LA PRÉSENTE DEMANDE DU DÉFENDEUR, UN JUGEMENT PEUT ÊTRE INSCRIT CONTRE VOUS SANS AUTRE AVIS.*

TYPE OF CLAIM / *NATURE DE LA DEMANDE*

☐ Unpaid Account *Compte impayé*	☐ Promissory Note *Billet*	☐ Damage to Property *Dommages causés à des biens*
☐ Contract *Contrat*	☐ Services Rendered *Services rendus*	☐ Lease *Contrat de location*
☐ Motor Vehicle Accident *Accident de véhicule automobile*	☐ N.S.F. Cheque *Chèque sans provision*	☒ Other __Product Liability__ *Autre* __Contribution/Indemnity__

REASONS FOR CLAIM AND DETAILS / *MOTIFS DE LA DEMANDE ET PRÉCISIONS*
Explain what happened, where and when **and** the amounts of money involved.
*Expliquer ce qui est arrivé, indiquer le lieu et le moment de l'incident **et** préciser les sommes d'argent en cause.*

SEE ATTACHED SCHEDULE 'A'

If more space is required, attach separate sheet(s)./Si vous avez besoin de plus d'espace, annexez une feuille supplémentaire.

If the claim is based in whole or in part on a document(s), **you must attach** a copy of the document(s) to the defendant's claim, or if the document(s) is lost or unavailable, **you must explain** why it is not attached in the space provided below.
*Si la demande est fondée en tout ou en partie sur un document, **vous devez annexer** une copie de celui-ci à la demande du défendeur. Si le document est perdu ou n'est pas disponible, **vous devez expliquer** ci-dessous pourquoi il n'est pas annexé.*

> NOTE: You may attend at the nearest Small Claims Court and obtain "Your Guide to Making a Defence."
> *REMARQUE : Vous pouvez vous rendre à la Cour des petites créances la plus proche pour vous procurer un exemplaire du Guide sur la défense.*

_____   _____
(Date)   (Signature of clerk/*Signature du greffier*)
SCR 10.01-10A (REV. 99/10) *(formerly/anciennement SCC 0076)*

© Queen's Printer for Ontario, 2000. This is an unofficial version of Government of Ontario legal materials.

Defendant's Claim for Commission of a Tort

SAMPLE DEFENDANT'S CLAIM	EXPLANATIONS

Schedule 'A'
Defendant's Claim
 	
The Relief Sought: *(Headings are optional)*
 	
1. The plaintiff seeks the following relief:
 	
   a) General damages in the amount of $450;
 	
   b) Special damages in the amount of $500;
 	
   c) Punitive damages in the amount of $500;
 	
   d) Prejudgment interest under the Courts of Justice Act;
 	
   e) Postjudgment interest under the Courts of Justice Act; and
 	
   f) Its costs of this action.
 	
1. This claim is related to Plaintiff's Claim No. T-99999, issued on June 7, 200–. The plaintiff in that action, Monty Fall, is a resident of Windsor, Ontario. The defendant, Ilya Pushdim, is a resident of Essex, Ontario, and is bringing a defendant's claim against Aladdin Ladder Inc., Incorporated under the statutes of Ontario, and carrying on business in Hamilton, Ontario.
 	
2. Aladdin Ladder Inc. was the manufacturer and distributor of the ladder referenced in the plaintiff's claim, purchased by Monty Fall.
 	
3. Monty Fall was using a ladder when, on May 30, 200–, he sustained injuries in a fall. The fall occurred when the locking mechanism gave way and caused the ladder to move, thereby throwing Monty Fall down a ravine.
 	
4. The claimant states that were it not for the negligence of the defendant and its employees, the ladder would not have had a defect in its locking mechanism.
 	
5. The claimant further states that Aladdin Ladder Inc. is solely responsible for the injuries alleged by Monty Fall in the plaintiff's claim.
 	
6. The claimant in this defendant's claim states that the fall and resulting injuries were solely the result of the negligence as follows:
	► State the remedy being sought — general, special, punitive damages, pre-judgment interest. Postjudgment interest is usually pleaded even though it is awarded upon judgment pursuant to the Courts of Justice Act.
	
	► Identify the parties.
	
	► State the facts with respect to liability in chronological order.
	
	► State the allegations of negligence.
	
	► State any alternative allegations such as intentional torts.

(a) Aladdin Ladder Inc. owed a duty to the plaintiff to provide him with a ladder that meets all safety regulations;

(b) it, its employees, or both it and its employees failed to take the reasonable care in manufacturing the ladder in failing to ensure that:

    (i) the ladder was properly made;

    (ii) the ladder was properly inspected;

    (iii) the ladder was properly tested; and

    (iv) the ladder met all industry safety regulations.

7. The claimant herein claims as against the defendant Aladdin Ladder Inc. in the amount of the plaintiff's claim for general and special damages.

    ▶ State the general damages.

    ▶ State the special damages.

    ▶ State the punitive damages.

8. The plaintiff pleads that, if the court finds this to be a case of negligence, this is a proper case for the defendant to pay punitive damages in the amount of $500, considering the circumstances.

Legislation

9. The plaintiff pleads and relies upon the relevant provisions of the Negligence Act, R.S.O. 1990, c.N.1.

    ▶ List any legislation on which the plaintiff relies.

CHECKLIST 8
CHECKLIST FOR PREPARING DOCUMENTS

DEMAND LETTERS

❑ **Does your demand letter contain the following elements:**

   ❑ the writer's name, address, telephone number, and fax number, if available, all clearly printed or typed?

   ❑ the recipient's name, address, telephone number, and fax number, if available, all clearly printed or typed?

   ❑ the date that you sent the letter?

   ❑ the manner in which the letter will be sent (by regular mail, by fax, by registered mail, by courier, by hand)?

   ❑ a paragraph that identifies the writer and the recipient?

   ❑ a paragraph that outlines the problem and includes an invoice number, cheque number, contract number, or other document at the core of the alleged wrongdoing?

   ❑ a paragraph that makes the demand?

   ❑ a paragraph that states the consequences for failing to respond to the demand?

   ❑ a paragraph that ends the letter in a tone that will encourage the recipient to meet the demand?

   ❑ a signature?

LETTERS OF COMPLAINT

❑ **Does your letter of complaint contain the following elements:**

   ❑ the writer's name, address, telephone number, and fax number, if available, all clearly printed or typed?

   ❑ the recipient's name, address, telephone number, and fax number, if available, all clearly printed or typed?

   ❑ the date that you sent the letter?

   ❑ the manner in which the letter will be sent (by regular mail, by fax, by registered mail, by courier, by hand)?

   ❑ a paragraph that identifies the writer and the recipient?

   ❑ a paragraph that specifies the complaint?

   ❑ a paragraph that offers a solution for the recipient's consideration?

   ❑ a paragraph that ends the letter in a tone that will encourage the recipient to respond favourably or make their own suggestions?

   ❑ a signature?

LETTERS TO THE COURT

❑ **Do your letters to the court contain the following elements:**

    ❑ the writer's name, address, telephone number, and fax number, if available, all clearly printed or typed?

    ❑ the court file number?

    ❑ the names of the parties, or style of cause (e.g., *Bif v. Mif Enterprises*)?

    ❑ the court's address clearly printed or typed?

    ❑ the date of writing or typing?

    ❑ the manner in which the letter will be sent (by regular mail, by fax, by registered mail, by courier, by hand)?

    ❑ a paragraph that identifies the writer as a plaintiff or defendant?

    ❑ a paragraph that outlines the problem or request?

    ❑ a signature?

PLAINTIFF'S CLAIM

❑ **Did you complete the form, if required?**

❑ **Did you do the following on a separate sheet to attach to the form:**

    ❑ state the remedy being sought — general, special, punitive damages, prejudgment interest?

    ❑ identify the parties?

    ❑ state the facts in chronological order?

    ❑ state the allegation the defendant's wrongdoing?

    ❑ state the allegation that damages resulted from the wrongdoing?

    ❑ list any legislation upon which the plaintiff relies?

    ❑ show that damages resulted from the breach (specifically state the reasons punitive damages apply, if alleged)?

    ❑ Show that there was mitigation (reduction of loss through plaintiff's actions), if there was?

❑ **Did you include as attachments to the claim the following:**

    ❑ a photocopy of the contract?

    ❑ a photocopy of any demand letters that were sent?

    ❑ a photocopy of the sections of legislation on which the plaintiff relies?

CHECKLIST 8 — Continued

DEFENCE

❑ **Did you complete the form?**

❑ **Did you do the following on a separate sheet and attach it to the form:**

    ❑ state that the defendant admits the allegations contained in certain paragraphs?

    ❑ state that the defendant denies the allegations contained in certain paragraphs?

    ❑ state that the defendant knows nothing about the allegations contained in certain paragraphs?

    ❑ plead that the claim is statute-barred, if applicable to your case?

    ❑ state the defendant's version of events for each allegation that the defendant denies?

    ❑ provide a defence for each allegation about liability that the defendant denies?

    ❑ state that the defendant denies or knows nothing about the damages the plaintiff claimed?

    ❑ state that the plaintiff failed to mitigate damages, if this is applicable to your case?

    ❑ plead any legislation on which the defendant is relying?

    ❑ plead any costs that the defendant wishes to recover?

❑ **Did you include as attachments to the defence the following:**

    ❑ a photocopy of the contract (if written and if the plaintiff has not attached it to the claim)?

    ❑ a photocopy of any letters sent to the defendant about this action (if the plaintiff has not attached them to the claim)?

    ❑ a photocopy of the sections of legislation on which the defendant relies?

DEFENCE-RELATED CLAIMS

❑ **Did you do the following on a separate sheet and attach it to the form:**

    ❑ state the remedy being sought — general, special, punitive damages, prejudgment interest?

    ❑ identify the parties and, particularly, explain that the claimant is a defendant in a particular plaintiff's claim?

    ❑ state the facts in chronological order?

    ❑ state the allegations that are the source of this claim?

    ❑ state the allegation that damages resulted?

    ❑ list any legislation on which you rely?

❑ **Did you include as attachments to the claim the following:**

    ❑ a photocopy of the contract?

    ❑ a photocopy of any demand letters that were sent?

    ❑ a photocopy of the sections of legislation on which the plaintiff relies?

CHECKLIST 8 — Continued

AFFIDAVIT

❑ **Did you include the following in the affidavit:**

   ❑ Court File No. (claim number)?

   ❑ name of the small claims court?

   ❑ names of the parties?

   ❑ title: "Affidavit"?

   ❑ statement of oath or affirmation?

   ❑ statement about who you are and why you have knowledge of the contents of the affidavit?

   ❑ reason for preparing affidavit using the following standard line or a variation:

      "I make this affidavit in support of the relief sought and for no other or improper purpose."

   ❑ jurat consisting of:

      ❑ deponent?

      ❑ signature of commissioner of oaths or lawyer?

❑ **Is your affidavit logical and well organized?**

   ❑ Did you tell the story in your own words?

   ❑ Did you begin at the beginning, give the facts in the order they occurred, and end at the end?

   ❑ Did you use one thought per paragraph?

   ❑ Did you number all the paragraphs after the oath or affirmation?

❑ **Did you swear the affidavit before a commissioner of oaths or a lawyer?**

SUPPLEMENTARY AFFIDAVIT

❑ **Did you include all the elements listed above?**

❑ **Did you include a paragraph that states that this affidavit is a supplement to a previously sworn affidavit?**

AFFIDAVIT FOR DAMAGES ASSESSMENT HEARING

❑ **Did you include all the elements listed above?**

❑ **Did you include the following:**

   ❑ statement about the cause of action?

   ❑ statement about the damages?

   ❑ statement about the cost to repair or replace damaged items or land?

   ❑ statement that repair estimates contain no element of betterment or profit?

❑ **Did you include as exhibits the estimates for repairs or replacement of goods?**

❑ **Did you make a photocopy for yourself?**

13
Serving Court Documents

Service or *serving a document* means that a copy of a court document is delivered to the actual party or witness named on the document. Proper service is critical since court documents must properly come to the attention of the person named on the document. When that happens, service has been carried out or *effected*. However, the date on which service is deemed (considered) to have been effected may differ depending on the manner in which service was carried out.

Court documents can be served in a number of ways. These may, however, be limited when the rules specify that a court document must be served in a particular way. Always check your provincial or territorial rules to ensure that you choose the right method of service for a particular court document. The following options are available:

▸ *Personal service.* Serving a document personally means leaving a copy of the court document with the actual party or witness named on the document. Service is effected when the person named on the document receives it.

▸ *Mail or registered mail.* When a document is served by mail or registered mail, service is generally effected a certain amount of time after the mailing rather than on the day the mailing took place.

▸ *Courier.* When a document is served by courier, service is effected when the person named on the document receives it.

▶ *Fax.* When a document is served by fax during business hours, service is generally considered effected that same day. When a document is served by fax outside of business hours, service is generally considered effected the next business day. The number of pages that may be faxed during business hours may be restricted.

▶ *Other methods of service.* The small claims court rules may provide for other service methods. An example includes serving a document on a person who has contact with the person named on the document or putting an advertisement in a newspaper. Court approval of an alternate method is usually required and may be obtained by bringing a motion or application.

The following people can generally serve court documents on a party or witness:

▶ Your lawyer

▶ A process server

▶ Your friends, relatives, and business associates

▶ You

When to use a process server

When personal service is required, in certain situations it may be preferable to have a process server or party other than a party to the proceeding serve a court document. These situations include the following circumstances:

▶ There is potential for violence or animosity between the parties or their families.

▶ The address for service is in an area known to have a high rate of crime.

▶ The address for service is a long distance away from the serving party.

When service by mail is allowed, it is often a good alternative to personal service.

This chapter will now turn to the particular service rules of individual provinces and territories. Some provinces and territories lay out these rules in great detail. Others may not mention service rules at all. In that case, you will have to inquire about local practice with your court office. For all provinces, read through the entire section before deciding how to proceed. Once you have determined what constitutes proper service of your particular document, proceed to section **12** to learn how to prove that service has been effected.

Acknowledgement of receipt

The acknowledgement of receipt card is a postcard-type item with a stamp. It is served with a claim only when the claim is served on a defendant by leaving it with the defendant's lawyer. The lawyer then signs and dates the card as proof that service was effected. Law firms usually use this method when serving other law firms. For simplicity, it is best to use an affidavit of service.

1. British Columbia

1.1 Notice of claim

A claimant must serve each defendant with the defendant's copy of the notice of claim and a blank reply form (available from your courthouse). If the notice of claim is not served within 12 months after it was filed, the claim expires. The claimant, however, may apply to have claim renewed.

When the defendant is an *individual*, serve the document claim by leaving a copy of it with the defendant, or by mailing a copy of it by registered mail to the defendant and obtaining the post office proof of delivery card.

If the defendant is an *individual outside British Columbia*, serve the document on that individual in one or more of the following circumstances:

▸ The individual normally resides in British Columbia.

▸ The transaction took place in British Columbia.

▸ The registrar gives permission.

When the defendant is a *corporation*, serve the document by mailing a copy of it by registered mail to the registered office of the company and obtaining the post office proof of delivery card, or by leaving a copy of the document —

▸ at the registered office of the company,

- at the place of business of the company, with a receptionist or the person who appears to manage or control the business there, or

- with a director, liquidator, trustee in bankruptcy, or receiver manager of the company.

When the defendant is an *extraprovincial company*, serve the document by mailing a copy of it by registered mail to the attorney of the company and obtaining the original signed acknowledgment of receipt card in return, or by leaving a copy of the documents with the attorney. If no attorney is appointed, mail a copy of the document by registered mail to the registered office of the company and obtain the original signed acknowledgment of receipt card, or leave a copy of the document —

- at the registered office of the company,

- at the place of business of the company, with a receptionist or the person who appears to manage or control the business, or

- with a director, liquidator, trustee in bankruptcy, or receiver manager of the company.

When the defendant is a *partnership*, serve the document by mailing a copy of it by registered mail to a partner and obtaining the original signed acknowledgment of receipt card, or by leaving a copy of the document —

- with a partner,

- at the place of business of the partnership, with a person who appears to manage or control the partnership business, or

- with a receptionist who works at a place of business of the partnership.

When the defendant is a *society* incorporated under the Society Act, serve the document by mailing a copy of it to the address for service on file with the Registrar of Companies and obtaining the original signed acknowledgment of receipt card, or by leaving it —

- at the address for service on file with the Registrar of Companies and obtaining the original signed acknowledgment of receipt card, or

- with a director, officer, receiver manager, or liquidator of the society.

If the defendant is an *unincorporated association*, including a trade union, serve the document by —

- mailing a copy of it by registered mail to the registered office of the association and obtaining the original signed acknowledgment of receipt card, or

- by leaving a copy of it with an officer of the association or, in the case of the trade union, with a business agent.

When the defendant is an *extraprovincial society*, serve the document by mailing a copy of it by registered mail to the attorney appointed under the Society Act and obtaining the original signed acknowledgment of receipt card, by leaving a copy of it with the attorney, or, if there is no attorney, by mailing the document to the address for service on file with the Registrar of Companies and obtaining the original signed acknowledgment of receipt card, or by leaving it —

- at the address for service on file with the Registrar of Companies and obtaining the original signed acknowledgment of receipt card, or
- with a director, officer, receiver manager, or liquidator of the society.

1.2 Alternative methods of service

If the notice of claim cannot be served using the methods described earlier, the claimant may apply to the registrar, who may permit another method of service to be used and set the time limit for filing the reply. If another method of service is permitted, a copy of the registrar's order must be served with the notice of claim, unless the registrar —

- orders otherwise, or
- orders that notice be given by advertisement.

If a copy of the registrar's order is not included, service is not valid.

When the registrar permits notice by advertisement, the person who obtains the order must pay for the advertisement.

1.3 Reply

The registrar must serve a copy of the reply within 21 days after the reply is filed with the court.

1.4 Third party notice

The defendant must serve a third party with the following:

- A copy of the third party notice
- A blank reply
- A copy of the notice of claim

- A copy of the reply to the notice of claim

- A copy of the notice of settlement conference or trial, if one has been issued, in the same way as is required for service of the notice of claim

The defendant must file a certificate of service within 30 days of filing the notice of third party claim, or else the third party notice expires. However, the defendant may file an application with the court to request that the third party notice be renewed.

1.5 Service by mail

When a document is served by mail, service is deemed to have been effected 14 days after it was mailed unless there is evidence to the contrary.

1.6 Address for service

A party must, on the claim or reply, give the party's address for service, which must be —

- the party's residence, place of business, or solicitor's office, if the party is not incorporated and not a partnership, or

- its registered office, place of business, or solicitor's office, if the party is incorporated or is a partnership.

2. Alberta

2.1 Civil claim

When serving the civil claim, the claimant must serve each defendant with the defendant's copy of the civil claim and a blank dispute note. The civil claim may be served on any day of the week.

When the defendant is an *individual*, serve the civil claim by —

- leaving a copy of the documents with the defendant,

- leaving a copy of the documents at the defendant's usual place of residence with a resident who is apparently 16 years of age or older, or

- mailing a copy of the documents by registered mail to the defendant and obtaining an affidavit of service with the postal receipt and the "Signature Copy" acknowledgment of receipt.

When the defendant is a *corporation*, serve the civil claim by:

- giving a copy of it to the chairperson, head officer, or a director of the corporation;

- giving a copy of the documents to the manager, agent, or officer of the corporation located where the civil claim was issued; or

- leaving the documents at, or sending the documents by registered mail to the registered office of the corporation.

2.2 Reply

If the defendant files a dispute note, the clerk will serve a copy of it on the plaintiff by mail.

3. Saskatchewan

3.1 Summons

The plaintiff must serve the summons on the defendant at least 10 days before the trial date stated in the summons. When a summons has not been served on time and there is not enough time before the trial date stated in the summons to comply with the 10-day time limit, a judge may set a new trial date. The summons would then have to be amended to reflect the new trial date.

3.2 Service generally

When the defendant is an *adult*, serve the document by leaving a copy of it with the defendant.

When the defendant is a *minor*, serve the document by leaving a copy of it with the minor defendant and the defendant's parent or guardian or another adult with whom the minor defendant resides.

When the defendant is a *municipality*, serve the document by leaving a copy it with the mayor, reeve, clerk, or secretary of the municipality, or with the deputy of any of those persons.

When the defendant is a *Crown corporation*, serve the document by mailing a copy of it by registered mail or certified mail to the chief executive officer of the Crown corporation, or by personal service on the chief executive officer of the Crown corporation.

When the defendant is a *corporation*, serve the document by leaving a copy of it with any officer, director, agent, or liquidator of the corporation or the clerk, manager, agent, or other representative at, or in charge of, any office or any other place where the corporation carries on business in Saskatchewan; or by mailing a copy of it by registered mail or certified mail, or delivering a copy of the document to the registered office of the corporation, or to any attorney of the corporation appointed under the Business Corporations Act.

When the defendant is the *Government of Saskatchewan*, service of the document is effected by leaving a copy of the document with —

> the attorney general or the deputy attorney general, or

> any barrister and solicitor who is designated by the attorney general for the purposes of the Proceedings Against the Crown Act.

When the person is *represented by a lawyer*, serve the document on that party's lawyer by leaving a copy of it with the lawyer. Service will be effected only if the lawyer accepts service by signing a copy of the document and indicating that he or she is the lawyer for the person.

3.3 Service outside of Saskatchewan

A document may be served outside Saskatchewan if the matter is one in which service outside Saskatchewan would be allowed without a court order if the action were commenced in the higher court (Court of Queen's Bench).

3.4 Service by registered or certified mail

When service is effected by registered or certified mail, the document is deemed to have been served —

> on the delivery date shown on the original signed acknowledgment of receipt card or the post office proof of delivery card, or

> on the date that the signed original acknowledgment of receipt card or proof of delivery card is returned to the sender.

3.5 Third party claim

The third party claimant must serve copies of the issued notice of third party claim on the third party and on the other parties to the action at least 10 days before the trial date stated in the third party claim.

3.6 Alternative methods of service

If you cannot serve a document using the methods described earlier, the judge may make an order permitting an alternative method of service. When the judge makes an order for alternative methods of service, service is deemed to have been effected if the document is served in accordance with the order.

3.7 Deemed service

A *summons* is deemed to have been served if the defendant takes any action or step to participate in the proceedings without having been served.

A *notice of third party claim* is deemed to have been served if a third party takes any action or step to participate in the proceedings without having been served.

A judge may order that a document is deemed to have been served if the judge is of the opinion that the document came to the attention of the person to be served without having been served by method that meets the requirements of the small claims legislation.

The defendant must file with the court a notice of counterclaim served on the plaintiff. The other option is for the defendant to raise a counterclaim orally at trial.

4. Manitoba

4.1 Claim

The plaintiff must file a claim with the court and serve a copy of it, along with a blank copy of the notice of intention to appear, on each defendant named in the claim.

4.2 Counterclaim

When the defendant files a counterclaim, the defendant must immediately serve a copy of it on the plaintiff.

4.3 Bench warrant

A bench warrant is a warrant authorizing the police to bring a witness who disobeyed a subpoena (summons to witness) before the court.

You must file an affidavit of personal service with the court indicating that the subpoena was served on a witness at least three days before the hearing before a judge will issue a bench warrant for the witness who did not attend the hearing.

5. Ontario

Depending on the court document being served, service may be effected by either personal service, alternatives to personal service, or substituted service.

Ontario's rules are very detailed and can best be dealt with in the summary that appears as Table 17.

The day on which you serve a document is important because certain restrictions limit the *day of service*. Ontario legislation provides the following definitions:

> ▸ *Holiday* means any Saturday or Sunday, New Year's Day, Good Friday, Easter Monday, Victoria Day, Canada Day, Civic Holiday, Labour Day, Thanksgiving Day, Remembrance Day, Christmas Day, Boxing Day, and any special holiday proclaimed by the Governor General or the Lieutenant Governor.

> ▸ If New Year's Day, Canada Day, or Remembrance Day fall on a Saturday, the following Monday is a holiday.

> ▸ If Christmas Day falls on a Friday, the following Monday is a holiday.

> ▸ If Christmas Day falls on a Saturday or Sunday, the following Monday and Tuesday are holidays.

If you are serving a document by regular mail, service is deemed effective on the fifth day following the date of mailing. There is one exception to this rule: alternative service of a claim by mail to last known address is effective on the 20th day after mailing.

When is a letter considered served?

The postmark on an envelope is the only indicator, save for the sender's word, of the date of mailing. Sometimes, however, you may mail a letter after the mail was collected for the final time that evening. In that case, the envelope would be postmarked the following day. Therefore, be watchful of the date that the letter is postmarked when preparing your Affidavit of Service as well as when calculating the effective date of service.

TABLE 17
SERVICE IN ONTARIO

Note: Since Ontario are so detailed, this chart helps to distill them.

(UNLESS OTHERWISE STATED, THE PERSON WISHING TO SERVE THE DOCUMENT IS RESPONSIBLE FOR SERVICE, NOT THE COURT)

COURT DOCUMENT	WHOM TO SERVE	HOW TO SERVE	WHEN TO SERVE
1. **Plaintiff's Claim**	All Parties Named in Claim	• Personal Service or or Alternative to Personal Service	Within six months of issuing the claim, UNLESS a judge orders otherwise
2. **Defendant's Claim**	All Parties Named in Claim	• Personal Service or Alternative to Personal Service	Within six months of issuing the claim, UNLESS a judge orders otherwise
3. **Defence**	All Parties Named in Plaintiff's or Defendant's Claim	• The court clerk will fax or mail the defence	
4. **Notice of Default Judgment**	All Parties Named in Plaintiff's or Defendant's Claim	• The court clerk will mail the Notice of Default Judgment	
5. **Summons to Witness**	Witness and All Parties Named in Claim	• Witnesses: Personal Service — attendance money must be attached • Parties: By Mail or By Fax	
6. **Notice of Garnishment**	Debtor or Garnishee	• Personal Service or Alternative to Personal Service	
7. **Notice of Judgment Debtor Examination**	Debtor	• By Mail or • By Personal Service or • By Alternative to Personal Service	At least 30 days before the date fixed for the examination
8. **Notice of Contempt Hearing**	Debtor	• Personal Service	
9. **Other Documents**		• By Mail or • By Fax or • By Personal Service or • By Alternative to Personal Service, unless the court orders otherwise	

If the fax transmission takes place before 5:00 p.m. on a day that is not a holiday, as defined by the rules, service is deemed to be effective that day. However, if the transmission takes place after 5:00 p.m. on any day or at any time during a holiday, service will be deemed effective the first day that is not a holiday.

If you require an extension of time, you must bring a motion to request an order for an extension of time. Such an order is discretionary on the part of the court.

5.1 Personal service

Personal service involves leaving an original copy of the court document with the actual party or witness named on the document.

When an *individual* is named on the court document, leave the document only with that individual; do not deliver it by mail or leave it with another individual.

When a *municipality* is named on the document, leave a copy of the document with the chair, mayor, warden, reeve, clerk or deputy-clerk, or lawyer of the municipality.

When a business or *corporation* is named on the document, then take one or more of the following steps:

▸ The document must be served at the place of business.

▸ Personally leave the document with an officer, director, or agent of the corporation.

▸ Personally leave the document with an individual who appears to be in control or management of the place of business.

When a *board or commission* is named on the document, leave a copy with a member or officer of the board or commission.

When a *person outside Ontario* carrying on business outside Ontario is named on the document, leave a copy of the document with anyone carrying on business in Ontario for the person named on the document.

When the *Crown in the Right of Canada* is named on the document, leave a copy of the document with the deputy attorney general of Canada or the chief executive officer of the agency in whose name the proceedings are taken.

When the *Crown in the Right of Ontario* is named on the document, leave a copy of the document with a solicitor in the Crown Law Office (Civil Law) of the Ministry of the Attorney General.

When an *absentee* (someone whose whereabouts are unknown) is named on the document, leave a copy of the document with the absentee's committee if one has been appointed, or leave a copy of the document with the public guardian and trustee, if a committee has not been appointed.

In Ontario, a minor is a person who has not reached the age of majority (age 18).

When a *minor* is named on the document, leave a copy of the document with the minor; and if the minor resides with a parent or person with lawful custody, leave another copy of the document with that person.

When a *mentally incapable person* is named on the document, take one or more of the following steps:

▸ If there is a guardian or attorney acting under a validated power of attorney for personal care with authority to act in the proceeding, leave a copy of the document with that person.

▸ If there is no guardian or attorney acting under a validated power of attorney for personal care with authority to act in the proceeding, leave a copy of the document with any other person acting under a validated power of attorney.

▸ If there is neither a guardian nor an attorney with authority to act in the proceeding, leave a copy of the document bearing the name and address of the mentally incapable person with the public guardian and trustee, and leave a copy with the mentally incapable person.

When a *partnership* is named on the document, leave a copy of the document with any one or more of the partners at the principal place of business; or leave a copy of the document with a person at the principal place of business of the partnership who appears to be in control or management of the place of business.

When a *sole proprietorship* is named on the document, leave a copy of the document with the sole proprietor; or leave a copy with any person at the principal place of business of the sole proprietorship who appears to be in control or management of the place of business.

5.2 Alternatives to personal service

You may attempt to serve a court document personally at a person's place of residence but may not be able to carry that service out. This may be because the person you are trying to serve is evading service or is not home when service is attempted. In such cases, you may serve the document by taking all of the following steps:

(a) Place a copy of the document in a sealed envelope showing the address of the person whom you wish to serve.

(b) Leave the sealed envelope with anyone who appears to be an adult member of the same household as the person whom you wish to serve.

(c) On the same day or on the following day, mail to the same address another copy of the court document, addressed to the person whom you wish to serve. This can be done by regular mail or registered mail.

If you serve the document in the manner described, the service is effective on the fifth day after the document is mailed.

If a person is *represented by a lawyer*, you may serve such a person by taking all of the following steps:

(a) Leave a copy of the document with the person's lawyer or an employee in that lawyer's office.

(b) Have that lawyer or employee write on the document or a copy of that document:

(i) that he or she accepted service,

(ii) the date that service was accepted, and

(iii) his or her name, printed and signed.

Serving the document in this manner makes service effective as endorsed by the lawyer or employee who accepted service. By accepting service the lawyer is deemed to represent to the court that he or she has the client's authority to accept service.

Typically, you serve a *corporation* by leaving a copy of the court document with one of its officers, directors, or agents at the head office or principal place of business. If you discover that the last address recorded with the Ministry of Consumer and Commercial Relations is not the same as that of the head office or principal place of business of that corporation, you may serve the document by taking one of the following steps:

(a) Mail a copy of the document to the corporation if you believe that the corporation is carrying on business in Ontario.

(b) Mail a copy of the document to the corporation's lawyer (attorney for service) if the business is that of a province or territory other than Ontario.

Serving the document in this manner makes service effective on the fifth day after the document is mailed.

To properly serve a plaintiff's claim or defendant's claim on the defendant *at the defendant's last known address*:

(a) Prepare an envelope showing the last known address of the person whom you wish to serve and the sender's return address.

(b) Use that envelope to mail a copy of the plaintiff's claim or defendant's claim and note the date of mailing.

(c) On the 20th day after mailing the document (not before), prepare an affidavit of service indicating the following information, if it is true —

   (i) that the address to which the claim is sent is one you believe to be the last known address of the person to be served, and

   (ii) that the claim has not been returned to you, and

   (iii) that you have no reason to believe that the person to be served did not receive the claim.

Service in this situation is effective on the 20th day after mailing, provided that you comply with all three steps listed earlier.

5.3 Substituted service

If you are unable to carry out personal service or an alternative to personal service or if such service is impractical, you may file a motion with the court requesting an order permitting substituted service. This will allow you to leave with or send by registered mail an original copy of the court document to a person who is not the actual party or witness named on the document.

When making the motion for substituted service, the plaintiff should be prepared to show that service was attempted and has failed. It is important that, before the motion, you plan how you might effect service, should an order for substituted service be granted. For example, substituted service may be accomplished by —

➤ posting an advertisement in a newspaper,

➤ posting the document on the door to a residence or business of the person to be served, or

➤ serving another person such as a spouse or parent, landlord, or roommate whom you have reason to believe resides at the same address as the person to be served.

The number and timing of attempts that the court may deem sufficient to warrant such an order is up to the judge who will assess all the facts presented in support of the motion. In hearing your motion, the court will read your affidavit, hear your arguments, and make a decision. In most cases, the court order will provide the effective date of the substituted service as well as the details of how it is to be effected.

6. New Brunswick

6.1 Claim

The claimant must serve a copy of the claim and a copy of the dispute note on each defendant and each plaintiff by ordinary mail at the address noted on the claim.

If the claim is not served within 12 months after it was filed, the claim expires. The claimant, however, may apply to have the claim extended a further 6 months if the defendant has not been served and the plaintiff requests an extension from the court.

6.2 Service generally

When the party is an *individual*, except an individual under a disability, serve the document by —

> leaving a copy of it with the party,

> mailing a copy of it by prepaid registered or certified mail, or prepaid courier, to the party and obtaining the original acknowledgment of receipt card signed by the party, or

> leaving a copy of it with an adult occupant of the dwelling in which the individual to be served resides, and by mailing a copy by ordinary mail on the same day to the individual to be served.

When the party is *under 19 years of age*, serve the document by leaving a copy of it with the party's parent or guardian or another adult with whom, or in whose care, the young person resides.

When the party is a *corporation*, serve the document by —

> leaving a copy of it with a director or officer of the corporation,

> leaving a copy of it with a person at a place of business of the corporation who appears to manage or control the place of business,

> leaving a copy of it at a place of business of the corporation with a receptionist who works at the place of business,

- leaving a copy of it at the registered office of the corporation, or
- sending a copy of it by prepaid registered or certified mail, or prepaid courier, to the registered office of the corporation and obtaining the original signed acknowledgment of receipt card.

When the party is an *extraprovincial company*, serve the document by mailing a copy of it by prepaid registered or certified mail, or prepaid courier, to the address of the attorney for service of the corporation and obtaining the original signed acknowledgment of receipt card.

When the party is a *partnership*, serve the document by —

- leaving a copy of it with a partner,
- leaving a copy of it with a person at the place of business of the partnership who appears to manage or control the partnership business,
- leaving a copy of it with a receptionist who works at a place of business of the partnership, or
- sending a copy of it by prepaid registered or certified mail, or prepaid courier, to the registered office of the corporation and obtaining the original signed acknowledgment of receipt card.

When the party is a *sole proprietorship*, serve the document by —

- leaving a copy of it with the sole proprietor,
- leaving a copy of it with a person at the place of business of the sole proprietor who appears to manage or control the partnership business,
- leaving a copy of it with a receptionist who works at a place of business of the sole proprietor, or
- sending a copy of it by prepaid registered or certified mail, or prepaid courier, to the proprietor and obtaining the original acknowledgment of receipt card signed by the proprietor.

When the party is a *municipality*, serve the document by leaving a copy of it with the mayor, deputy mayor, clerk, assistant clerk, or with any solicitor for the municipality.

When the party is an *unincorporated association*, serve the document by leaving a copy of it with an officer of the association or with any other person at any office or premises occupied by the association who appears to be in control or management of the premises.

When the party is a *board, tribunal, or commission*, serve the document by leaving a copy of it with the secretary, an officer, or a member of that body.

When the party is the *Crown in Right of New Brunswick*, serve the document by leaving a copy of it with any lawyer who is designated by the attorney general for the purposes of the Proceedings Against the Crown Act.

When the party is the *Crown in Right of Canada*, serve the document by leaving a copy of it with any lawyer who is designated by the attorney general for the purposes of the Crown Liability Act.

When the party is the *Attorney General*, serve the document by leaving a copy of it with the Attorney General or with any lawyer employed in the office of the Attorney General at Fredericton.

When the party is an *estate*, serve the document on the administrator of estates, the committee by virtue of the Mental Health Act, by leaving a copy of the document with that committee.

When the party has been declared *mentally incompetent* or incapable of managing his or her own affairs, serve the document by leaving a copy of it with the committee of that person's estate.

When the party is *mentally incompetent* or incapable of managing his or her own affairs, not so declared, serve the document by leaving a copy of it with that party and with the person in whose care that party resides.

When the party has been declared to be an *absentee* under the Presumption of Death Act, serve the document by leaving a copy of it with the absentee's committee.

When the party is *represented by a lawyer*, serve the document by leaving a copy of it with the lawyer, provided the lawyer endorses a copy of the document indicating his or her acceptance of the document and the date of acceptance.

6.3 Deemed service

If the claim is mailed, service is deemed to have occurred within 35 days after the date of mailing. If the claim is returned, the clerk will notify the plaintiff, who may provide another mailing address for the defendant.

When the document is sent by prepaid registered or certified mail or prepaid courier, service will be deemed to be effected on the date noted on the original signed acknowledgment of receipt card.

6.4 Alternative methods of service

If you cannot serve the document using these methods or the rules have not provided for a particular type of service, you may request a court order to —

> permit another method of service to be used, and

> specify when service in accordance with the order is deemed effected.

7. Nova Scotia

7.1 Claim

On filing and issuing the claim, the claimant must serve a certified copy of the original claim and a defence form on each defendant.

7.2 Defence and counterclaim

On filing the defence, counterclaim, or both, the clerk will issue a certified copy of it, which the defendant must serve on the plaintiff either personally or by registered mail.

8. Prince Edward Island

8.1 Notice of claim

The plaintiff must serve the notice of claim on each defendant together with the defendant's copy of the notice of claim and a blank dispute note. If the notice of claim is not served within 12 months of the date of issuance, it expires. The registrar may, however, extend the time for service for another six months if the plaintiff requires an extension.

When the defendant is an *individual*, serve the individual by —

> leaving a copy of the documents with the defendant,

> leaving a copy, in a sealed envelope addressed to the person, at the place of residence with anyone who appears to be an adult member of the household; and on the same day or the following day mailing another copy of the document to the defendant at the place of residence, or

> by mailing a copy of the document by registered mail to the defendant.

When the defendant is a *company*, serve the document by mailing a copy of it by registered mail to the registered office of the company, or by leaving a copy of it —

> at the registered office of the company,

> at the place of business of the company, with a person who appears to manage or control the business, or

> with a director, officer, liquidator, trustee in bankruptcy, or receiver manager of the company.

When the defendant is a *partnership*, serve the document by —

> mailing a copy of it by registered mail to a partner,

> leaving a copy of it with a partner, or

> leaving a copy of it at the place of business of the partnership, with a person who appears to manage or control the partnership business, or with a receptionist who works at a place of business of the partnership.

8.2 Reply

The registrar will notify the plaintiff once the dispute note has been filed.

8.3 Service by mail

When a document is served by mail, service is deemed to have been effected on the fifth day after it was mailed.

9. Newfoundland

When the defendant is an *individual over 19 years of age*, serve the document by leaving a copy of it with the defendant or by mailing a copy of it by registered mail to the defendant's last known address and obtaining the original signed acknowledgment of receipt card.

When the defendant is an *individual under the age of 19*, serve the document by —

> mailing a copy of it by registered mail to the last known address of the defendant and a next friend (litigation guardian), and obtaining the original signed acknowledgment of receipt card, or

> by personal service on the defendant and the next friend of the defendant.

In Newfoundland, the litigation guardian is known as the *next friend*.

When the defendant is a *partnership*, serve the document by —

▸ mailing a copy of it by registered mail to a partner and obtaining the original signed acknowledgment of receipt card,

▸ leaving a copy of it with a partner, at a place of business of the partnership, with a person who appears to manage or control the partnership business, or

▸ leaving a copy of it with a receptionist who works at the place of business of the partnership.

When the defendant is a *corporation* incorporated or continued under the Corporations Act, the plaintiff must file with the document a printout of a corporation search showing the most recent address of the registered office of the corporation on file with the Registrar of Companies, and serve the document by mailing a copy of it by registered mail to the registered office of the corporation and obtaining the original signed receipt card, or by leaving it —

▸ at the registered office of the corporation,

▸ at the place of business of the corporation, with a receptionist or a person who appears to manage or control the corporation's business, or

▸ with a director, officer, liquidator, trustee in bankruptcy, or receiver manager of the corporation.

When the defendant is an *extra-provincial corporation*, serve the document by mailing a copy of it by registered mail to the attorney of the corporation appointed under the Corporations Act and obtaining the original signed acknowledgment of receipt card, leaving it with the attorney, or when an attorney has not been appointed, by leaving it —

▸ at the registered office of the corporation,

▸ at the place of business of the corporation, with a receptionist or a person who appears to manage or control the corporation's business, or

▸ with a director, officer, liquidator, trustee in bankruptcy, or receiver manager of the corporation.

When the defendant is a *municipality or local service district*, serve the document by mailing a copy of it by registered mail or by giving a copy to the court, town manager, or someone acting in a similar capacity.

When a defendant is an *incorporated association*, including a trade union, serve the document by —

- mailing a copy of it by registered mail to the registered office of the association and obtaining the original signed acknowledgment of receipt card,
- leaving a copy of it with an officer of the association, or
- in the case of trade union, leaving a copy of it with a business agent.

When the defendant is *Her Majesty in Right of Newfoundland* you must comply with the Proceedings Against the Crown Act and serve the document on the Ministry of Justice or the Deputy Minister of Justice.

10. Yukon

10.1 Claim

The claimant must serve each defendant with the defendant's copy of the notice of claim and a blank reply form.

Service may be effected by the plaintiff, the plaintiff's solicitor or agent, the sheriff or the sheriff's agent, or by sending the document by certified mail.

No document need be served by personal service unless otherwise provided by the regulations.

When the party is an *individual*, serve the document by leaving a copy of it with the individual.

When the party is a *minor*, serve the document by leaving a copy of it with the minor. When the minor resides with a parent or other person having care of lawful custody of the minor, leave another copy of the document with the parent or other person.

When the party is a *corporation* other than a municipal corporation, serve the document by leaving a copy of it with —

- an officer, director or agent of the corporation,
- any person at any place of business or registered office of the corporation, or
- a person who appears to be in control or management of the place of business.

When the party is a *partnership*, serve the document by leaving a copy of it with —

> any partner, or

> a person at any place of business of the partnership who appears to manage or to be in control of the partnership business.

When the defendant is a *sole proprietorship*, serve the document by leaving a copy of it with —

> the sole proprietor, or

> a person at any place of business of the sole proprietor who appears to manage or to be in control of the partnership business.

When the party is a *municipal corporation*, serve the document by leaving a copy of it with —

> the chairperson, mayor, warden, reeve, clerk, or deputy clerk of the municipality, or

> the solicitor of the municipality.

When the party is an *individual outside Yukon* who carries on business in Yukon, serve the document by leaving a copy of it with anyone carrying on business in Yukon for that person.

When the party is a *board or commission*, serve the document by leaving a copy of it with a member, officer, or secretary of the board or commission.

When the party is *Her Majesty the Queen in the Right of Canada*, serve the document in accordance with the Crown Liability Act.

When the party is the *Government of Yukon*, serve the document by leaving a copy of it with a solicitor for the Government of Yukon at the Andrew Philipsen Law Centre, Whitehorse, Yukon.

When the party has been declared *mentally incompetent* or incapable of managing his or her own affairs, serve the document by leaving a copy of it with —

> the committee of the person's estate if there is one or, if not, with the committee of the person.

When the party is mentally incompetent or incapable of managing his or her own affairs, not so declared, serve the document by leaving a copy of it with the public administrator, and by leaving another copy with that party. When the public administrator is the committee of the person's estate, and the person is a patient or out-patient of a hospital under the Mental Health Act, and the attending physician is of the opinion that leaving a copy with the party would be likely to cause the person serious harm, serve the document on the committee only.

When the party has been declared to be an *absentee*, serve the document by leaving a copy of it with his or her committee if one has been appointed or, if not, with the public administrator.

10.2 Alternative service

When personal service is required by the rules or regulations of the court and personal service cannot be effected, serve the document by leaving a copy of it addressed to the person at the place of residence with anyone who appears to be an adult member of the household and, on the same day or the following day, mailing another copy to the person.

If a corporation cannot be found at the last address on record at the Registrar of Corporations, serve the document by mailing a copy of it to the corporation or to the attorney for service in Yukon at the corporation's last address, recorded at the Registrar of Corporations.

Alternative service is effective on the 10th day after the document is mailed.

10.3 Reply

On filing the reply with the clerk of the court, the defendant must mail a copy of the reply to every party within 20 days if the party resides in Yukon, or within 30 days if the party resides outside Yukon.

10.4 Third party claim

A third party claim must be filed with the court and served with two copies for each third party and a copy for each party to the action using the same service rules that apply to the claim.

10.5 Substituted service

If personal service is impractical, the court may permit substituted service.

10.6 Service outside Yukon

When the defendant resides outside Yukon, the plaintiff may serve the claim on the defendant if the defendant normally resides in Yukon or if the transaction or event that resulted in the claim took place in Yukon.

When the defendant lives outside of Yukon, the court may allow for reasonable costs for serving the document.

10.7 Service by mail

When personal service is not required, service may be effected by mail to the party or by mail to the party's agent, to the last known address for service provided by the party, if no address has been provided.

When service is effected by mail, the document is deemed to have been served on the 10th day after the document is mailed.

10.8 Service by fax

When personal service is not required, service may also be effected by fax, by sending a fax cover memo and a copy of the document.

11. Northwest Territories

11.1 Claim

Serve a copy of the claim together with a blank copy of the defence on every party in the action. You may do this by personal service or by mailing a copy of the claim to each defendant by registered mail, with an original acknowledgment of receipt card, to the defendant's last known post office address.

11.2 Substituted service

If personal service is impractical, the court may allow substituted service.

11.3 Defence

On receipt of the defence, the clerk of the court will mail a copy of it to the plaintiff and to every party to the main action, other than the defendant filing the defence.

12. Proof of Service

Regardless of how or on whom you serve a court document, you must be able to prove that service was effected (carried out according to the rules). The methods available for proving service in the various provinces and territories are summarized in Table 18.

13. Failure to Receive a Court Document

Sometimes, even though a document was served or deemed to have been served, it may not have come to your attention. It may also be that a document came to your attention some time after it was served or was deemed to have been served.

These events can be quite unfortunate if the document is a claim, because failure to file a defence in a timely manner may ultimately mean having default judgment entered against you. If this has happened to you, you may be able to overcome it by bringing a motion to set aside default judgment.

Even though service was carried out according to the rules, you may request by motion or application that —

(a) the noting in default or default judgment be set aside,

(b) the time for filing a defence or other court document or payment be extended, and/or

(c) an adjournment be granted.

The court may grant or deny an adjournment, an extension of time, or a setting aside of the noting in default or default judgment, based on the evidence it has before it.

TABLE 18

PROVING SERVICE

PROVINCE	PROVING SERVICE
British Columbia	**Written Proof of Service** Service may be proven by filing at the registry any or all of the following: ► for personal service of a document except a summons to a payment hearing, a certificate of service, with a copy of the document attached; ► for service by registered mail, a certificate of service with the original signed acknowledgment of receipt card and a copy of the document attached to the certificate; ► for personal service on a lawyer or articled student, a copy of the document signed by the lawyer or articled student or by a partner or employee of the firm; or ► for personal service of a summons to a payment hearing, an affidavit of service.
Alberta	**Oral Proof of Service** A judge or registrar may allow a person to prove by sworn oral evidence that a person has personally served a document **Written Proof of Service** Service may be proven by filing at the Civil Division Office the following: ► for personal service of the Civil Claim, an affidavit of service; or ► for service by single registered or certified mail, an affidavit of service with the postal receipt attached to the affidavit; ► for service by registered mail, an affidavit of service with the postal receipt and the "Signature Copy" acknowledgment of receipt attached to the affidavit.
Saskatchewan	**Written Proof of Service** A document may be served by any means that permits the person serving the document to produce proof of service including: ► where service is effected by personal service, by filing with the court an affidavit sworn by the person delivering the document; ► where service is effected by registered mail, by filing with the court the post office acknowledgment of receipt card purporting to be signed by or on behalf of the addressee; ► where service is effected by certified mail, by filing with the court the post office proof of delivery card purporting to be signed by or on behalf of the addressee;

TABLE 18 — Continued

	► where service is effected by fax, by filing with the court the transmission record or journal generated by the fax machine that indicates the date of transmission and that the transmission was successful; ► where service is effected by a sheriff, a deputy sheriff, or a sheriff's bailiff, by filing a copy of the document endorsed with the certificate of service in the prescribed form; or ► where service is effected by leaving a copy with the person's lawyer, by filing a copy of the document endorsed with the acceptance of service by the lawyer. **Oral Proof of Service** The rules also permit a person to prove by sworn oral evidence that a person has personally served a document.
Manitoba	**Written Proof of Service** Service may be proven by filing at the court any or all of the following: ► where service of the small claim is effected by personal service, by filing with the court a declaration of service, or ► where service of the counterclaim is effected by personal service, by filing with the court a declaration of service.
Ontario	**Written Proof of Service** Service may be proven by filing at the court any or all of the following: ► where service is effected by personal service or by substituted service, by filing with the court an affidavit of service sworn or affirmed by the person delivering the document with a copy of the document attached; ► where service is effected by fax, by an affidavit of service, by attaching a copy of the fax memo and a copy of the document attached; ► where service is effected by a bailiff or an agent of the bailiff, by a certificate of service of the person effecting the service with a copy of the document attached.
New Brunswick	**Written Proof of Service** Service may be proven by filing at the court any or all of the following: ► where service is effected by personal service, by filing with the court an affidavit of service sworn or affirmed by the person delivering the document; ► where service is effected by registered or certified mail or prepaid courier, and service is proved by an affidavit of service, by attaching a copy of the original signed acknowledgment of receipt card to the affidavit; or ► where service is effected by leaving a copy with the person's lawyer, written admission or acceptance of service need not be verified by an affidavit.

TABLE 18 — Continued

Nova Scotia	**Written Proof of Service** Service may be proven by filing with the court, ► a letter certifying the fact of service and the mode of service, or ► where service was by registered mail, attaching the registration receipt The rules are silent with respect to proof of service. Check your court office for local practice or prepare an affidavit of service.
Prince Edward Island	**Written Proof of Service** Service may be proven by filing at the court any or all of the following: ► for personal service, a certificate of service with a copy of the document attached ► for service by registered mail, a certificate of service with the original signed acknowledgment of receipt card and a copy of the document attached to the certificate; or ► for personal service on a lawyer or articled clerk, a copy of the document signed by the lawyer or articled clerk or by a partner or employee of the firm.
Newfoundland	**Oral Proof of Service** A judge may allow a person to prove by sworn oral evidence that a person has personally served a document.
Yukon	**Written Proof of Service** Service may be proven by filing at the court any or all of the following: ► where service is effected by personal service or by substituted service, by filing with the court an affidavit of service sworn or affirmed by the person delivering the document with a copy of the document; ► where service is effected by fax, by an affidavit of service, by attaching a copy of the fax memo and a copy of the document; or ► where service is effected by a sheriff or an agent of the sheriff, by a certificate of service of the person effecting the service with a copy of the document attached.
Northwest Territories	The rules are silent about proof of service. Check your court office for local practice or prepare an affidavit of service.

APPENDIX 1
OVERVIEW OF A LAWSUIT

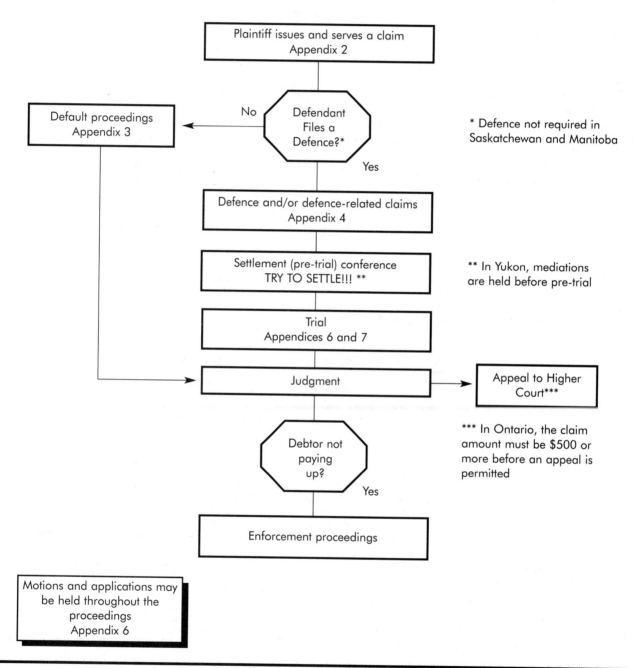

Plaintiff issues and serves a claim
Appendix 2

Defendant Files a Defence?*

No → Default proceedings Appendix 3

Yes

* Defence not required in Saskatchewan and Manitoba

Defence and/or defence-related claims
Appendix 4

Settlement (pre-trial) conference
TRY TO SETTLE!!! **

** In Yukon, mediations are held before pre-trial

Trial
Appendices 6 and 7

Judgment → Appeal to Higher Court***

*** In Ontario, the claim amount must be $500 or more before an appeal is permitted

Debtor not paying up?

Yes

Enforcement proceedings

Motions and applications may be held throughout the proceedings
Appendix 6

These procedures are discussed throughout *Small Claims Court for the Everyday Canadian*

APPENDIX 2
THE PLAINTIFF'S CLAIM

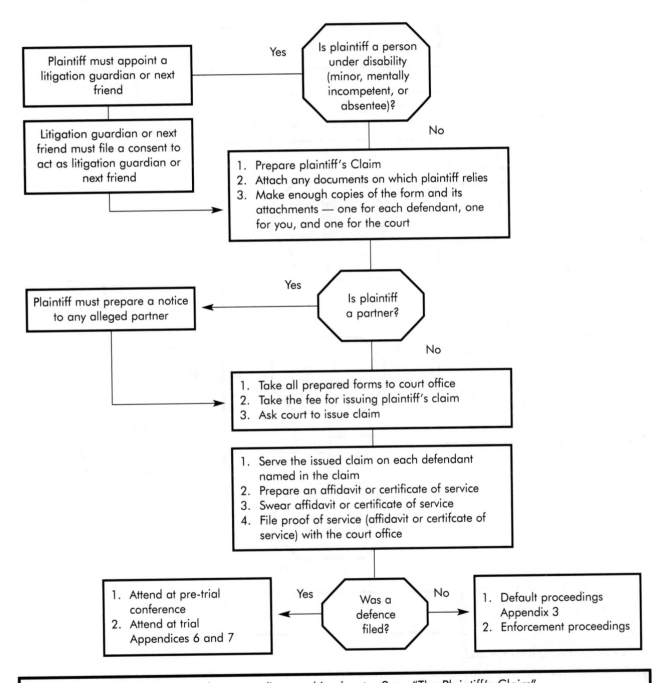

Plaintiff must appoint a litigation guardian or next friend

Litigation guardian or next friend must file a consent to act as litigation guardian or next friend

Yes — Is plaintiff a person under disability (minor, mentally incompetent, or absentee)?

No

1. Prepare plaintiff's Claim
2. Attach any documents on which plaintiff relies
3. Make enough copies of the form and its attachments — one for each defendant, one for you, and one for the court

Plaintiff must prepare a notice to any alleged partner

Yes — Is plaintiff a partner?

No

1. Take all prepared forms to court office
2. Take the fee for issuing plaintiff's claim
3. Ask court to issue claim

1. Serve the issued claim on each defendant named in the claim
2. Prepare an affidavit or certificate of service
3. Swear affidavit or certificate of service
4. File proof of service (affidavit or certifcate of service) with the court office

1. Attend at pre-trial conference
2. Attend at trial Appendices 6 and 7

Yes — Was a defence filed? — **No**

1. Default proceedings Appendix 3
2. Enforcement proceedings

These procedures are discussed in chapter 3 on "The Plaintiff's Claim"

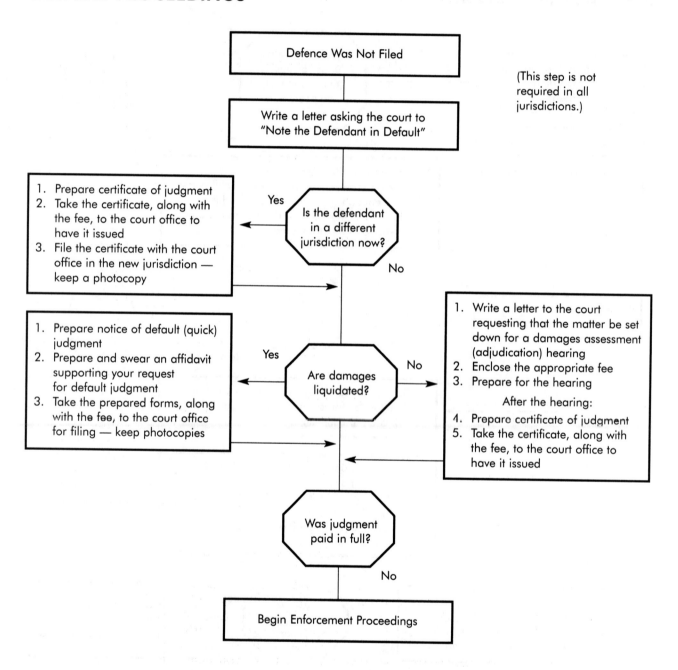

(This step is not required in all jurisdictions.)

Defence Was Not Filed

Write a letter asking the court to "Note the Defendant in Default"

Is the defendant in a different jurisdiction now?

Yes
1. Prepare certificate of judgment
2. Take the certificate, along with the fee, to the court office to have it issued
3. File the certificate with the court office in the new jurisdiction — keep a photocopy

No

Are damages liquidated?

Yes
1. Prepare notice of default (quick) judgment
2. Prepare and swear an affidavit supporting your request for default judgment
3. Take the prepared forms, along with the fee, to the court office for filing — keep photocopies

No
1. Write a letter to the court requesting that the matter be set down for a damages assessment (adjudication) hearing
2. Enclose the appropriate fee
3. Prepare for the hearing

   After the hearing:
4. Prepare certificate of judgment
5. Take the certificate, along with the fee, to the court office to have it issued

Was judgment paid in full?

No

Begin Enforcement Proceedings

These procedures are discussed in chapters 3, 4, 10, and 11

APPENDIX 4
DEFENCE AND DEFENCE-RELATED CLAIMS

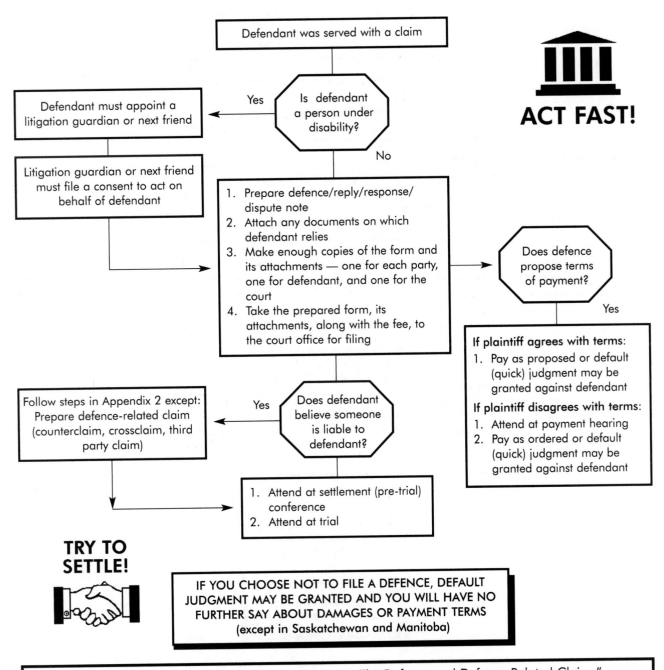

Defendant was served with a claim

Is defendant a person under disability?

Yes → Defendant must appoint a litigation guardian or next friend

Litigation guardian or next friend must file a consent to act on behalf of defendant

No

1. Prepare defence/reply/response/dispute note
2. Attach any documents on which defendant relies
3. Make enough copies of the form and its attachments — one for each party, one for defendant, and one for the court
4. Take the prepared form, its attachments, along with the fee, to the court office for filing

ACT FAST!

Does defence propose terms of payment?

Yes

If plaintiff agrees with terms:
1. Pay as proposed or default (quick) judgment may be granted against defendant

If plaintiff disagrees with terms:
1. Attend at payment hearing
2. Pay as ordered or default (quick) judgment may be granted against defendant

Does defendant believe someone is liable to defendant?

Yes → Follow steps in Appendix 2 except: Prepare defence-related claim (counterclaim, crossclaim, third party claim)

1. Attend at settlement (pre-trial) conference
2. Attend at trial

TRY TO SETTLE!

IF YOU CHOOSE NOT TO FILE A DEFENCE, DEFAULT JUDGMENT MAY BE GRANTED AND YOU WILL HAVE NO FURTHER SAY ABOUT DAMAGES OR PAYMENT TERMS
(except in Saskatchewan and Manitoba)

These procedures are discussed in chapter 4 on "The Defence and Defence-Related Claims"

APPENDIX 5
SUMMONSING WITNESSES

```
┌─────────────────────────────────────────────────────┐
│   Prepare for each witness a summons to witness or    │
│   subpoena, as required by your province or territory │
└─────────────────────────────────────────────────────┘
                          │
┌─────────────────────────────────────────────────────┐
│  Check fee schedule for:                              │
│  1. Attendance fee for each witness                   │
│  2. Fee for issuing each summons to witness or subpoena│
└─────────────────────────────────────────────────────┘
                          │
┌─────────────────────────────────────────────────────┐
│  1. Place attendance fee as certified cheque or exact │
│     cash amount in a separate envelope for each summons│
│     to witness or subpoena                            │
│  2. Prepare the issuing fee for all witnesses as one sum│
└─────────────────────────────────────────────────────┘
                          │
┌─────────────────────────────────────────────────────┐
│   Take the form or forms and fees to the court office │
│      in the location where the action will be tried.  │
│  Court staff will issue the summons to witness or subpoena│
└─────────────────────────────────────────────────────┘
                          │
┌─────────────────────────────────────────────────────┐
│            Serve each witness personally with         │
│        the issued summons to witness or subpoena      │
└─────────────────────────────────────────────────────┘
                          │
┌─────────────────────────────────────────────────────┐
│  Prepare an affidavit of service for each witness you served│
│  with a summons to witness (Newfoundland, British Columbia,│
│  and Saskatchewan will accept proof of service orally at trial)│
└─────────────────────────────────────────────────────┘
                          │
┌─────────────────────────────────────────────────────┐
│  Remind each witness a few days before trial about the date,│
│  time, and location of trial and where you will be meeting them.│
└─────────────────────────────────────────────────────┘
```

**Summons only those
witnesses you
absolutely need for trial**

This procedure is discussed in chapter 8 on "Preparing for Trial"

BRINGING A MOTION OR APPLICATION

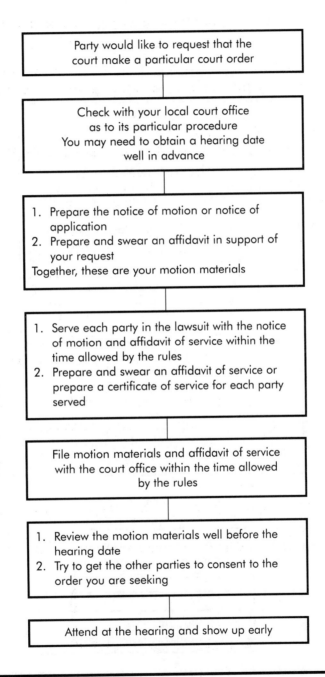

Party would like to request that the court make a particular court order

Check with your local court office as to its particular procedure
You may need to obtain a hearing date well in advance

1. Prepare the notice of motion or notice of application
2. Prepare and swear an affidavit in support of your request

Together, these are your motion materials

1. Serve each party in the lawsuit with the notice of motion and affidavit of service within the time allowed by the rules
2. Prepare and swear an affidavit of service or prepare a certificate of service for each party served

File motion materials and affidavit of service with the court office within the time allowed by the rules

1. Review the motion materials well before the hearing date
2. Try to get the other parties to consent to the order you are seeking

Attend at the hearing and show up early

This procedure is discussed in chapter 11 on "Other Appearances"

TRIAL PROCEDURE

This flowchart illustrates the order of events at trial

Opening Statements
Plaintiff gives opening statement
Defendant gives opening statement

Motions or Applications, if any

Plaintiff's Case
Plaintiff calls a witness
Clerk swears or affirms witness
Plaintiff examines witness in chief
Defendant cross-examines plaintiff's witness
Plaintiff re-examines own witness, if warranted
Plaintiff announces that this is the close of evidence
for the plaintiff

If the plaintiff has more than one witness, the events in this box are repeated, except last point

Motions or Applications, if any

Defendant's Case
Defendant calls a witness
Clerk swears or affirms witness
Defendant examines witness in chief
Plaintiff cross-examines defendant's witness
Defendant re-examines own witness, if warranted
Defendant announces that this is the close of
evidence for the defendant

If the defendant has more than one witness, the events in this box are repeated, except last point

Parties may request recesses or adjournments throughout the flow of events
The judge may or may not grant such requests

Motions or Applications, if any

Closing Arguments (Summation)
Plaintiff makes closing arguments
Defendant makes closing arguments

Judgment
Judge renders verdict or reserves decision

These events are discussed fully in chapter 9 on "Trial Procedure"

Glossary

(What That Legal Jargon Really Means)

Absentee	A person whose whereabouts are unknown and as to whom there is no knowledge as to whether he or she is alive or dead.
Adjourn	When a proceeding is delayed or rescheduled to a date in the future, it is adjourned.
Adjournment	When you wish to reschedule the date of a proceeding, you seek an adjournment.
Adjudication hearing	Same as **damages assessment**.
Affidavit	A written statement of facts which the person making the statement swears is true. The affidavit must be sworn by a commissioner of oaths or a lawyer.
Affidavit of service	A sworn document that states when, how, and upon whom a court document was served.
Agent	An agent may be a law student, articling student, or any other person. The agent represents either the plaintiff or defendant in the action.
Alternative to personal service	A method of service used when personal service is not possible.
Amended	When a court document is changed in any way, re-served on the parties, and filed with the court, the document has been amended.
Appeal	A request to a higher court to review the decision of a lower court. All appeals from the small claims court are heard in the higher court.
Application	Same as **motion**.
Bailiff /court enforcement officer	The court officer responsible for enforcing court orders.
Balance of probabilities	Evidence in a small claims court trial must be proved on the balance of probabilities. That is, the plaintiff must show that it is more likely than not that the cause of action occurred as alleged in the claim.
Cause of action	The reason for bringing the claim. The cause of action may be comprised of one or more events and refers to the whole cause of action, not portions of it.

Certificate of service	A document endorsed by the bailiff or court enforcement officer signifying that certain documents were served by that individual.
Chambers	The judge's office, usually positioned close to the courtroom.
Claim splitting	Claim splitting occurs when the elements of one claim are divided into two or more separate actions. If the plaintiff is claiming damages for several items arising out of the same act of wrongdoing, the items cannot be claimed on separate claims.
Closing argument	The last statement made by each party at trial. The closing argument is a brief summation of the case and includes arguments as to why the law supports your claim or defence. Same as **summation**.
Commissioner of oaths	This may be a person designated by the government as a commissioner of oaths or a lawyer. You will be able to find a commissioner of oaths at the court office.
Consent	Agreement by a party regarding some step in the proceeding initiated by another party.
Contempt of court	A penalty for not abiding by a court order. A person will be found in contempt when he or she is served with a summons to witness or subpoena but deliberately disregards the summons or subpoena and fails to testify at trial.
Counter offer	Once served upon the party who made the offer, that party can accept it, counter it, or reject the counter offer.
Court officer or court staff member	The court officer or court staff member works in the court office. He or she process claims, defences, and other court documents, schedules appearances, and deals with other administrative matters.
Counterclaim	A claim brought by a defendant against the plaintiff.
Court reporter	A court staff member who is present at trials and motions. The court reporter records the players in attendance, takes notes at or records the proceedings, and keeps transcripts. In some jurisdictions, the court reporter performs the duties of a court clerk as well.
Creditor	Same as **judgment creditor.**
Crossclaim	A claim brought by a defendant against another defendant.
Cross-examination	The mode of questioning used on witnesses called by an opposing party. The questions are short and generally require a short answer. The purpose is to test the testimony given by the witness during their examination-in-chief.
Damages	The monetary loss specified in the plaintiff's claim.
Damages assessment	A trial on the issue of damages. The plaintiff must prove his or her unliquidated damages to the court. A damages assessment is typically ordered when the defendant has failed to file a defence.
Debtor	Same as **judgment debtor.**

Default judgment	Judgment granted when the defendant fails to file a defence. Same as **quick judgment.**
Default proceedings	Proceedings initiated when the defendant fails to file a defence. Default proceedings start when the defendant is noted in default (this step is omitted from some rules) and ends when judgment is obtained.
Defence	The document filed by the defendant in reply to the allegations made in the plaintiff's claim. Same as **reply** and **response.**
Defence-related claim	A fictitious term the authors created to represent any one of the following claims that may be brought by a defendant against another party: defendant's claim, counterclaim, crossclaim, or third party claim.
Defendant	The person being sued. The defendant may also be referred to as a *party to the action.*
Defendant's claim	The document filed by the defendant in which he or she wishes to make a claim against another party.
Demand letter	A letter written by the plaintiff in an effort to recover the losses or to prevent an event from continuing or occurring. It is written to prevent the need for court action.
Deponent	The person swearing that the contents of an affidavit are true.
Deputy judge	A practising lawyer who performs the duties of a judge in the small claims court.
Discoverability rule	A common law rule that states that the limitation period does not begin to run until the plaintiff discovers that a wrong has been committed. This is a tricky concept best left to a lawyer to advise a claimant.
Dismiss	A claim may be dismissed by the court if it is frivolous, scandalous, vexatious, or an abuse of process. A claim that is dismissed cannot be tried in any other court.
Endorsement	An official entry in the court file outlining any orders made and, possibly, judges' reasons for them. When a judge makes an entry in the court file, he or she is said to endorse the record.
Equity	Equity is the principle of fairness. While the law may support a particular party's set of facts, the judge may decide to rule in favour of the other party or in favour of both parties on separate issues if he or she feels that such a decision would be fair.
Evidence	Any documents, photographs, objects, or testimony of the parties, witnesses, and expert witnesses that prove that the facts occurred as alleged.
Ex parte	A proceeding that is brought and conducted without notice to the other party who, therefore, does not attend the proceeding.
Expert	A person with expertise in a certain field such as medicine, auto mechanics, engineering, and other technological or academic areas. Such a person is generally consulted on an issue to be presented at trial and may appear as a witness in addition to producing a report providing his or her expert opinion on the issue in question.

Examination-in-Chief	The mode of questioning used on witnesses called by the party doing the questioning. The style is open-ended with the purpose of asking questions to allow the witness to tell his or her story in clear, complete manner.
File	A document is filed with the court when it is left in your court file held at the court office.
Garnishee	An individual or corporation that owes money to the debtor.
Garnishment	A procedure that allows a creditor to demand money from a business or person whom the creditor expects will owe money to the debtor.
Garnishor	The creditor demanding that money owed as a result of a judgment be paid to the court.
General damages	General damages refers to an award of money meant to reinstate the loss (and no more) resulting from the defendant's conduct.
Hearsay	When a witness repeats a statement spoken or written by someone who is not a witness at the trial, it is considered hearsay. Such statements are generally inadmissible.
Interim recovery of property	Personal property may be returned prior to the final decision of the court on a motion. In such cases, the court generally requires the individual seeking return of the goods to pay a sum of money to the court which is equal to the amount of the property to be returned.
Issue	A question of fact or law to be resolved during the lawsuit.
Issue	A court document is issued when the court clerk dates, signs, seals, and assigns it a court file number.
Judge	The decision-maker who presides over motions, hearings, examinations, pre-trial conferences, and trials.
Judgment	The judgment is the final decision in the case. It can be oral or written. It may be reserved; that is, left to be delivered at some point after the day of trial.
Judgment creditor	A person who is owed money as a result of a small claims court judgment.
Judgment debtor	A person who owes money as a result of a small claims court judgment.
Judgment-proof	If the defendant cannot afford to pay if judgment is given against him or her, than the defendant is said to be judgment-proof.
Jurisdiction	The court's authority to deal with a matter. See also **territorial jurisdiction** and **monetary jurisdiction**.
Jurisdictional hearing	A court hearing held during the early stages of a lawsuit to determine whether the plaintiff brought the action in the appropriate territory or whether the trial ought to be held elsewhere.
Legislation	A statute or regulation.

Limitation period	The time limit for commencing an action. You can lose your right to sue if you miss the limitation period.
Liquidated damages	Amounts that are easily determined by the court, thereby allowing the court to grant damages without further proof by the party.
Litigant	A party to the lawsuit.
Litigation guardian	A person who stands in place of the party suing or being sued. Generally, the litigation guardian is required where the party is a youth, is mentally incompetent, or is an absentee. Same as **next friend.**
Material facts	Material facts are those that will help prove your case.
Mediator	A neutral third party who officiates at the mediation.
Minor	A person who has not reached the age of majority (presently age 18).
Minutes of settlement	A document that is a written record of the terms of settlement and the consequences of not adhering to them.
Mitigate/mitigation	The act of minimizing your losses or damages. The plaintiff has a duty to minimize losses.
Monetary jurisdiction	Monetary jurisdiction refers to maximum amount of a claim allowed under the small claims court rules for a particular province or territory.
Motion	A request made to the court at any time before judgment. The request is for an order requiring that an act be carried out or money be paid.
Next friend	Same as **litigation guardian.**
Noted in default	A notation made by the court clerk suggesting that the defendant may no longer file a defence without the approval of the court. When a defendant fails to file a defence, that defendant may be noted in default at the request of the plaintiff or court clerk.
Notice of examination	A document that puts the debtor on notice that he or she is to appear for an examination respecting his or her assets and liabilities.
Notice of garnishment	A document which places the debtor and garnishee on notice that money is owing to the creditor.
Notice period	The time period within which the defendant must receive written notice that an action will be commenced. If notice is not given, the plaintiff may lose the right to sue.
Oath	A solemn promise that the facts a person is providing in court or in an affidavit are true.
Offer to settle	A proposal made by a party to a lawsuit with a view to resolving it.
Opening statement	The opening statement is made by each party near the outset of a trial to outline their positions.

Order	An order is a demand made by a judge at any point up to judgment. The order may require a party to perform an action, stop doing something, or make a payment.
Partnership	A business comprised of two or more partners. Both the partnership and partners should be named as parties in a lawsuit.
Payment into court	A payment arrangement by which either party deposits money with the court in accordance with a court order or an agreement between the parties.
Perjury	A false statement that is knowingly made under oath, either in court or in an affidavit. It is a criminal offence.
Person under disability	A person under disability is a minor, someone who is mentally incapable, or someone who is an absentee.
Personal service	The method by which an original copy of the court document is left with the actual party or witness named on the document.
Plaintiff	The plaintiff is a person who initiates an action and may also be referred to as a party.
Plaintiff's claim	The document in which the plaintiff explains the dispute and the events surrounding it. The plaintiff's claim puts the defendant on notice that he or she is now a party in a lawsuit.
Pleadings	Official court documents that outline the parties and their positions in the lawsuit. These are the plaintiff's claim, the defence, and defence-related claims.
Postjudgment interest	Interest which may be awarded by the court from the date of judgment.
Prejudgment interest	Interest which may be payable from the date of the cause of action until the date of judgment.
Pre-trial conference	A meeting that takes place after the pleadings have been filed with the court and before a trial is scheduled. It is an informal discussion between the parties, their lawyers or agents, and a pre-trial official (a judge, deputy judge, or referee) with a view to settling the case. Same as **settlement conference.**
Proceeding	An event that forms part of the lawsuit. The term includes trials, motions, applications, and settlement or pre-trial conferences.
Process server	An individual or business responsible for serving court documents.
Prothonotary	A senior clerk of the court.
Punitive damages	These are damages over and above general and special damages. They are awarded only to punish and deter the defendant from engaging in similar behaviour in the future.
Quick judgment	Same as **default judgment.**
Record	The official court notation of the proceedings.

Referee	A court official who may preside over pre-trial conferences, judgment debtor examinations, and hearings as ordered by a judge. The referee is usually a lawyer or mediator.
Registrar	A senior official of the registry office or court.
Release	A release is a document, a written record, that outlines the terms of settlement and specifies that the defendant is released from further payments or court actions for the same events upon which the action was based.
Relief	The remedy or judgment set out in the claim.
Reply	Same as **defence.**
Requisition	A written request to the court to perform a certain action required in the lawsuit.
Reserved judgment	When judgment is not given at the end of a trial, but is given at a later date, it is said to be a reserved judgment.
Response	Same as **defence.**
Service	Delivery of a copy of a court document to the party or witness named on the document.
Settlement	An agreement that resolves and brings an end to the lawsuit.
Settlement conference	Same as **pre-trial conference.**
Sole proprietorship	A business owned by one individual.
Special damages	Damages which the plaintiff will incur in the future as a result of the defendant's conduct.
Statute-barred	No longer legally enforceable by reason of the lapse of time.
Stay	An order by the court halting the proceedings. The proceedings may be reinstated following the occurrence of a certain event or an order of the court.
Strike	When a judge orders that a plaintiff's claim, defence, defendant's claim, or any portions of those pleadings be deleted, the pleading or section of the pleading is said to be struck.
Style of cause	The title of proceedings or the title of the lawsuit.
Subpoena	A document which demands the appearance before the court of a specified party or document. Same as **summons to witness.**
Substituted service	A method of serving a party ordered by the court when the methods allowed by the rules cannot be carried out.
Summation	Same as **closing argument.**
Summons to witness	Same as **subpoena.**

Supplementary affidavit	An affidavit which is written in addition to a previous affidavit to clarify the facts originally set out or to detail new facts.
Swear or affirm	To solemnly promise that the facts a person is providing in court or in an affidavit are true.
Terms of payment	The payment agreement reached by the parties or ordered by a court official following settlement, judgment, or admission of all or parts of the claim.
Territorial jurisdiction	Territorial jurisdiction refers to the geographical location in which a claim may be brought. The court can only deal with a claim brought in the appropriate jurisdiction.
Third party claim	A claim brought by the defendant against a person who is not a party in the lawsuit.
Tort	A wrong causing damages to a person or property. It could be an infringement of a statutory right or obligation. It could involve the failure to do something that would avoid harm or an act committed that caused harm. This is different from a breach of contract. Examples are defamation, trespass to property, trespass to land, false imprisonment, assault, battery, negligence, and others.
Trial	The court procedure which allows the parties and their witnesses to present their versions of the events that led to the lawsuit.
Trial list	The trial list is the court's schedule of trials which are to be heard on the specified day.
Unliquidated damages	Amounts that are not easily determined by the court.
Verdict	Judgment or decision following trial.
Warrant	The court document that gives the police the right to apprehend an individual and bring him or her before the court.
Witness	A person who tells the story to support one or more of the parties in the lawsuit.
Writ of delivery	A court document that allows the bailiff or other enforcement officer to seize the items listed on the writ of delivery and deliver them to the person who had the writ issued.
Writ of seizure and sale	The court document that allows the sheriff, bailiff, or court enforcement officer to seize the items listed on the writ, then sell them with a view toward paying the debt owed to the creditor.